VIOLENCE
AGAINST
WOMEN IN
CONTEMPORARY
WORLD
RELIGIONS

violence against women in contemporary world religions

R o o t s   a n d   C u r e s

DANIEL C. MAGUIRE
and
SA'DIYYA SHAIKH
editors

PILGRIM PRESS
CLEVELAND

This book is dedicated to **GRACE JANTZEN**, who, with heroic effort, completed her chapter in the final weeks of her life. She leaves us a stirring legacy of gentleness and unwavering courage in the pursuit of justice and truth.

The Pilgrim Press
700 Prospect Avenue
Cleveland, Ohio 44115-1100
thepilgrimpress.com
© 2007 by Religious Consultation on Population, Reproductive Health, and Ethics

♻ Printed in the United States of America on acid-free paper with post-consumer fiber.

11   10   09   08   07   5   4   3   2   1

Library of Congress Cataloging-in-Publication Data
Violence against women in contemporary world religion : roots and cure / Daniel C.
   Maguire and Sa'diyya Shaikh, editors.
      p. cm.
   ISBN 978-0-8298-1767-6
      1. Women and religion.   2. Women—Religious aspects.   I. Maguire, Daniel C.
II. Shaikh, Sa'diyya.
BL458.W56385 2007
200.82—dc22   2007025034

Contents

Contributors

LIORA GUBKIN is assistant professor of religious studies at California State University, Bakersfield. She currently serves as chair of the Women and Gender Studies program, American Academy of Religion.

CHRISTINE E. GUDORF is professor and chair in the Department of Religious Studies, Florida International University. She is currently president of the Society of Christian Ethics. Among her writings is *Body, Sex, and Pleasure: Reconstructing Christian Ethics.*

HSIAO-LAN HU is a PhD candidate at the Religion Department at Temple University. She is an adjunct instructor for the Religion Department, the Women's Studies Program, and the Asian Studies Program at Temple University.

GRACE M. JANTZEN, deceased, was affiliated with Centre for Religion, Culture, and Gender, Department of Religions and Theology, University of Manchester, United Kingdom.

REGINA SOARES JURKEWICZ, a co-author in this volume with Maria José Rosado-Nunes, has done major research in Latin America on issues of concern to this project, including studies on the sexual abuse of women by priests in Brazil.

DAVID R. LOY is Besl Family Professor of Ethics, Religion, and Society at Xavier University in Cincinnati, Ohio. His field of specialization is Buddhist and comparative philosophy. A Zen practitioner for many years, he is qualified as a teacher in the Sambo Kyodan lineage. He is the author of *A Buddhist History of the West: Studies in Lack.*

DANIEL C. MAGUIRE is professor of ethics at Marquette University and president of the Religious Consultation on Population, Reproductive Health, and Ethics, the organization sponsoring this project. Among his writings is *Sacred Choices: The Right to Contraception and Abortion in Ten World Religions.*

MUTOMBO NKULU-N'SENGHA currently teaches in the Department of Religion at California State University Northridge. He grew up in the Democratic Republic of the Congo. He studied philosophy and theology in Lubumbashi and Kinshasa (Congo), the Jesuit Gregorian University in Rome, and Temple University.

VEENA TALWAR OLDENBURG is professor of history at the Graduate Center and Baruch College, City University of New York, with a specialty in British colonial history and women's history in India. She has authored several scholarly books and articles, including *Dowry Murder: The Imperial Origins of a Cultural Crime.*

OUYPORN KHUANKAEW is a Buddhist feminist activist working on the issue of women, gender, and peace building. She is a founder and director of the International Women's Partnership for Peace and Justice (IWP), which trains women leaders in South and Southeast Asian communities based on the framework of feminism, spirituality, and nonviolence for social change.

JOHN RAINES is professor of religion at Temple University as well as senior advisor for the Center for Religious and Cross-Cultural Studies at Gadjah Mada University in Yogyakarta, Indonesia. His writings include *What Men Owe to Women: Men's Voices from World Religions* (co-authored with Daniel C. Maguire).

MARIA JOSÉ ROSADO-NUNES is professor of sociology of religion at the Catholic University of São Paulo. She is also a senior research associate of the National Council of Scientific and Technological Development. She investigates the situation of women in the Catholic Church in Brazil as well as the relationship between the gender-religion linkage and reproductive rights.

SA'DIYYA SHAIKH is a lecturer in the Department of Religious Studies at the University of Cape Town, South Africa. Working at the intersection of Islamic Studies and Gender Studies, she has a special interest in Sufism and its implications for Islamic feminism and feminist theory. Currently she is also initiating a research project that focuses on sexuality, marriage, HIV/Aids and reproductive choices among South African Muslim women. She is a member of the interfaith feminist organization "The Circle of Concerned African Women Theologians" and the faith-based organization "Positive Muslims," which works on raising awareness regarding HIV/Aids.

ARVIND SHARMA is the Birks Professor of Comparative Religion in the Faculty of Religious Studies at McGill University in Montreal, Canada. He has published more than seventy-five books and is currently engaged in promoting the adoption of Universal Declaration of Human Rights by the World's Religions.

Introduction The Religiously Induced Illness of Women's Subordination and Its Cure

DANIEL C. MAGUIRE

The *Oxford Dictionary of World Religions* states it bluntly: "The subordination of women to men became widespread in all religions."[1] This subordination is the primal violence from which other forms of antiwoman violence are spawned. The *Oxford Dictionary*'s "all religions" has suggested to some that religion is by its nature sexist and invariably the underwriter of the abuse of women. That overstates the case, as the authors of this volume demonstrate, but it is searingly true that the world's religions contain some easily diagnosed— and some not so easily diagnosed—inducements to violence against women. Those judged inferior are more liable to abuse and, when their "inferiority" is numenally blessed, the prejudice sinks deep, well-fed roots.

This book puts world religions on the stand as defendants and then, by a kind of homeopathic medicine, the authors show how those same religions contain the cures for the misogyny they have caused and abetted. Religiously nourished illnesses require religious cures. There is nothing that so enlivens the will as the tincture of the sacred. Religiously grounded prejudice is most lethal. The poet Alexander Pope said that the worst of madmen is a saint gone mad. John Henry Cardinal Newman wrote that people will die for dogma who will not stir for a conclusion. Both the poet and the cardinal made the same point: religion is uniquely powerful and not to address it when it is at the core of a problem is analytically and sociologically naive.

---

1. John Bowker, ed., *The Oxford Dictionary of World Religions* (New York: Oxford University Press, 1997), 1041.

Blunt accusations against religions are unpalatable to many, but until the guilt of religions is known and accepted, these symbolic powerhouses will be more of a problem than a solution to the panhuman suffering of girls and women. The world religions, those that are theistic and those that are not, are flawed classics and sometimes it is their flaws that thrive and become most influential. The constructive moral revolutions they house get lost in the swirl and morass of history. Nothing is more anti-dotal to religious prejudice than the recovery of the ideals and sense of justice that gave those religions birth. The authors in this book mine the lost moral treasures in their traditions and marshal them against the violence of sexism. Calling people before the bar of their professed ideals is jolting and eye-opening. There are renewable moral energies in all these religious classics, and the scholars of this volume seek them out and apply them to the healing of women and of men—and to the healing of the religions themselves.

There are many advantages to approaching this problem in a collaborative way, as this volume does, with scholars from Hinduism, Buddhism, Taoism, Confucianism, Judaism, Protestant and Catholic Christianity, Islam, and native indigenous religions. Facing together faults that all share dismantles tenured defenses and dissolves some barriers to hard analysis. Ecumenical dialogue too often suffers from overweening politeness, as though ecumenism requires the fudging of criticism of one's own religious tradition and, more certainly, criticism of other religions. True dialogue can break your heart, but the pain is prelude to the delight of growing in truth.

Thanks to a grant to the Religious Consultation on Population, Reproductive Health, and Ethics from the Windhover Foundation, we recruited scholars from around the world and, over a two-year period, brought them together twice for four days of vigorous and honest sessions. This kind of collegium-building could not occur by e-mail, fax, and telephone, though we also used all of these communication modes. Candor grows in face-to-face sessions like these, and mutual critiquing improves and becomes more effective.

REMOVING BLINDERS

As someone trained as a Catholic theologian at the Pontifical Gregorian University in Rome, I was baptized by immersion in many of the classical treasures of the Christian West. This was a gift. However, I was also equipped with blinders that all religions impose on their devotees. Somehow I was able to ignore embarrassments and skip around land mines in the Catholic tradition. Love is blind not just in romance but also in the study of one's religion, and this is common to all religions.

I visited the Dachau camp ten years after World War II. I was keenly aware of the Nazi crimes but not sensitive to Catholic complicity. I attended Mass in the lovely church in the village of Dachau, some eighteen kilometers from the camp and within earshot of the railroad. Mass was celebrated there all during the war thanks to a Concordat between the Vatican and Nazi Germany. Pope Pius XII felt this necessary to keep the sacraments, the media of salvation, operative. He was not unaware of Nazi atrocities but felt this compromise necessary to keep Catholic liturgy alive. Only later did I acknowledge—with belated pain—that there were times during that war when the smoke of incense from the Catholic altar rose in the sky and commingled in unholy union with the smoke of the murdered dead. None could call those liturgies worship. Later yet I realized that there are areas in Latin America and elsewhere where there are no Catholic liturgies because there are no Catholic priests. Women and married men in those areas are prepared and ready for ordination but the Vatican will not accept them due to its celibacy requirement. Thus the Holocaust could be tolerated to keep liturgy going but the sacramental system can be shut down sooner than allow a woman or a man married to one to celebrate Mass. The implications of that are stark. All this illustrates the art of strategic blindness skillfully practiced by nations and religions.

For a long time, I was able to avoid moral shock that my beloved Thomas Aquinas joined Aristotle in teaching that women were a biological mistake. In the process of generation, these men averred, nature intended male perfection but obviously that does not always happen—there are women. This is due to accidents in the conception process. Thus a woman is *aliquid deficiens et occasionatum*, as Thomas put it, something deficient and misbegotten.[2] Thomas followed through on this. He taught that children and even the insane could be validly ordained as priests—as long as they were male—but adult and healthy women could not be![3]

DESCRIPTION VERSUS PRESCRIPTION

It is the role of religious scholars to identify the noxious debris that has accumulated in the passage of time. The narratives, myths, and scriptures of the religions never filter out all the accrued errors. Therefore, religious scholarship proceeds most effectively by looking for the mistakes and

2. Thomas Aquinas, *Summa Theologiae*, I q. 92, a.1, ad 1.q. 99, a.2, ad 2.
3. Thomas Aquinas, *Summa Theologiae*, Supplementum, q. 39, a.2.

then finding correctives, when possible, right within the same tradition. This is illustrated in Christian scriptures by the contrast between two epistles: Ephesians and Galatians. The Epistle to the Ephesians tells women: "Be subject to your husbands as you are to the Lord. For the husband is the head of the wife just as Christ is the head of the church . . . wives ought to be [subject], in everything, to their husbands" (Eph. 5:22–24). Much in the literature of religions is *descriptive* of the way things were, not *prescriptive* of the way things ought to be. Ephesians' instructions on the servile status of women accurately described the customs and gender injustice of that day. The value of scriptures is in their prescriptive breakthroughs, which represent a correction of the status quo. Thus, in Galatians 3:28, the announcement is made that in the new and revolutionary perspectives of the Jesus movement all hostile divisions between male and female, slave and free, Greek and Jew are washed away. There is no longer any need to be "enslaved to the elemental spirits" of the time (Gal. 4:3). It is these *creative discontinuities* that are the main targets of creative religious scholarship.[4]

The Buddhist saying that all belief systems are illnesses in need of a cure may overstate the case but it has a point. Religions that cannot admit and work to correct their lethal errors and flawed heroes do not deserve to survive.

The authors of this volume do not shy from this challenge.

Christine Gudorf, a Catholic theologian and world religionist, shows how the history of the religious assault on women takes us back to the fringes of prehistory where a multifaceted patriarchy prevailed. Thus "even the oldest of the contemporary world religions" arrived in a world where patriarchal controls were already in place, often "legitimated by prior religious traditions now extinct." Gudorf notes that the control of women was justified as protection "from supposedly incurably violent and sexually predatory males," the irony being that this "protection" made women "the economic and social dependents of these same males."

Grace Jantzen of the University of Manchester in England, writing as a Christian theologian, calls it all too "obvious" that "the texts and traditions used to justify or condone violence against women be dismantled one by one and liberatory alternatives explored." This, however, she says, is not enough. Some of the basic "conceptual foundations of traditional Christian thought" need radical surgery, alteration, or rejection. She cites

---

4. For a method for reading sacred texts, see Daniel C. Maguire, *The Moral Core of Judaism and Christianity* (Minneapolis: Fortress Press, 1993), 58–84; Daniel C. Maguire, *A Moral Creed for All Christians* (Minneapolis: Fortress Press, 2005), 22–26.

covenant, theories of atonement through bloody sacrifice, and the substitutional birthing through baptism as among some of the doctrines requiring revision. In the spirit of this volume she points to neglected themes and symbols in the biblical tradition as curative alternatives needing development.

David Loy, a Buddhist, who has been teaching at Bunkyo University in Japan, challenges the common interpretation of karma, especially as related to women. Loy sees Buddhism as "not what the Buddha taught, but what he started." He notes that the Buddha encouraged "intelligent, probing doubt," meaning that "we should not believe in something until we have established its truth for ourselves." Thus the common and literal understanding of rebirth dependent on karma needs critical attention and that is what he gives it. This too-common understanding makes karma teaching a kind of "moral determinism," used, for example, to tell sex workers that their ignoble calling is due to bad karma from a past life. This obviously paralyzes social reform. Better and revolutionary readings of the Buddha's insight can be had, and Loy offers them here.

Sa'diyya Shaikh, a Muslim theologian at the University of Cape Town, is among the pioneers doing reinterpretations of the Qur'an and Muslim traditions through the lens of women's experience. She addresses the problem of "an intellectual legacy formulated in the context of premodern gender norms" that entrenched in much of Islam "a stagnant, ahistorical perspective of gender born from patriarchal readings of the text." She proposes "an active engagement with Islamic gender ethics as a living, dynamic, and contextually unfolding phenomenon." In this heartening view, Islam is not to be seen as "a handmaiden of patriarchy," since faithful "Qur'anic exegesis is woven intricately with ever-expanding human conceptions of justice and equality that sculpt the living, emerging, social texts of Islam." She treats "women's experiences as a conceptual category to redress the historical gender imbalance."

John Raines of Temple University writes that religions are gendered entities, although often presenting themselves as something simply natural or God-ordained and therefore universally true. The gendering of many religions is oppressively male. The creator in Genesis is presented as a "Sovereign Outsider" who relates to the world by way of command. "It is a male story of power, a story of hierarchical command and control" affecting the Abrahamic religions of Judaism, Christianity, and Islam. Without romanticizing any one religion, gentler models, such as those found in some streams of Taoism, can be corrective, as can a return to more promising symbols in the Abrahamic religions themselves. Raines cites the tendency in religions to caricature women's sexuality and to blame them for everything including our mortality, since they give birth to a life destined to die.

Hsiao-Lan Hu, in studying the Chinese religions, shows how all religious and cultural symbols can be abused, with women as losers. "Philosophical Taoism's elevation of the feminine will not help much as long as women are considered the embodiment of the *yin* force" and are then expected to be servile, accepting, and subject to violence if they do not comply with this caricature. The best Taoist contribution, she argues, lies in "its dynamic understanding of seeming opposites." This can be a solvent for the hostilities implicit in rigid dimorphism, which casts male and female into competitive opposition. Hsiao-Lan Hu shows the Chinese culture is in fact four teachings in one, including Taoism, Confucianism, Buddhism, and the Legalist tradition, a fact often not understood by Western commentators. She also illuminates the ambiguity of the word "religion" as we move from culture to culture.[5]

Mutombo Nkulu-N'Sengha looks at the indigenous African religions and finds there the ubiquitous problem of violence against women braced by religion and various "patriarchal cultural plagues." He focuses on the much discussed problem of female genital excision, noting that "excision has survived and even gained momentum despite more than one hundred years of war to outlaw it." Well-intentioned Western commentators often see it as simply a matter of male control of women. It is more complex than that and, until the full and depressing panoply of causes entrenched in African culture is faced, this devastating practice will not be rooted

---

5. The term "religion" is not univocal and indeed is not tidily mirrored in many other languages. Chinese scholars say there is no word in the Chinese languages that perfectly parallels the common usage in English. In the world of ancient Israel, as Morton Smith writes, there was no "general term for religion"; "philosophy of life" would come closer to its understanding. (Morton Smith, "Palestinian Judaism in the First Century," in *Israel: Its Role in Civilization* [New York: Jewish Theological Seminary of America, 1956] 67–81.) The Religious Consultation on Population, Reproductive Health and Ethics has worked with the idea of religion as a response to the sacred, whether that sacred is theistically or nontheistically explicated. (Cf. Daniel C. Maguire, "Introduction," *Visions of a New Earth: Religious Perspectives on Population, Consumption, and Ecology,* ed. Harold Coward and Daniel C. Maguire [Albany: State University of New York Press, 2000], 1–7). As Hsiao-Lan Hu writes in footnote 5 in chapter 6:

> Traditionally Chinese people did not have exact equivalents for 'religious' or 'sacred.' They honored some teachings and schools of thoughts and saw them as grasping, to some extent, the operating principle of the universe that should also be guiding human behaviors (i.e. the Tao/Dao). None of these teachings, however, was taken as a self-contained 'religion' with monopoly of truth. In this line of thinking and conceptualizing, Confucianism and Legalism, though lacking apparent 'religious' elements, were put in the same category as Taoism and Buddhism, which bear elements that would be more readily recognized as 'religious' by Westerners.

out. Professor Nkulu-N'Sengha goes on to demonstrate that excision is actually opposed by many of the central ideas of native African religions. Many of those ideas are corrective not just of mutilation of women but are also instructive for Western society's biases against women.

Veena Talwar Oldenburg, author of *Dowry Murder: The Imperial Origins of a Cultural Crime* (Oxford University Press, 2002), explicates how in Hinduism—in ways that parallel attitudes in Buddhism, Judaism, Christianity, Islam, and other religions—"female sexuality is seen as dangerous, fickle, polluting, and potent, even emasculating, and in strong need of male control." Religion reveals a perverse virtuosity in its assault on women. Often it stimulates violence, and at other times it is employed as an effective cover-up. Professor Oldenburg looks at "the bewilderingly vast set of ideas, beliefs, philosophies, epics, and legal and social treatises that constitute the Hindu canon" and chooses the epic *Ramayana* story because of how pervasive it has been and still is in Indian culture. Indeed the ancient myths still play out in modern film and media, and Professor Oldenburg does redemptive surgery on many of their perversely enduring messages.

Ouyporn Khuankaew is a Buddhist educator and practitioner living in Thailand. She conducts workshops and retreats for Buddhist women in South and Southeastern Asia, in Thailand, Cambodia, Burma, India, Nepal, Bhutan, and Tibet. Her broad experience shows how culturally ensconced male dominance has perverted Buddhist teaching, particularly around the notion of karma. Buddhism is often romantically viewed as the gentlest of religions, and it is true that it is not conducive to crusades or jihads, but its teachings can be used and are used to torture women in cruel ways that rob them of their spirit and hope. Ouyporn Khuankaew counters all of this in her work and her writing with the traditional teachings of the Four Noble Truths and the Eightfold Noble Path, giving these traditional teachings a new and healing meaning for women.

Liora Gubkin sheds antiseptic light on a subject that has enjoyed undue immunity, domestic violence in the American Jewish community. Citing the fact that one out of every three U.S. women reports being physically or sexually abused by a husband or boyfriend at some point in her life, she shows that Judaism is no protection from this horror, in spite of widespread belief—even among Jews—that this is not the case. She recognizes that not all abusers are men but that men are the main abusers and she concentrates on the suffering of women. She has researched the number of helpful ways that the Jewish community is finally and forcefully reacting to this situation in promoting education and training to help abused women and girls, and she explores some of the biblical texts used to justify violence against women.

Maria Jose Rosado-Nunes, professor at the Pontifical Catholic University of São Paulo, Brazil, reports on sexual violence in the Catholic Church, citing studies from twenty-three countries. Joining professor Rosado-Nunes is Regina Soares Jurkewicz, who has conducted research on the sexual abuse of women by priests in Brazil. The authors document the extent of this abuse and the cynical care taken by Catholic authorities to cover up this criminal violence. Frequently the women are blamed for the sexual assaults of priests. The authors argue that forced celibacy is a failed experiment and an invitation to pathology. Many communities do not believe this and so cooperate in persecuting these victimized women. The authors show that the tragic Brazilian experience is illustrative of problems in other countries also, including the United States. They find their slim hope only in the fact of ongoing exposure.

Throughout this volume, the authors do not want merely to deal with problem texts and obviously damaging practices in the world's religions. They go two steps beyond that, first by questioning some of the sacrosanct fundamentals of these belief systems, and then by reaching into these traditions for antidotal medicine. The world's religions are classical, though flawed, efforts to develop in humanity the essential art of cherishing. The respect they deserve is candid criticism and then a retrieval and application of their neglected moral energies and healing powers. That is the mission of the authors of this volume.

1

Violence against Women in World Religions

CHRISTINE E. GUDORF

A great deal has been written on the subject of violence against women in one world religious tradition after another. This literature focuses on various kinds of violence, from physical violence, such as wife beating, through sexual violence, including marital rape and sexual harassment, even to violence called "structural," inflicted on girls and women by the placement of religiously legitimated limits on their freedom, activities, and ambitions—limitations that stunt the self-image of girls and women. Most of the critical literature on violence against women in religions is done from an extrareligious perspective, but some of it has been authored not only by members of the religion in question, but even by religious *authorities* within the religion, as in the case of the Assembly of Quebec [Catholic] Bishops in Canada, who wrote the excellent treatise, *A Heritage of Violence? A Pastoral Reflection on Conjugal Violence,* in 1989.[1]

As the chapters of this book show, religions have blessed and legitimated various forms of violence perpetrated on women. Yet it would be a mistake for women to simply write off religions as antifemale, as an artifact from the distant past that has outlasted whatever social utility it once had. As the chapters of this book also show, many millions of women across many religions have relied and still rely on their religious faith and practice, not only to survive the violence aimed at them as women, but also

---

1. Social Affairs Committee of the Assembly of Quebec Bishops, *A Heritage of Violence? A Pastoral Reflection on Conjugal Violence,* trans. Antoinette Kinlough (Montreal: L'Assemblee des eveques du Quebec, 1989).

as the source of hope and power that helps them resist that violence and to continue their struggle to eradicate such violence from the lives of their daughters and granddaughters.[2] Religious traditions are multifaceted, and include both liberating and oppressive elements.

It is not difficult to list the most common forms of violence against women legitimated in world religions. They would be:

1. Marital rape and/or enforced pregnancy. Many traditions—Christianity, Hinduism, and Islam, but not Judaism, Bahai, or a number of local religions—have understood a, if not the, primary purpose of women as reproduction,[3] and marriage as conferring control of women's bodies—or at least their sexual bodies, as in Islam[4]—to husbands. While this understanding has begun to change in some traditions, religions have not disavowed past teachings or laws that embody this understanding.

2. Wife beating. In many traditions, male headship of the family is assumed, if not demanded, and that headship includes the right of husbands to discipline wives as well as children, using corporal punish-

---

2. Examples abound across a huge range. It is sometimes difficult to draw the line between, for example, women mystics and meditators whose personal experiences of divine communion sustain and even nourish them within oppressive religious institutions, as in the case of the nun and Beguine mystics Dorothee Soelle describes in *The Silent Cry: Mysticism and Resistance* (Minneapolis: Fortress, 2001), and women who have been so cowed and stunted by religious authorities that they cannot leave even the most oppressive religious institution, as with the lifelong Magdalens in Frances Finnegan's *Do Penance or Perish: Magdalen Asylums in Ireland* (New York: Oxford University Press, 2004).

3. In Hinduism, reproduction is not the principal purpose of women—that honor goes to serving her husband—but reproduction, particularly of sons, clearly stands in second place, especially as it is a central part of serving the husband (Anantanand Rambachan, "A Hindu Perspective," in John C. Raines and Daniel C. Maguire, *What Men Owe to Women: Men's Voices from World Religions* [Albany: SUNY Press, 2001], 21). In Christian theology, women's nature is understood as determined by her reproductive purpose (Rosemary Ruether, "Virginal Feminism in the Fathers of the Church," and Eleanor Como McLaughlin, "Equality of Souls, Inequality of Sexes: Women in Medieval Theology," both in Rosemary R. Ruether, ed., *Religion and Sexism: Images of Women in the Jewish and Christian Traditions* [New York: Simon and Schuster, 1974]). In Islam, the situation is more complicated, in that while the Qur'an includes many more treatments of women as made from the same substance as men, equal to men and called to the same religious duty, it also has some verses that refer to women as sexual property of men, and the legal interpretations of women's role have focused on subordination, reproduction, and seclusion (Ayesha M. Imam, "The Muslim Religious Right and Sexuality," and Pinar Ilkkaracan, "Islam and Women's Sexuality: A Research Report From Turkey," in Patricia B. Jung, Mary E. Hunt, and Radhika Balakrishnan, eds., *Good Sex: Feminist Perspectives from the World's Religions* [New Brunswick, N.J.: Rutgers University Press, 2001]; Ziba Mir Hosseini, "The Construction of Gender in Islamic Legal Thought and Strategies for Reform," Hawwa: *Journal of Women in the Middle East and the Islamic World* 1.1[2003]: 1–28).

4. Mir Hosseini, "Construction of Gender," 7.

ment among other types of discipline. These traditions have come under fire in late modernity, with various Muslim, Christian, Hindu, and Buddhist religious authorities attempting to reinterpret sacred texts, but the practice is still legitimated by other authorities.

3. Limitations on, or exclusion from, property ownership. Many religions have legitimated unequal inheritance rights for daughters vis-à-vis sons, and some have excluded women from ownership of land. In many parts of the developing world, women who had had land tenure and/or inheritance rights lost them under colonial Christian administrators.

4. Sexual harassment and/or the restriction of women to domestic space. Many religions in the past, and still parts of a number of religious traditions today, have defined the nature of men as requiring that women either be victims of harassment (even including sexual violence) or be restricted to the domestic sphere for their own protection. "Protective" restrictions include the extreme of purdah, in which women must be fully covered and escorted by a male relative in order to leave the home for any purpose, which almost always rules out employment in the public sphere altogether. Thus women are, for their own "protection" from supposedly incurably violent and sexually predatory males, made the economic and social dependents of these same males. It should be, then, no wonder that around the world more women are raped and beaten in their own homes by their "protectors" than anywhere else.

5. Religious exclusion. Within religions themselves, women have been largely excluded from both positions of leadership and access to religious knowledge. Until the last century and a half, all the Abrahamic religions excluded women from leadership and usually from scholarship. Though some versions of Hinduism (e.g., in Bali) still have women among the holy elites who preside at celebrations, those women were generally only consorts, not independent leaders. In Buddhism some nations still retain female *sangha*; some have never had female *sangha*. Due to the eight heavy rules imposed on female members of the *sangha*, the status, and usually the education, of nuns has been inferior to that of monks.

These exclusions have enabled male leaders and scholars of religions to manipulate the rules and interpret the texts in myriad ways that victimize women. As women in the last decades gained access to religious scholarship (often over the objections of male religious authorities), they have pointed out in tradition after tradition the selective and inconsistent interpretation of sacred texts by male scholarly elites, noting that such biased interpretations could never have been promulgated had women been included among the learned.

6. Spiritual inferiority. As if it were not enough that women have been excluded from all decision making and interpretation within most world religions, women have usually been interpreted in religious thought as inferior to men in important ways, usually ways crucial to holiness, thus casting doubt on women's ability to be saved. In Brahmanic Hinduism, for example, a woman's salvation—her ability to reach *moksha*—is tied to her role as a wife to her husband. This is why widows are not to remarry, and why the custom of *sati* could develop as it did.[5] Most religions include some statement from an authoritative, venerated figure that echoes the conclusion of Augustine on why women but not men are to cover their heads: "the woman, together with her own husband, is the image of God, so that the whole substance may be one image, but when she is referred to separately in her quality as helpmeet, which regards the woman alone, then she is not the image of God, but as regards the man alone, he is the image of God as fully and completely as when the woman is joined with him in one."[6] A divine view that holds females in lower esteem than males not only encourages women to accept violence, but also fails to impede those inclined to violence against women. In many traditions women are not only excluded from leadership and scholarship, but are also not allowed to attend or are strongly discouraged from attending public ritual, for the purported reasons of either protecting female modesty or fulfilling domestic duties—and then their absence from public ritual, scholarship, and leadership are proposed as evidence for women's lesser holiness!

FACTORS SUPPORTING VIOLENCE AGAINST WOMEN

Obviously, a variety of factors has influenced support for violence against women in religions. It is important to note that these factors do not, for the most part, originate directly in humanity's impulse to religiosity, though religion has often had an important role in legitimizing and sustaining various factors supporting violence against women. Patriarchy preceded the origins of even the oldest of the contemporary world religions, so that contemporary religions came into being in cultures already

---

5. Rambachan, "A Hindu Perspective," 22; James Freeman, "The Ladies of Lord Krishna: Rituals of Middle Aged Women in Eastern India," in Nancy Falk and Rita M. Gross, *Unspoken Worlds: Women's Religious Lives* (Belmont, Calif.: Wadsworth, 1989); Veena Talwar Oldenburg, *Dowry Murder: The Imperial Origins of a Cultural Crime* (New York: Oxford, 2002), 179–80.
6. Augustine, *De Trinitate*, 7.7, 10.

imbued with patriarchy, a patriarchy that had often been legitimated by prior religious traditions now extinct. Not only did contemporary religions "inherit" a patriarchy that included tolerance for violence against women, but religion also tends to be conservative, in that it passes on, both orally and in texts, accounts of divine activity in the historical world. Those accounts are always socially and culturally situated. Religion's role of preserving revelation, mixed as it is with its historical and cultural context, and the difficulty of distinguishing revelation from context, together incline religion to conserve the cultural context along with the revelation, though this tendency is not absolute.

As mentioned above, there has been a clear universal historical tendency to exclude women from access to religious texts by excluding them from the clerical/monastic roles that required textual expertise, by excluding them from roles as scholars who interpret the texts, and/or by excluding them from roles as judges who apply the texts in given social situations. These denials of religious roles to women have left women without a voice in reading, interpreting, and applying sacred texts. Women have been largely defenseless within religion, and violence against women in religions seems to be closely linked to this powerlessness of women within the traditions, though the movement of women into religious leadership today, as in the movement of women into all manner of secular leadership today, has itself been accused of provoking violence. It is frequently pointed out by critics in other nations that the United States, which is often pointed to as the most egalitarian of societies, also has the world's highest level of violence—of rape and murder, as well as assault—against women. In the last three decades, conservative political currents in the United States have been attempting to check, or even reverse, decades of earlier advances in women's rights not only in sexuality, but in religion (e.g., ordination) as well. These conservative currents are closely tied to the history of Christian religious fundamentalism in the United States, which rejected nineteenth-century Victorian domesticity and the elevation of the home, presided over by women, to "near sacramental status in mainline Christian denominations," and instead touted Christ as the "most manly of men," the Bible as "virile literature."[7] Historian of the American family Margaret Lamberts Bendroth writes that the shift of Christian conservatives from fundamentalism to the profamily neo-evangelical movement contains a number of historical

---

7. Margaret Lamberts Bendroth, "Fundamentalism and the Family: Gender, Culture, and the American Pro-Family Movement," in Betsy Reed, ed., *Nothing Sacred: Women Respond to Fundamentalism and Terror* (New York: Nation's Books, 2002), 263.

contradictions, but that "a dedicated group of neo-evangelical leaders discovered that family matters resonated with churchgoers, providing clear lines between the godly and the unrighteous. Such issues allowed preachers to invoke personal and social morality; and they laid down moral boundaries that differentiated believers from nonbelievers, without rendering religion socially irrelevant. Opposing abortion, divorce, homosexuality, or teenage pregnancy permitted evangelical leaders to evoke a separatist, fundamentalist past and speak a prophetic word to present-day American culture."[8] By the late seventies and early eighties, this movement saw itself as the only bulwark against the "post-Christian" spirit of the age, signified most deeply in the feminist movement, and saw abortion as the boundary issue.[9]

According to a number of Muslim feminist scholars, there have been recent increases in public violence against women in a number of Muslim majority nations, especially increases in gang rapes and honor killings, as well as religious fundamentalist attempts to retain women in domestic realms under the control of men. A number of Middle Eastern nations as well as Pakistan[10] have experienced a resurgence of honor killings. In recent years, rapes have risen exponentially in Pakistan, and one in four of these are gang rapes, aimed at women who move outside the home. Such violent acts have at their roots religious and familial disquiet over rising rates of secondary education for girls, which requires unmarried young women past adolescence to travel in public.[11] In Muslim cultures in which puberty traditionally signaled the need to arrange daughters' marriages to avoid risk of sexual impurity, the postponement of marriage by a decade or more to make room for education, and the fact that education for women necessarily takes girls and young women out of their homes, creates totally new public and domestic living arrangements.[12]

Critics of Hindu fundamentalism have pointed out that in the February 2002 massacre of Muslims in Gujarat, women were singled out for especially horrible treatment among the more than two thousand dead and the hundred thousand left homeless.[13] In an editorial in *Hindu*, India's

---

8. Ibid., 272–73.
9. Ibid., 272.
10. See the two half-hour *Nightline* tapes with Riffat Hassan on honor killings in Pakistan.
11. Anita M. Weiss, "The Slow yet Steady Path to Women's Empowerment in Pakistan," in Yvonne Haddad and John Esposito, eds., *Islam, Gender, and Social Change* (New York: New York University, 1997), 124–43; and Fatima Mernissi, "Muslim Women and Fundamentalism," in Reed, *Nothing Sacred*, 141–48.
12. Mernissi, "Muslim Women,"145–46.
13. Ruth Baldwin, "Gujarat's Gendered Violence," in Reed, *Nothing Sacred*, 186.

national daily newspaper, Raka Roy, sociologist at Berkeley, argued that the root of such treatment was that the creation "'of the inferior Other in India begins with the divisive caste system that has allowed the principle of inequality to become embedded in Hindu culture, continuing the belief that women are not only inferior, but also that women's sexuality has to be patrolled so that it is legitimately accessible to some men and inaccessible to others.'[14] If a woman's body belongs not to herself, but to her community, then the violation of that body signifies an attack upon the honor (*izzat*) of the whole community. Hindu nationalist fundamentalists raped and burned minority women to destroy not only their bodies, but also the integrity and identity of Muslim society."[15]

Thus in some places (India) public, religiously validated, physical violence against women of other communities is based on inherited views of women as representatives of their owners, the men of the community; in other places (the United States) women are victims not only of high rates of domestic and sexual violence by intimates, but also of political, legal violence that is a backlash against (secular) modernity by religious groups who see themselves as the only hope for preserving religious culture; and in yet others (Muslim) women are victims of both physical and legal/political violence, based on both inherited views of women as inferior and reified, and on the backlash against secular modernity that opens new roles for women.

Such analysis only pushes us to another level of questioning concerning the motivations for violence against women. Why is it that [male-dominated] society and religion have sought to assign inferior status to women and use violence to enforce that status? While a brief answer to this question is not difficult—fear of difference is a common global cause of violence, much less discrimination—the question calls for further explanations, and there are many, some complementary, and some conflicting. Here we will assume that we can dismiss those theories that maintain that the inferiority of women is real, not imagined, and that male possession and control of women is appropriate. However, differences of all kinds have created tensions and conflict in history—racial, ethnic, linguistic, class, religious, and sexual differences, to name just the major ones. Difference spawns theories of difference, and theories of difference are weighted, for the most part, in terms of the interests of the more powerful group, able to establish ideological supremacy over the weaker groups.

---

14. Raka Roy, as quoted in Baldwin, "Gujarat's Gendered Violence," 186.
15. Baldwin, "Gujarat's Gendered Violence, 186–87.

Until very recently in human history, reproduction has been a front and center concern of virtually every human society. Plagues, famines, and wars wiped out ten to more than thirty percent of local populations at least every century or two for millennia.[16] Death rates remained high even apart from these disasters, especially for infants and children. In most societies, only a quarter to a half of live births survived to reproduce, which meant that those who did needed to reproduce in large numbers if societies were to recover from the periodic disasters.[17] Societies thus tended to be very focused upon reproduction, and this focus tended to emphasize sexual difference and to suggest sexually differentiated roles.

But sexual difference is almost certainly not the only source of inequality and violence toward women. Several theories can support inequality and even violence toward women. Freudian psychological theories continue Aristotelian theories of women as defective men (compare to female penis envy in Freud's work). Conservative sociobiological theories understand men and women as necessarily employing different reproductive strategies to maximize the survival and spread of their genetic heritage, based on their different biologies. Since the birth of a single offspring usually accounts for a year or more of a woman's reproductive life, while it may account for less than a day's investment of time and effort for a man, men can use a strategy of spreading their seed as widely as possible, with little attention to nurture or protection, while women try to ensure that their much smaller number of offspring are given every advantage, so that they will all survive and thrive. Female subordination, including sexual subordination, to men is thus viewed as strategically aimed at keeping males present and involved in protection and care for

---

16. While we might think of the thirteenth century bubonic plague in Europe in this regard, it by no means stands alone. In modernity we can point to the 1918–1919 worldwide influenza epidemic, which killed close to fifty million persons, or the current HIV/AIDS pandemic, which continues to kill millions and is depopulating much of Africa. There is great fear at the present moment that deadly avian flu, which has now spread from birds to humans, may soon mutate again to become transmittable from human to human.

17. Ryan Johansson gives the example, for instance of the average woman in early modern colonial America, who had 13 pregnancies, 8 live births, 5 children who survived infancy, and 2–3 who lived to adulthood. These statistics are surely more favorable than in many parts of the world, because the persistent labor shortage in the colonies kept employment rates and wages relatively high, so that starvation and malnutrition were much rarer than in many other parts of the world. (S. Ryan Johansson, "The Moral Imperatives of Christian Marriage: Their Biological, Economic and Demographic Implications in Changing Historical Contexts," in John Coleman, S.J., ed., *One Hundred Years of Catholic Social Teaching* [Maryknoll, N.Y.: Orbis Books, 1991]).

women's offspring, thus maximizing their survival chances.[18] Such theories have been well popularized.

One theory concerning male violence against women, distinct from sociobiology and yet related to it in that it links biology to sexual behavior, is based on medical research over the last decades. It is well known that aggression in both males and females is strongly correlated to testosterone levels. Levels of aggression can be raised or lowered by changing the level of testosterone. Physical violence is the extreme form of aggression, and thus the fact that testosterone levels are normally much higher in men than in women can be used to explain much higher levels of violence in men than in women. Such a theory does not necessarily require motivation: men will be more inclined to use violence to attain their ends because they are more aggressive, and some of those ends will involve women. The vast majority of male aggression, even violence, is aimed at other men, not women. If one accepts this explanation, then the remaining question becomes why religions have chosen to turn a blind eye to domestic violence by men against women, sometimes even justifying it, while going to great lengths to develop rules (such as "just war" theories) restricting and channeling male violence against other men both within and between civil societies.

In an interview, Robert Bly cites two roots for male violence against women, which pertain to male violence per se.[19] The first is historical conditioning, beginning four hundred thousand years ago with male hunting and killing of animals, and then extending, once food surpluses were established, into raiding others' food stores and defending one's own. The use of violence was, in effect, a major part of the role assigned to males. The second root is a different kind of cultural conditioning still common today, in which men are not allowed to express emotion. Relationships with women are the most common place for emotionally repressed men to express emotion. But repressed negative emotions, often from other areas of men's lives, often explode within the sexual/domestic space with

---

18. Sociobiology extends over a wide range and includes early works such as Desmond Morris's *The Naked Ape* (New York: Random House, 1967) through Edward O. Wilson's *On Human Nature* (Cambridge: Harvard University Press, 1978) and many more. The most common treatment of sexual difference focuses on differences in sexual behavior: that men's best strategy for their DNA to survive and spread is to sow as much seed in as many women as possible, which they have been biologically programmed to do, while women's best strategy is to see that her necessarily more limited number of offspring survive to reproduce, to which end she uses her sexuality to attract and keep the help of a male partner.
19. Interview with Robert Bly, "No Safe Place: Violence against Women," March 27, 1998, http://www.pbs.org/kued/nosafeplace/interv/bly.html.

women as targets, and become difficult to control. Bly's programs encourage men to regularly, even ritually, express emotions with other men, especially anger, and condition themselves not to take that anger home, in order to learn how to express emotions in a more controlled way and directed at the appropriate persons.

Another contemporary psychological theory from Dorothy Dinnerstein locates male possessiveness of women, which sometimes leads to violent behaviors including stalking, harassment, rape, wife-beating, or even murder, in the desire of men to recapture the bliss of fetal and infant life, which was grounded in the experience of the child's unity with the female (maternal) body which supplied all its needs.[20] The desire to recapture that early bliss, she says, takes a different form in women, who identify with the maternal figure and seek to *be* the body desired by the other.

A number of theorists, most notably Nancy Chodorow[21] and Carole Gilligan,[22] have suggested that in societies where women are assigned care of infants (whether their own, their kin, or the clients of nurseries or day care centers), children of both sexes may carry over memories of hostility to women as disciplinarians, as sources of frustrated infant and toddler desire (it being impossible for any caretaker to immediately satisfy all infant desires), while men often make their first significance into the lives of toddlers as representatives of the stimulating outside world, as symbols of freedom and special attention. More central in Chodorow's research is the proposal that in the task of identity formation, which the vast majority of toddlers face in a context of more or less exclusive female care, boys choose a strategy of separation from female caretakers that entails denying to themselves much nurture and intimacy, as well as traits associated with the female caretaker. Boys often use this same strategy of separation to meet other, later, social tasks, which may leave them with a disdain for femaleness and even an understanding of femaleness and intimacy as threatening to their (sexual) identity. Girls, on the other hand, reach gender identity through modeling their female caretaker(s), with whom they develop intimate relationships, and then continue to rely on intimate relationships in other social tasks.[23] In terms of sexual violence (which Chodorow did not discuss) the process of gender development in

---

20. Dorothy Dinnerstein, *The Mermaid and the Minotaur: Sexual Arrangements and Human Malaise* (New York: Harper and Row, 1977).
21. Nancy Chodorow, *The Reproduction of Mothering: Psychoanalysis and the Sociology of Gender* (Berkeley: University of California Press, 1978).
22. Carol Gilligan, *In A Different Voice: Psychological Theory and Women's Development* (Cambridge: Harvard University Press, 1982).
23. Chodorow, *Reproduction of Mothering*, 168–72.

boys thus may leave a disdain for femaleness, while the process of acquiring gender for girls may leave them devoted to the preservation of relationships, and thus reluctant to leave relationships in which there is abuse and danger of violence.

Gilligan points out that this sexually differentiated path to gender identity affects the moral decision making of males and females. Separation strategies lead to males relying on principles to make moral decisions, regardless of their effect on relationships, and females attempting to limit pain and spread both advantages and suffering widely, in order to preserve relationships. Perhaps the most relevant part of Gilligan's work to questions of violence against women is her finding that in the three-stage process of moral development typical of women, the highest and most elusive stage is for women to learn to integrate their own needs and desires into the circle of needs and desires to be taken into account in moral decisions.[24] Failure to learn this—failure to claim the right to consider one's own needs and desires as equal in weight to others—can lead women to understand their role in relationships as self-sacrificial, as in women who allow spouses to use them as punching bags for venting anger at job frustration or other difficulties, or mothers who accept abuse in order to deflect abuse from the children. Such self-sacrifice can prevent the development of self-esteem and therefore of self-protection. But failure to learn to integrate one's own needs and desires into the complex of needs and desire to be considered can also lead not to self-sacrifice, but to manipulation of others to get one's own needs met, as in women who emotionally abuse children and spouses in order to achieve personal ends and exercise the personal power they feel unable to claim directly.

Yet another more recent theory comes from a study of research on the gender of playmates chosen by children from birth to adolescence. Eleanor Maccoby in *The Two Sexes* reports that until age three children have no gender preference in playmates, but that at age three strong same-sex gender preferences are introduced initially by girls, but are picked up much more strongly by boys, who become the enforcers of sex separation until sexual pairing begins in adolescence. Maccoby presents human life from adolescence on as a struggle, often frustrating for both sexes, to learn the folkways of the other sex, of which one has been kept ignorant. Both Maccoby's and Dinnerstein's theories can easily be combined with the evidence connecting testosterone with physical aggression. Frustration with the other sex at either their differentness (Maccoby) or their refusal to be

---

24. Gilligan, *A Different Voice*, chap. 4.

possessed/seduced (Dinnerstein) would be more likely to take the form of physical violence in males than in females.

Most of these theorists, however, focus on explaining male/female difference, but all their theories have some implications for gendered violence—why men are more physically violent than women, why some male violence is aimed at women (but less than is aimed at men), and why so many women seem not to resist that violence. None of these theories deal explicitly with religion, on why religions would, in effect, take the part of men and support the subjection of women, much less support the use of violence to maintain that subjection.

HISTORICAL THEORIES

There are also larger social theories based on the history of human social development that focus on the development of religion itself. Religion as a human activity seems to be primordial: the archeological data suggests that Paleolithic and most of Neolithic religion was extremely nature-oriented, and that the earliest images of deity were female.[25] Those images included deities with both animal and human features, often mixed together. These peoples venerated various powers of nature, not only fertility, but water in the form of rivers or seas, as well as lightning, trees, and various animals. As far as archeologists can tell, various animals came to represent different powers of nature: for example, horses with power and speed, snakes with spring rebirth through the shedding of their skins, birds with water, since they congregate at water, and pigs with fertility because of their large litters, rapid weight gain, and high protein value. Many ancient representations of female deity, in fact, had female human bodies, but the heads of birds, or pigs.[26] We have discovered a number of cave paintings at sites of ancient ritual that depict herds of horses, deer, and buffalo, which appear to be objects of veneration, since the midden piles at these sites demonstrate that the animals hunted and eaten by these groups were not these large mammals, but much smaller animals such as rabbits, squirrels, and otter.[27]

About 8000 BCE in various sites of the Neolithic world, the agricultural revolution began to gradually change the human relationship with

---

25. Marya Gimbutas' *Language of the Goddess* (London: Thames and Hudson, 1989) assembles a massive amount of data attesting to this, including hundreds of photos of artifacts, which stand independent of her theories on the culture of Old Europe and the Kurgan invasion.
26. Ibid.
27. For example, see the famous caves at Lascaux, France. http://www.culture.gouv.fr /culture/arcnat/lascaux/en/.

nature.[28] Humans began to plant seeds instead of merely gathering whatever edible windborne seed randomly sprouted. They began to domesticate chickens, cows, goats, sheep, camels, buffalo, and horses instead of relying solely on hunting for protein. Domestication of cows, goats, and camels also provided dairy products, including milk, butter, yogurt, and cheese.

The agricultural revolution allowed human settlements not only to be permanent, but to enlarge exponentially by allowing control of the food supply. Human bands no longer needed to remain small and periodically move because local hunting and gathering had been exhausted. Urbanization began, and within urbanization, specialization of human labor developed. Agriculture became so productive that 5 percent of the population, and in some civilizations even more, could be spared for other work—as priests, kings, blacksmiths, masons, artists, warriors, and so on. In turn, intensive agriculture, urbanization, and labor specialization promoted technological development. Wheels, wagons, wells, city walls, dams, irrigation, ovens, aqueducts, plows, harnesses, and multiple-storied buildings—these new technologies not only made human lives easier and more secure, but they represented growing human control over many aspects of nature itself. And the central feature of nature that humans learned to control, which allowed all these other areas of control, was fertility, beginning with the fertility of plants and animals.

The reason that the earliest (Paleolithic) religious deity images we have found were female is the same reason that late Neolithic religious culture (and surviving tribal mythology in many areas of the world) carries multiple stories, images, and laws legitimating male control over women:[29] women and nature were understood as linked by reproduction. As the extension of human control over one aspect of nature after another continued over centuries, especially in animal husbandry, the idea that human societies should and could exert control over human reproduction, over

28. For an entrancing description of this process, see Jared Diamond, *Guns, Germs and Steel: The Fates of Human Societies* (New York: W.W. Norton, 1997).

29. To name just a few examples, we would certainly cite the Enuma Elish, the oldest written myth, in which the god Marduk led a rebellion against his grandmother Tiamat, queen of the Gods, killed her, and created the world out of her corpse. Marduk was the patron of the city of Babylon. While the Genesis account of Adam and Eve did not begin with female control (doubtless because the deity was already male), it tells how through the sin of the first parents men came to be in control of women. Today, in the myths of Australian Aborigines, the Djanggawu sisters first carried the sacred emblems and performed the tribal rituals, but later their brother stole them. This explains, for the Aborigines, how men gained control over women (Rita M. Gross, "Menstruation and Childbirth as Ritual and Religious Experience," in Nancy Falk and Rita M. Gross, *Unspoken Worlds: Women's Religious Lives* [Belmont, Calif.: Wadsworth, 1989], 262). According to Yolanda and

those bodies that reproduced the species, became irresistible. Human female bodies were only dimly and intermittently understood as separable
from the rest of nature over which humans were exerting control. Human
women came to be understood as having a dual membership—part of the
human race destined to control the natural world, but also part of the natural world to be controlled. Religions of the world today reflect, but did
not invent, this dual membership of women.

The history of women's dual membership is not simply linear; the
analogy between human women and nature itself was a dynamic one, and
like any good analogy, it could be worked from either end. Human experience of innovative *techne* controlling otherwise disordered nature
could be and was used to justify religious sanction for male control of
women, who were often imaged as disorderly. In Judaism, women were
understood as requiring strict supervision, especially during moments of
transition (from a father's home to a husband's, from married woman to
either single [divorced] woman or widow).[30] In Hinduism, women were
understood in terms of *shakti*, a hot, vital energy that had the power to
create or destroy, and required the "cool" control of men if chaos was to
be avoided.[31] In other religions, too, women are imaged in terms of their
potential for disorder, as opposed to men's "cooler," more rational, more
controlled essence.

But sometimes the analogy between women and nature was used
from the other end. For example, Carolyn Merchant recounts that the
background for much of Francis Bacon's philosophy of science was the
witchcraft trials in the crackdown under James I. The interrogations of
the witch trials and the mechanical devices used to torture confessions
from witches became the imagery Bacon used for the new industrial tech-

---

Robert Murphy in *Women of the Forest*, 2nd ed. (New York: Columbia University Press,
1989), 114–30, the Mundurucu of Para state in the Brazilian Amazon share a mythology
in which the sacred trumpets, the source of sacred power and authority, once belonged to
the women, but were stolen by the men, who now claim the right to control society. Such
tribal myths are interesting, because they often exist in societies where from a late modern
technological perspective there is little evidence of control over nature. Jared Diamond
would point out that most of these groups live in inaccessible and often undesirable locations, and that many have been pushed into such locations either in the distant past or
more recently by "modern" societies. Their very survival in such places called for a rigid
discipline, or order, and techniques for extracting from local nature the basics for human
life. Some of those techniques reflect advanced technology, some of which, for example, in
botany and pharmacology, are being imitated in the developed world (Diamond, *Guns,
Germs and Steel*).
30. Judith Plaskow, *Standing Again at Sinai: Judaism from a Feminist Perspective* (New
York: Harper Collins, 1990), chap. 2.
31. Lucinda Joy Peach, *Women and Religion* (Upper Saddle River, N.J.: Prentice-Hall,
2002), 17.

nologies extracting natural riches from a selfish "mother earth."[32] Bacon asserts that the method for discovering nature's secrets replicates the investigation of the secrets of witchcraft in the Inquisition, referring to the methods used by James's inquisitors:

> For you have but to follow nature and as it were hound nature in her wanderings, and you will be able when you like to lead and drive her afterward to the same place again. Neither am I of the opinion in this history of marvels that superstitious narratives of sorceries, witchcrafts, charms, divinations and the like, where there is an assurance and clear evidence of the fact, should be altogether excluded . . . howsoever the use and practice of such arts is to be condemned, yet from the speculation and consideration of them. . . a useful light may be gained, not only for a true judgment of the offenses of persons charged with such practices, but likewise for the further disclosing of the secrets of nature. Neither ought a man to make scruple of entering and penetrating into these holes and corners, when the inquisition of truth is his whole object—as your majesty has shown in your own example.[33]

The scientist, then, is analogous to the torturer of the Inquisition, extracting secrets. In a similar way, Bacon compared the invention of the forceps, which he applauded, to new mining techniques, for the forceps allowed men to extract from selfish woman, as from nature, the fruit so reluctantly surrendered. Bacon, rejecting the traditional understanding of nature as organic, as a person, instead interprets nature both as female and yet as inert material to be manipulated at will. Merchant quotes Bacon as writing, "Matter is not devoid of an appetite and inclination to dissolve the world and fall back into the old Chaos. . . ."[34] The same chaos that women supposedly represent. Miners and smiths, he felt, were an example of the right relation between humanity and nature in that "nature takes orders from man and works under his authority"; miners and smiths had developed the two most important methods of wresting nature's secrets from her, "the one searching into the bowels of nature, the other shaping nature as an anvil."[35] Note that in this last sentence, Bacon shifts from an image of nature as an organism with bowels to nature as an inanimate thing to be shaped.

---

32. Carolyn Merchant, *The Death of Nature: Women, Ecology and the Scientific Revolution* (San Francisco: Harper and Row, 1980), 168–72.
33. Bacon, "De Dignitatem et Augmentis Scientiarum," as quoted in Merchant, 168.
34. Merchant, 171.
35. Ibid.

If the agricultural revolution began the shift of women from connection to nature as the source of all power to connection with nature as inert substance to be overpowered and controlled, the industrial revolution added new force to female subjection. In the industrial revolution, production was shifted out of the home, into factories. Men followed production into the factories, and women were left at home with children, in a new social role, no longer as producers (of food, cloth, clothing, soap, candles, and the like) but now as consumers and dependents upon male producers. The new economic dependency of women increased their subjection.

Unfortunately for many peoples of the world, modern European colonization coincided with European industrial revolution, so that the social model that Europeans exported to and imposed on the Americas, Asia, and Africa was an extremely patriarchal one, which by the early nineteenth century clearly reflected industrial gender relations. Females were understood as dependents of males—dependent upon males for economic support and protection, and therefore subject to males in all areas of life. Under this model of gender relations, women in Asia, Africa, and the Americas were denied land tenure rights, the ability to hold public office (or paid employment without spousal approval), access to divorce, and often even legal guardianship of their children, not to mention inequal access to education.

By the end of the colonial period in the middle of the twentieth century, a further change was taking place in late modern society that disadvantaged women, and that was the shift from extended to nuclear families. Women had always been vulnerable to domestic violence and abuse in virilocal exogamous social systems in which women marry out of the extended family and live with the husband's family. Matrilocal systems, in which husbands live with their wives' families, not surprisingly, have much lower rates of domestic violence against wives. But even the extended family of the husband offers a great deal more protection for wives than they have in the isolation of nuclear households.[36]

The view of women's dual membership in controller humanity and controlled nature endures yet today. It was not until the late-twentieth-century ecological movement that the human imagination began to be able to recognize that the human species, *male and female alike,* are part of nature, part of the divine creation, part of the biosphere, and not separate, semidivine rulers independent of natural processes. Today, as bioethics and ecological ethics merge, we see that human stewardship is

---

36. Weiss, "Slow yet Steady Path."

stewardship not only of the material resources that support human life, but of human life itself as an intimate part of the biosphere. In our contemporary world this realization is still slowly sinking into various political circles and popular masses: both male and female humans are a part of nature, of the biosphere, just as both are stewards. The ecological movement has thus allowed us to see more clearly how the philosophy of science underlying the industrial revolution transformed earlier human understandings of nature, and by analogy, women.

THE TECHNOLOGY OF TEXTS

Religions were peculiarly suited for absorbing and maintaining this view of women as part of the natural world that mankind was destined to control, because one part of the technologies that developed out of human labor specialization was writing: texts. In many areas of the world, the earliest known texts are sacred texts. This makes sense, in that writing was a specialized feat usually limited to a specific group, who were often priest/scholars. The development of sacred texts proved to be perhaps the most devastating weapon involved in historic violence against women, because as texts became more and more central to religion, it became an easy matter to restrict access to the texts to men, which meant that men became the experts in the texts, not only the sole interpreters of sacred texts, but the only authors or redactors of those sacred texts that continued to appear. Thus, although at least three women, Ghosa, Apala, and Visvavara are credited with writing parts of the Rig Veda, Vedic commentators redefined women as unworthy of Vedic education.[37] In fact,

> For the Vedic Commentators, however, both class and sex are crucial: sudras and women are excluded from all religious ritual. From now on, women are openly grouped with the lowest class. The lawbooks make this quite plain: the three higher classes are defined as having the right to study the Vedas and offer sacrifice; women, regardless of the class they were born into, are forbidden to do either.[38]

In Islam, Khadija, the first wife of Mohammed, was the first to believe in his revelations, and Aisha, the youngest of Mohammed's wives, was responsible for contributing many of the *hadith* concerning the words and deeds of the Prophet, yet women in successive generations until very recently have been excluded from studying sacred texts. Mary

---

37. Julia Leslie, "Essence and Existence: Women and Religion in Ancient Hindu Texts," in Peach, ed., *Women and Religion*, 28–29.
38. Leslie, 30.

Magdalene was not only a disciple of Jesus but also the first witness and first preacher of the resurrection as well as a great missionary, yet Catholic women are still today excluded from ordained ministry, and thus from all decision making in the Catholic Church, since governance is restricted to the ordained.[39] In many Buddhist nations, the lack of a female *sangha* has a similar effect on women. It is no accident that many monks, women activists, and commentators in Thailand today connect the lack of a female *sangha* with the prevalence of prostitution and sex tourism in that nation. They argue not only that the lack of female *sangha* degrades the worth of women, supporting the selling of daughters into prostitution, but also that the lack of public support for convents of Buddhist nuns denies poor families whose sons receive education in monasteries the ability to educate daughters, and denies unmarried daughters the refuges that are available for "excess" sons in Thailand.[40]

Across the traditions, the sacred texts from which women have been largely excluded treat violence against women more or less cavalierly. Rambachan treats examples of Hindu texts, such as Tulsidas's *Ramcharitmanas*, which includes not only extended denigration of women, but even lumps women together with "drums, rustics, animals, and members of the lowest caste and all of these are described as objects that are fit to be beaten."[41] Muslim feminists such as Amina Wadud attempt to restrain the implications of the Qur'anic verse 4:34 by insisting that it is limited by the rest of the Qur'an, which insists on the equality and dignity of women.[42] But the verse says, "And those who you fear may be rebellious admonish, banish them to separate beds, and beat them. And if they then obey you, look not for any way against them; Allah is all-high, all-great." Perhaps one of the most brutal sacred regulations inflicted on women was the Mosaic law's requirement[43] that rapists be forced to marry their unmarried victims—and that their further punishment for the rape (besides having to pay her father the brideprice) was that the husband would not be allowed to divorce this wife, unlike the normal case. What a consolation this must have been to the rape victim, to be tied to the rapist with no hope of release!

---

39. Christine E. Gudorf, "Probing the Politics of Difference: What's Wrong with an All-Male Priesthood?" *Journal of Religious Ethics*, vol. 27.3 (1999): 377–406.

40. Tavivat Puntarigvivat, "A Thai Buddhist Perspective," in Raines and Maguire, eds., *What Men Owe to Women*; "Female Ordination: Senate Panel Visits Temple in Lop Buri," *The Nation,* 7/19/2002.

41. Rambachan, "A Hindu Perspective,"20–21.

42. Amina Wadud, *Qur'an and Woman: Reading the Sacred Text from Women's Perspective* (New York: Oxford University Press, 1999), chap. 4.

43. Deuteronomy 22:28–29.

Across the world religions, feminists are clear that the dignity and welfare of women within religions and within their larger communities requires the development of women clergy, judges, and religious scholars. Religion should be more than simply a source of comfort for women resisting degradation and violence aimed at them; it should be, and could be, a support for women liberating themselves from all kinds of violence against women—whether we speak of wife beating, marital/stranger/date rape, domestic seclusion of women, arranged marriages of minors, or women's inaccessibility to divorce, not to mention women unable to develop physically, spiritually, and intellectually because they are given less food, respect, education, and other resources than men. But in order for religion to be a source of liberation, it must develop the ability to critically examine its history and development and the impact that it has had on the lives of girls and women. This indeed is one major goal of this book.

Today the most serious sexual challenge to religions comes from those groups pressing to end the narrow dimorphism in traditional religious views of sexuality. Gay, lesbian, transgender, and sexually ambiguous persons question the division of all humans into male and female, behaviors into masculine and feminine, and sexual orientation into homosexual and heterosexual. Together with many feminists and sexuality researchers in biology and medicine, they point out that none of the six biological markers for sex is clearly dimorphic—even chromosomal sex includes not only XX and XY, but also XXX, XYY, XXY, XO, and even rarely XXXX. Our dimorphic view of sexes is clearly socially constructed, just as are all understandings of gender. Sexual orientation, too, seems to be at least partly socially constructed, as well as influenced by genetic predisposition.[44] The Sambia of New Guinea, for example, assign all adolescent boys roles in fellatio: younger boys regularly fellate older boys in the understanding that only the ingestion of semen will turn them into men.[45] When older boys reach the ages of nineteen and twenty, they marry women and practice heterosexual sex only. In this social construction, there is no enduring heterosexual or homosexual orientation, and thus not much ability to influence core identity.

44. J. M. Bailey, M. P. Dunne, and N. G. Martin, "Genetic and Environmental Influences on Sexual Orientation and Its Correlates in an Australian Twin Sample," *Journal of Personality and Social Psychology* 78 (2000): 524–36; J. M. Bailey and R. C. Pillard, "Genetic Study of Male Sexual Orientation," *Archives of General Psychiatry* 48 (1991): 1089–96; J. M. Bailey, R. C. Pillard, M. C. Neale, and Y. Agyei, "Heritable Factors Influence Sexual Orientation in Women," *Archives of General Psychiatry* 50 (1993): 217–23.
45. Gilbert Herdt, *Guardians of the Flutes: Idioms of Masculinity* (Chicago: University of Chicago Press, 1994), and Gilbert Herdt and Robert J. Stoller, *Intimate Communications: Erotics and the Study of Culture* (New York: Columbia University Press, 1990).

Thus, when we consider violence against women, we cannot ground the category "women" securely in biology, and can wonder if perhaps this very category is a patriarchal construct, an act of violence parallel to that perpetrated on gay, lesbian, transgender, transsexual, and sexually ambiguous persons, that imposes narrow, degrading, and subordinate definitions on the majority of humans in the interests of a small elite. Religions of the world need to reject this narrow sexual dimorphism that has characterized all human history in the past, in order to meet the needs and expectations of the millions of women and other sexual groups, who continue to look to religion for hope and support.

2

The Courtroom and the Garden: Gender and Violence in Christendom

GRACE M. JANTZEN

Deliver me, O Lord, from evil men;
Preserve me from violent men,
who plan evil things in their heart,
and stir up wars continually . . . (Psa. 140:1–2)[1]

The words of this psalm echo the cry of women throughout the centuries of Christendom, women who have been abused, raped, and killed in violence that is disproportionately gendered.[2] In the world of Christendom and its secular off-shoots, by far the greatest amount of violence is engaged in by men. This is true of wars and international violence and true also of murder, rape, and domestic violence. In all of these, women (and often children) bear the brunt, their lives and homes and families destroyed, their self-esteem and sense of bodily integrity crushed.

All this is obvious. It is obvious too that when it comes to gendered violence Christendom has much to answer for, as men have appealed to the Bible to justify their treatment of women. Women are descendants of Eve, it is claimed, and surely it was Eve who first seduced Adam into sin. She is therefore a temptress who must be kept firmly in her place. Alternatively it is claimed that women are the weaker sex, inferior to men in both mind and body, so that men have the right—even the duty—to as-

---

1. Scripture quotations for this chapter are from the Revised Standard Version of the Bible.
2. In the context the words are, of course, those of a man involved in a situation of male–male conflict.

sert their God-given authority, violently if need be, since women may not be duly submissive unless coerced. Through many centuries of Christendom men have been seen as God-like in their rationality and mastery, while women have been conceptually linked with the body, sexuality, reproduction, and the earth—in short, with everything that would draw men away from their spiritual well-being.

There are, of course, plenty of voices in Christendom and in the Bible itself that complicate this picture and make it possible to argue that violence against women is an aberration or perversion of Christianity: true Christianity would condemn such attitudes and actions. Feminist scholars (and others) have argued that Eve, with Adam, was made in the divine image; that Jesus included women among his closest followers; that Paul insisted that "in Christ there is neither male nor female"; that the relation between husband and wife should be as loving as that between Christ and the church. In almost every area of biblical studies, theology, and the history of Christendom, feminists have challenged the prevailing patriarchy and its culture of violence and have pointed the way to a liberatory and egalitarian theory and practice rooted in the Bible and the teachings of Jesus.

All this work is of immense importance. It is crucial that the texts and traditions that have been used to justify or condone violence against women be dismantled one by one and liberatory alternatives explored. In addition to this, however, I suggest that there is a further task to be undertaken. I believe that some of the conceptual foundations of traditional Christian thought generate a construction of gender, both masculine and feminine, that in turn makes gender violence virtually inevitable. Until these conceptual models are destabilized, reinterpretation of this or that biblical passage or Christian practice will deal with symptoms rather than causes. What I propose to do in this chapter, therefore, is to look at some of these foundational concepts, those revolving around the courtroom and the covenant, and show how the implicit construction of gender leads to violence against women. I shall then offer an alternative organic account in which resources for mutuality and peace become the criteria of validity. Obviously I can do no more, in this space, than offer a sketch, but even a sketch can suggest possibilities whose detail can be developed in further work.

THE COVENANT AND THE COURTROOM

At the very heart of Christianity, and affecting its whole conceptual structure, is the idea of covenant, and with it a model of a courtroom and its forensic metaphors. Christians reached back to the stories and teaching of covenant that they found in the Old Testament.[3] In the Old Testament God repeatedly initiates a covenant with special men of his choice: Noah, whom he saves from the flood (Gen. 9:8); Abraham, who becomes the father of the people of Israel (Gen. 17:8); David, who is their greatest king (2 Sam. 7:10–16). Most important of all is his covenant through Moses with the people of Israel, when God gave them the Ten Commandments and the rest of the law, and the people pledged themselves to obey. God says,

> If you will obey my voice and keep my covenant, you shall be my own possession among all peoples; for all the earth is mine, and you shall be to me a kingdom of priests and a holy nation. (Exod. 19:5–6)

When Moses relays God's words to the people, they promise that "All that the Lord has spoken we will do" (Exod. 19:8). Forensic metaphors dominate: God is the judge and the redeemer, people keep or break the law. It is this narrative, more than any other, that constitutes the self-identity of Israel as God's chosen people, specially selected for divine favor and committed to divine law.

A patriarchal gender structure is at the very heart of this narrative. First and most obviously, God is represented as a male deity, as indeed he is routinely in the Old Testament. He is "God the Father," but also the God of Battles, the Lord of Hosts, the King, the paradigm of mastery, power, and all masculinist virtues. Moreover, as the story is told in Exodus, the covenant is made only with the *men* of Israel: the women are not invited. Indeed, even to go near a woman would pollute a man and render him unfit to participate in the encounter with God. Moses goes to prepare the people and says, "Be ready by the third day; do not go near a woman" (Exod. 19:15). As Judith Plaskow has pointed out, in this "root experience of Judaism" only the men are addressed.

> At the critical moment of Jewish history, women are invisible. Whether they too stood there trembling in fear and expectation, what they heard when the men heard these words of Moses, we do not know.[4]

---

3. The Christian "Old Testament" is, of course, the Hebrew Bible, which Christendom appropriated as its own scripture. The legitimacy of that appropriation and of Christendom's interpretation of key ideas is beyond the scope of this chapter; it has been contested from the start. The terms "Sacred Testament" and "First Testament" are now often used by Jewish and Christian scholars.
4. Judith Plaskow, *Standing Again at Sinai: Judaism from a Feminist Perspective* (San Francisco: Harper Collins, 1990), 25.

Whatever the women were doing, and even if they were in some sense included in the covenant (as in a second telling of the story in Deuteronomy 29:10–15), the token or symbol of the covenant is unambiguously reserved to men. All males are to be circumcised, their very masculinity inscribed with the sign of their covenant with God, which shows them as his special people. What about the women? Are women not special to God? If not—or if they take second place to men—then this gender construction at the very heart of the connection between God and people already signals the legitimation of, if not outright violence against, women, or at least differential treatment.

The idea of the covenant was taken up by early Christian writers and given as important a place in Christendom as it had in the Hebrew Bible. Indeed, even the names by which the two parts of the Christian Bible are named, the Old and New Testaments, are, strictly, the Old Covenant and the New Covenant. Whereas the central ingredient of the Old Covenant is the law, in the New Covenant it is a relationship with God mediated by the blood of Christ. Its symbolic enactment is the Eucharist:

> The Lord Jesus . . . took . . . the cup, after supper, saying, "This cup is the new covenant in my blood. Do this, as often as you drink it, in remembrance of me." (1 Cor. 11:25)

It is that new covenant with God through the blood of Christ that is the foundation of Christian theology, already in the New Testament and extending through Christian writing from that day to this. From Paul to Augustine, from the writer of Hebrews to Calvin and Karl Barth, the doctrine of the covenant, though variously interpreted, has always been central to their theologies. It has had endless repercussions on the formation of Western civilization, as one group after another conceived themselves as a people of the covenant, the new chosen people especially favored by God: the seventeenth century Puritans under Oliver Cromwell, the Scottish Covenanters, the Boers in South Africa, the framers of the American Constitution all saw themselves as reenacting the ancient covenant between God and Israel ratified by the new covenant of Christ's blood, which redeems from the debt of sin or disobedience to divine law.

Once again, however, a masculinist gender construction lurks just below the surface. As with the Mosaic covenant, the God of the new covenant is the Father God, and Christ is his son: there is no balancing female deity. Even though in Christian theology God's embodiment and hence God's gender are regularly denied, they are as regularly recuperated in the determined refusal to use any but masculine pronouns for God. The fuss that results when someone, exceptionally, goes against this convention—as Julian of Norwich on the Motherhood of God, or Edwina Sandys' Christa figure—shows just how deeply entrenched are the assumptions that God is (genderless!) male. Moreover, as with the Mosaic covenant, the rituals of its reenactment have been firmly in male hands. It has been argued that women were among the first followers of Jesus, but the New Testament gives the twelve disciples—all male—pride of place. They are the ones who are prominent when the new covenant is first ritually instituted in the Last Supper, and they are the ones who take charge of the organization of the church and the enactment of the sacraments. These are religious activities, but they are also technologies of power and hierarchies of control from which women have been excluded. Although as with the Mosaic covenant this male domination is not of itself a licence for gender violence, by constructing a gender dualism in which women are inferior (or invisible), the new covenant, like the old, sets up a structure in which gender violence becomes plausible in attitude and action.

In the writings of Paul, even circumcision is reinterpreted as part of the new covenant.

> For he is not a real Jew who is one outwardly, nor is true circumcision something external and physical. He is a Jew who is one inwardly, and real circumcision is a matter of the heart, spiritual and not literal. (Rom. 2:28–29)

Although the ritual is spiritualized, the imagination is still in masculine mode: what would it mean for a woman to undergo circumcision of the heart? Whatever the answer, it was not circumcision but new birth that became a prominent metaphor in Christendom—and here the misogyny is hardly veiled. The new birth, symbolized by baptism, which is a death to the life begun by birth from a woman, is a birth that has nothing to do with mothers or sex or bodies. Rather, it is a birth from the Father, not of the body but of the spiritual person, and its rites are regulated by the Father's earthly representatives, who, over the millennia, have been men. Does this constitute gender violence? Not in the overt sense of calling for specific acts of violence against women. But in its relegation of women to inferior or even harmful status, and in blotting out women and women's contributions (even to reproduction) from consciousness, it develops a structure in which gender violence will hardly cause surprise.

MILITIA CHRISTI

The consequences of being the chosen people of God bound to him by covenant have been both externalized and internalized in Christendom, in each case following from the Christian reading of the Old Testament, and in each case with massive implications for the structure of gender and consequent gender violence. In this section I shall discuss the externalization of the covenant, the holy war that is declared against those who are excluded, and the construction of ideal masculinity as a warrior. In the following section I shall discuss the internalizing of the covenant, its enactment in ritual sacrifice, and the implications for gender. I believe that taken together, these two aspects of covenant constitute the deep structures of gender in the West and render violence against women endemic in Christianity. In each case, forensic metaphors underpin the whole conceptual structure.

In many passages of the Old Testament, the representation of Israel as the chosen people is linked with the exclusion of others. Others are perceived as a threat. Difference is dangerous. And the way of dealing with this danger is not by becoming friends with these others and thus neutralizing the danger, but by exterminating those who are different. As represented in the Hebrew Bible, this is God's requirement, the condition of being his chosen people. Before they come to their "promised land," the Israelites are repeatedly warned that they must exterminate those who already live in the land: "you must utterly destroy them; you shall make no covenant with them, and show no mercy to them" (Deut. 7:2). To make a covenant with them, to enter into arrangements of peace and friendship, would threaten the exclusive relationship with God. Why this should be so—why the bond between God and Israel should be thought so weak that any other friendship would undermine it—is not questioned: the emphasis is rather on getting rid of all others. When the Israelites do finally enter the land, stories are told of their obedience and disobedience to this divine command, and the respective consequences. When, for example, they took the city of Jericho, "they utterly destroyed all in the city, both men and women, young and old, oxen, sheep, and asses, with the edge of the sword" (Josh. 6:21); this action received divine blessing. On the other hand, when the Israelites befriended the people of the land, they quickly succumbed also to worshipping their gods and goddesses, Baal and Asheroth: "therefore the anger of the Lord was kindled against Israel, and he sold them into the hands of [the enemy]" (Judg. 3:8).

Very large sections of the Hebrew scriptures can be read as lessons in this exclusivism and its expression in merciless violence. Again, the gender construction—this time of masculinity—is not far to seek. Men who, like Joshua and David, are renowned for their heroism in battle are lifted up as ideal. To be a real man is to be a warrior, to follow the Lord of Hosts into battle against "others," any who might pose a threat to wholehearted and exclusive loyalty to the Father God. All that would be needed for that violence to turn against women is that women should be seen as "others," a construction implicit in Christendom's gender dualism.

It was of course hardly possible for Christendom to declare war on women: men needed women for reproduction, nurture, and care. But just as circumcision was spiritualized in Pauline writings, so also was warfare. The battle, now, is not with physical armies but with "the world, the flesh, and the devil," against which the newly baptized declare themselves ready to fight as "a good soldier of Christ"; the words are still used in the baptismal rite of Catholic and Anglican churches. As Adolph Harnack characterized Paul's writings,

> The apostle is deeply convinced that each Christian must be a warrior and must endure fearful though certainly victorious battles. There are battles against flesh and blood, but those are the lesser ones, or rather their significance disappears when compared with the battles against the powers of the demons . . . Only an unrelieved warfare carried out with all the powers of the good and the holy will be able to defend against them.[5]

The good Christian is the spiritual warrior, engaging in battles that all too quickly turn literal again, when the "demons" are personified as heretics or infidels: the Crusades and the Inquisition are notorious examples.

Where does this leave women? Since women can be Christians, women too, presumably, are Christian soldiers. Yet the mental gymnastics are parallel to those required to conceptualize women undergoing circumcision of the heart. To be a person, to be a Christian, to be a soldier, is to be normatively male. Women are inferior; they are "misbegotten males," as Aristotle infamously put it in a phrase taken up by medieval churchmen like Thomas Aquinas. Thus when women did show great courage, like the martyr Perpetua, or were considered to have "conquered the demons" by maintaining their chastity like Mary of Egypt, they were thought of as exceptional, and labeled "honorary males."

The link between masculinity and active violence was deepened as Christendom adopted many of the thought forms of the Roman Empire. In Rome, the truly manly man was labeled *vir*, as contrasted with *homo*, men who because of their status or behavior did not come up to the ideal. A *vir*—the word from which English derives both "virile" and "virtue"—was above all a man of power and authority, one who asserts active manliness and does not submit to another. The opposite of *vir* is *mollitia*, the

---

5. Adolph Harnack, *Militia Christi: The Christian Religion and the Military in the First Three Centuries*, trans. David McInnes Gracie (Philadelphia: Fortress Press, 1981), 36.

effeminate, the one who did not have independence but must submit to another. To penetrate, whether by sword or by penis (both were called a *gladius*, the tool of a gladiator), was the act of a real (virile) man; to be penetrated was womanly. Violence, whether military or sexual, is thus inscribed into the construction of gender: "militarism, masculinity, and morality are inseparable in Roman thought."[6] As this construction of active manly virtue was taken up in the centuries of Christendom, the "soldiers of the cross" were valorized and their violence seen as part of a holy war. Since women were conceptually linked with the flesh (through the body and reproduction) and with the devil (because Eve was the first to sin), the warfare against these evils was construed in gendered terms.

Thus violence against women was built into the basic constructions of gender that lie at the heart of foundational Christian thinking. This was acted out in many forms. Whole territories were feminized—Africa, the Americas—seen as "virgin territory" ready to be subjected and penetrated by European men. Whole groups of women were demonized and persecuted as witches. And individual women in their millions were kept in "voluntary" subjection to their fathers and then their husbands in patriarchal Christendom, in which rebellion against that subjection gave the husband or father the right—even the duty—to beat the woman until she was ready to submit.

SACRIFICE

If such overt violence against women was in most cases unnecessary (though always available), it was because both women and men had internalized the gender constructions upon which it was based. Crucial to this was the idea of sacrifice, the aspect of the doctrine of covenant that turned inward to the community rather than outward in holy war. Again it was the Christian reading of the "Old Testament" that provided the paradigms, especially the story of Abraham's sacrifice of Isaac, and the ritual slaughter of animals in Israelite worship. Abraham's sacrifice of Isaac was taken as the example of perfect obedience; the ritual slaughter of animals was the means of purification and atonement for sins. Together, they indicate in Christian theology what is necessary for right standing before God, and they come together in Jesus' death. Jesus was the "only begotten son of God" who gave his life in perfect submission to the will of the Father, as Isaac had been willing to do. At the same time, he was the "Lamb of God, who takes away the sins of the world." Thus,

---

6. Susanna Morton Bruand, *Latin Literature* (New York and London: Routledge, 2002), 83.

for example, the writer of the book of Hebrews develops a theology in which Christ is the mediator of the new covenant, a covenant not now related to an earthly promised land but to an eternal life in a new kingdom, the kingdom of heaven. "Without the shedding of blood there is no forgiveness of sins" (Heb. 9:22), but Christ offers himself as the perfect sacrifice, in fulfilment of his Father's will.

> By that will we have been sanctified through the offering of the body of Jesus Christ . . . (Heb. 10:10)

> So Christ, having been offered once to bear the sins of many, will appear a second time, not to deal with sin but to save those who are eagerly waiting for him. (Heb. 9:28)

There are many variations on the doctrine of atonement, as it came to be called, both in the New Testament and in the history of Christendom. What they all have in common is the combination of forensic ideas: perfect obedience to divine law and blood sacrifice as the basis for redemption. It stands at the very center of Christendom; it is what the new covenant is at its very heart.

On the face of it, this does not seem to have anything to do with gender construction, let alone with violence against women. I suggest, however, that the opposite is the case; indeed, it builds a symbolic structure in which violence against women is legitimated into the central structure of Christendom. In the first place, note the importance, on this account, of blood and killing. As God is portrayed in most standard accounts of the doctrine of atonement, God desires blood and demands death. Without it, sins will not be forgiven. And unless God forgives sins, the penalty is, according to much Christian teaching across the centuries, eternal torment in hell. Christian teaching from the biblical writers onwards has placed the emphasis on divine love and mercy, God's rescue of humans from this dreadful fate by giving up his own son to take the penalty in substitution for them. But this emphasis evades the darker awareness that it is God who has set up the "courtroom" situation in the first place, instituting the requirement for blood before he will forgive sins and making the penalty of hell for those whose sins remain. Did God have to make such demands and penalties? What would we think of a parent or ruler who set up those under his authority in such a way, even if he then made special provision for a few favored subjects to live in bliss instead? I am of course not suggesting that this crude reading is the only way in which the Christian doctrine of atonement can be understood, let alone that this is what God is "really" like. But it cannot be denied that some such portrayal has domi-

nated Christendom through the centuries, and at its core is a God who legitimates—indeed requires—violence and blood. It is in fact the same God
as the one who requires the violent extermination of all who do not worship him: the doctrine of sacrifice is the inward expression of the doctrine
of holy war, and together they constitute the covenant.

If its violence thus becomes apparent, however, this still does not
show how it constructs gender. In fact, the sacrifices that the Bible emphasizes most are male: Isaac, the young lambs for ritual slaughter, and
above all Jesus himself. On the face of it, it would seem that what we
have here is institutionalized violence against men: how then did it come
to legitimate or condone violence against women?

Here again the critical move is the gender construction of the male as
active and the female as passive or, turning that around, of activity as masculine and passivity as feminine. To the extent that this became part of
Christian thinking, sacrifice itself was feminized. To be properly female is
to be self-sacrificial. There is not a one-to-one gender mapping here, but
the overarching picture sees the one who enacts the sacrifice—Abraham,
the Father God, the priest—as paradigmatically male, while the victim,
though literally male, is symbolically female. We can see this for example
in medieval paintings of Jesus' crucifixion, where he is portrayed giving the
blood/milk from his side/breast to nourish those who are newly born into
his church. The symbolism is complicated, as the convoluted pronouns indicate, but the trajectory is one in which suffering and sacrifice are constructed as feminine. When this was put together with the idea that men
are created to "have dominion" and that women are to be "help meet for
them," then it is obvious that women will be required to be subservient to
men, sacrificing themselves for men's needs, not least the selfless rearing of
children. Once again, this need not erupt into actual physical violence.
Both women and men could be socialized in such a way that female self-
sacrifice was taken for granted by all concerned. Women's suffering in
childbirth was assumed to be part of this self-sacrifice and interpreted both
as her punishment for Eve's sin and (not altogether consistently) as her natural selflessness, giving her very life, if need be, for her (husband's) child.

One could argue about whether this internalized gender construction
of women as sacrificial is violent: certainly most women devoted themselves to their husbands and children without having to be beaten or otherwise forced to do so. What women themselves might want or need, or
how these needs could be met, were questions that could scarcely arise:
there was not usually a separate or independent place from which such
considerations could be framed. But if a woman did assert herself against
male domination, if she was not sacrificial enough to satisfy her father or

husband, physical force could be used against her with relative impunity. She could be beaten or otherwise punished; forced into marriage or a convent. Rape within marriage was legitimate. Given the gender constructions of masculinity and femininity, gender violence was inevitable and to a large extent taken for granted by both sexes. And the deep structures of Christendom helped to make it so.

It is telling that marriage itself is described, in traditional Christian liturgy, as a *covenant* between a man and a woman, echoing the language of covenant of the Bible. In the sketch that I have presented, that covenant was represented as involving both externalized and internalized violence and bloodshed: violence against the threatening "other" and ritual violence in perpetual sacrifice. The gender constructions throughout are such that masculinity is geared toward acting out violence and women are conditioned to suffer it. Thus, it is hardly surprising if in the "covenant" of marriage the same gender roles have been taken for granted and sanctioned in Christendom.

RESOURCES FOR CHANGE?

Quite beyond discreet acts of gratuitous gender violence like rape, against which there have usually been laws and penalties, I have been focusing on the quotidian violence against women institutionalized in the deep structures of Christendom. Unless there is change in these structures themselves, it is unlikely that tinkering with individual biblical passages or stories will result in the shift in gender construction necessary for violence against women to be seen for what it is and its legitimation eradicated.

How is it, then, that there have been many Christians who have worked for a more just society and a more compassionate world, and have done so not in spite of their Christian commitment but precisely *because* of it? If the deep structures of Christendom are the framework for gender violence (including the violence of racism, colonialism, and many other forms of injustice supported by the construction of masculinity discussed above), then how can Christendom simultaneously provide the resources for change? And yet it cannot be denied that campaigns against oppression ranging from the suffragettes to the antislavery and civil rights movements have drawn upon the resources of the Bible and the churches to empower their work for justice.

Twentieth-century secular feminism tended to ignore this fact, seeing religion primarily as a problem to be overcome. But in the twenty-first century, in which the violent face of religion in the name of Allah and of "God bless America" is much to the fore, it is essential that we think again. It has become obvious that religion is not going to go away any time soon. If we do not want its violent structures to overwhelm the world, then it is crucial to destabilize those structures, to show that within Christendom itself there are resources for thinking otherwise. This task is all the more urgent because the covenant model with its sense of threat and its violent structures lies at the heart of the world's hyperpower, which considers itself the specially chosen and privileged people with a right—even a mandate—to impose its own way of salvation (now called "democracy") upon others using whatever force is necessary.

Those who have looked to the Bible and to Christian theology for resources for change have usually done so by pointing out that the Bible itself contains alternative understandings of covenant, warfare, and sacrifice, understandings that radically subvert their violence and exclusivity. The covenant, for instance, can be understood as reaching out to all peoples: if there are a "chosen few" they are chosen as those who have a special task of publishing the good news of the divine covenant to everyone, not of reserving it to themselves. Jesus is the Prince of Peace, the one who gives his life rather than stoop to the violence that excludes anyone, even those cast out by society, from his fellowship. And the sacrifice God requires is not a sacrifice of blood, but a contrite heart (Psa. 51:17), a heart that seeks integrity and social justice for all, especially those unable to seek it for themselves.

What to me is the multitude of your sacrifices? says the Lord . . .
Cease to do evil, learn to do good;
seek justice, correct oppression;
defend the fatherless, plead for the widow. (Isaiah 1:11, 16b–17)

There is much in the Bible, especially in the Hebrew prophets and in the life and teaching of Jesus, that thoroughly discredits the interpretations of covenant, war, and sacrifice outlined in the previous sections, and with them the gender constructions and the violence against women that they have supported.

It would be useful to study this in detail, and to show how such alternative understandings have enabled a wide range of groups and individuals from medieval mystics to contemporary liberation and feminist theologians to work for justice and an end to gender oppression in the name of Christianity. Without wanting for a moment to minimize the importance of such a study, however, I want to proceed in a different way in the rest of this chapter. What I propose to do is to show not simply that the conventional theological terms of covenant, sacrifice, and the rest can be understood differently, but that there is a whole set of *other* terms in the biblical writings themselves that, if taken seriously, generate a theological outlook in which violence against women has no place.

THE GARDEN

I shall label this set of terms "organic," in contrast to the legal or forensic mode of thought implicit in much of the vocabulary of covenant, warfare, and sacrifice. As these latter terms are used in biblical and theological thought, they are couched in the language of the law courts: there is guilt, debt, redemption, penalty, duty, and responsibility, to say nothing of the "law" itself or of the covenant understood as a legal treaty between two signatories. Even though there is plenty of scope for how these various terms should be read, the overall structure is forensic; the metaphors are legal metaphors.

This forensic symbolic is so completely taken for granted that it is regularly treated as literal, its metaphorical status forgotten. Even worse, because it is treated as literal, alternative metaphors are ignored or suppressed. Yet they exist, and they offer a significant antidote to the forensic terminology that has dominated Christian thought. Organic metaphors, drawn not from the law courts but from the nature and growth of living things, give us a whole different model for theology, a model that has implications for gender construction and therefore for issues of violence against women.

The Bible is full of such organic terminology, visions of life and growth and flourishing. The book of Genesis begins, not with a covenant or a law court but with the creation of a garden, full of diversity and beauty, in which trees—not stone tablets—are bearers of life and knowledge. This paradise is regularly invoked as the ideal place for humankind. When in Hosea God promises to heal Israel from the pain of faithlessness, for example, he says,

> I will be as dew to Israel;
> he shall blossom as the lily,
> he shall strike root as the poplar;
> his shoots shall spread out;
> his beauty shall be like the olive . . .
> They shall return and dwell beneath my shadow,
> they shall flourish as a garden . . . (Hos. 14:5–7)

The person who delights in God is likened by the psalmist to

> a tree planted by the streams of water,
> that yields its fruit in its season,
> and its leaf does not wither. (Psa. 1:3)

Again, God's work of justice in the earth is compared by Isaiah to a garden.

> For as the earth brings forth its shoots,
> and as a garden causes what is sown in it to spring up,
> so the Lord God will cause righteousness and praise
> to spring forth before all the nations. (Isa. 61:11)

In the New Testament, too, organic terminology is significant. In the Fourth Gospel, for example, Jesus uses an extended metaphor of vine and branches.

> I am the true vine and my father is the vinedresser. . . . Abide in me, and I in you. As the branch cannot bear fruit by itself, unless it abides in the vine, neither can you, unless you abide in me. (John 15:1–4)

In the Pauline letters there is an emphasis on being "rooted and grounded in love" (Eph. 3:17), on spiritual growth as a child or a plant would grow, on bringing forth "fruits of the Spirit," such as love, joy, and peace (Gal. 5:22). And the "new covenant" expressed in the Eucharist is based on organic elements: the bread and wine, whatever they become, are first of all "fruit of the vine and work of human hands."

It is true that these organic metaphors often occur side by side with forensic terminology, and that the latter often dominates in the biblical writings as it has in subsequent Christian theology. Nevertheless, the organic language is there, and not negligible, even though it has not been allowed to shape theological thought to anything like the same extent as the language of law and the courtroom. What if we were to lift up the model of life and growth, beauty and creativity and fruitfulness? In what follows, I want to begin to show how such an emphasis would yield gender constructions quite different from the masculinism of Western patriarchal Christendom and undermine its implicit support for violence against women.

CREATION AND FECUNDITY

Before the covenant there was creation: the heavens and the earth were made by God "in the beginning." It can be embarrassing for progressive Christians to take the creation stories seriously because of the literalist fuss made of them by the Christian right, but it is a pity not to recognize the resources in these stories just because they have been misused. On the whole, covenant stories are treated much more like literal or historical fact than are creation stories, though when we stop and think, there is little justification for this. It is after all no more likely that God wrote laws on stone tablets with his finger than it is that God created the world in six days. Both stories are there, not as flat-footed literal accounts, but as representations of what God is like and how God relates to humanity. We have seen how that representation has been taken with regard to the covenant and the law. But what sort of God is it who makes a garden? Especially the sort of garden that Eden was?

One thing that immediately strikes a reader of the Genesis creation stories is the sheer abundance and variety of what God makes. God is not content with just the light, but makes the sun and moon and all the vast array of stars. God makes "swarms of living creatures" to inhabit the seas, not just one or two kinds of fish but everything from sea monsters to the tiniest specks of life. God created all the winged birds, innumerable sorts of insects, every kind of flower and tree and plant, all the "cattle and creeping things and beasts of the earth" (Gen. 1:24). The sheer excessiveness of all this variety is striking. There is a huge outpouring of divine plenitude, a fecundity that is intended to continue as living creatures fulfil the divine mandate to "be fruitful and multiply." There is far more here than is necessary for a covenant.

What does this say about God? In the accounts of the covenant God is often represented as selecting only a chosen few, as though there is not enough love to go round and only those who are the covenant people can expect God's attention. They alone are given a "promised land," whether the land of Israel or the New Jerusalem or heaven after death: all others are excluded. And among these chosen people powerful men are to the fore, men who have been circumcised—in body or in heart—as a sign of their exclusive relationship with God. But if the God of covenant is a God of scarcity, the God of creation is a God of abundance. The theme of the Genesis story is generosity, overflowing of creative plenitude. Moreover, this divine fecundity expresses itself in diversity, an immense excessive variety of plants and animals, stars and seas. All the multitude of kinds of created things are given God's commendation, and man and woman together are the bearers of the "image" of God. This representation of the divine works against the narrow, exclusive idea that some created things are worth more than others, or that difference is dangerous or bad. All are created to be in harmony, and although at the end of the story humans are given "dominion," this is a "dominion" of "dressing and keeping" the garden, not trampling on it or treating it with violence. Quite the opposite: they are to foster and preserve the diversity of creation and find ways to help it to flourish.

In the Genesis story, too, there is repeated emphasis on the delight God takes in all this variety. In the forensic language of the covenant God is represented as a solemn lawgiver, a God of judgement. But in the Genesis story God is represented as enjoying himself, expressing his creativity and taking delight in it. There has been much in Christian theology about the wrath of God, but very little about the joy of God and almost nothing about God having fun. Yet surely that is part of what these stories of exuberant divine creativity are about. Anyone who can invent a penguin and a parakeet, a giraffe and a crocodile and a crab, must have a vivid imagination and a glorious sense of humor, and that is just what God is represented as doing. Indeed, there is repeated emphasis on the pleasure God takes in his creative activity and its results. Over and over comes the refrain, "and God saw that it was good": the Hebrew word connotes esthetic delight as well as moral goodness and utility. The picture of God in the creation stories is a picture of enjoyment and openness, pleasure and generosity, quite different from the picture of defensive and often violent exclusivity that emerges from the forensic language of covenant and law and judgement. And it is this creator God in whose image man and woman together are made. A theology that took this as central would give no endorsement to violence against women, or indeed to any attitudes of exclusiveness, threat, and the violence they breed. There is plenty of love to go 'round, and plenty of good humor and enjoyment with it.

FLOURISHING

In a courtroom, a judge presides. The main concern is to determine the guilt or innocence of those accused of wrongdoing and to mete out appropriate punishments to the guilty. A judge may be harsh or lenient, indictive or merciful. A particularly benevolent judge might even make alternative provisions for the payment of debts if a penitent debtor could not pay; but one way or another the law would have to be satisfied. There will be many assistants to the judge, who police and carry out these legal requirements, including the punishments and sanctioned violence that the judge decrees. All this is a familiar model for much Christian theology.

But what if we think of God as a gardener rather than a judge? Gardeners are not busy with accusations about their plants, or punishing them. Rather, gardeners are concerned with the welfare of their plants and how they flourish, with getting conditions right, and with the beauty and harmony of their garden. Gardeners cherish their plants, tend and prune and care for them, and take immense pleasure and enjoyment in their flourishing. It is a continuous process: a gardener's work is never done. But though there is weeding and pruning as well as planting and watering, there is no place for roughness or violence against the plants of the garden. It is a very different model than the forensic model, and hardly used in Christian theology, though as I have pointed out, it is well warranted by the biblical texts.

What does it mean for a garden to flourish? Most basically, it means that the trees and flowers are alive and growing, being themselves at their full potential. The life of a tree is not something alien or external to it, but of its very nature. It grows and flowers and produces fruit of itself. The gardener ensures appropriate conditions for its growth, adequate light and water and the rest, but having done that, the plant grows from its own inner resources. Compare this with the metaphors of the courtroom. Here the accused, if found guilty, can only be rescued or redeemed from the outside: by definition the guilty person's own resources are inadequate. There is a desperate situation, in which a savior—someone intervening from outside—is required. Left to themselves, those convicted of guilt can expect only punishment. Only if a savior comes to their rescue, paying the penalty on their behalf, will they be redeemed.

Again, these metaphors of salvation are so familiar in Christian thought that it is often forgotten that they are indeed just that: metaphors, not literal truth. And the interventionist model that they generate has been used to justify the actions of all manner of would-be "saviors" who believe themselves to know what constitutes wrongdoing and to have the right to make dramatic and often violent interventions: political, military, and economic interventions from the Crusades to the war in Iraq have appealed to this model of Christendom as a savior to inferior peoples, who should be both subordinate and duly grateful. The same, obviously, has applied to gender constructions within Christendom, where men are deemed superior to women and to have the right to intervene in women's lives so that they will be properly subservient, with the right to violence lurking as a threat against any who would dare to challenge that "law."

A whole different set of attitudes would be derived if we took flourishing rather than salvation as the central metaphor. For a garden to flourish it requires patient, gentle tending, not dramatic intervention, let alone violence, which would be much more likely to make things worse rather than better. A gardener cares for her plants, but they grow of themselves: unless they are alive and thriving she is no more able to get them to flower and fruit than if they were plastic, and no amount of force or violence could be of any possible use. Roses bloom and oak trees produce acorns because it is their nature to do so; they flourish from within themselves, and the gardener smells the fragrance and enjoys the shade and takes pleasure in what they are.

The diversity and variety of plants is again significant: a huge acreage with thousands of the same plant is a monoculture, not a garden. And here another contrast with forensic metaphors emerges. A plant does not flourish by itself alone, but within a whole ecosystem in which each is interdependent with others: plants, birds, insects all interact in the cycle of life. The courtroom, by contrast, concentrates on the individual: on a single person's rights, guilt, and punishment. Each one faces judgement alone. And a savior can save just one of those who are sentenced to death, leaving all the others to execution. Interdependence is not part of the picture. The model of the garden fosters appreciation for diversity rather than distrust of it, and recognition that vast differences of appearance and activity all contribute to the beauty and flourishing of the whole, each participating in the life of all the rest in a harmonious ecosystem.

Again, the whole distinction between active and passive that plays so large a part in Western constructions of savior and saved, as well as masculine and feminine, must be completely reconfigured in organic models. It is absurd to designate one plant as the active one and another as passive. All plants go through phases or cycles of activity and passivity, growth and decay, and their interaction depends upon it. Without death and decay a garden cannot flourish: it is part of the natural cycle. But this is a very different picture of death than that involved in a model of sacrifice, where the blood of a victim is required for the forgiveness of sin and where killing is inscribed into the heart of salvation. That model, as I showed earlier, has been used regularly in Christendom not only as an account of the death of Christ but also as a technology of gender oppression that makes women's self-sacrifice not only expected but holy. By contrast, the cycles of activity and passivity, growth and decay, of plants has nothing to do with killing or with violence or external intervention but is what the organism itself needs in its natural pattern, again with great diversity in the cycles of different plants. The binary distinctions of Western gender constructions simply do not map onto organic models in any intelligible way: indeed one might speculate that that is one reason why the masculinist tradition of Western Christendom has so largely ignored organic metaphors and emphasized forensic ones in a self-perpetuating pattern of oppression and violence.

BEAUTY

Gardens are grown for many reasons, some of them for their utility, for the fruit that they bear. But central to the idea of a garden, from the Garden of Eden to paradise, is beauty. The plants and trees of the garden are pleasant to the eyes, a delight to the senses. Now, beauty has not played a large part in Christian theology in modernity. This is true not only of conservative and masculinist theologies: where are the liberationist or progressive or feminist theologies that take beauty as a central theme?[7] Especially (but not only) Protestant theology has concentrated on truth

---

7. The notable exception is the multivolume *Herrlichkeit* of Hans Urs von Balthasar, but even this moves quickly to the language of covenant and does not explore organic metaphors.

and beliefs, to such an extent that the terms "believer" and "unbeliever" stand for "Christian" and "non-Christian" in contemporary discourse. There are many books on the arguments for the existence of God or the correct way to understand religious doctrines, but very little on beauty. Yet surely more people are drawn to the divine and to spirituality through the beauty of nature than are ever convinced by arguments or creeds. Churches and theologians have got things the wrong way around; and it is hard not to draw the conclusion that this is yet another manifestation of the implicit masculinism of Christendom. After all, truths and beliefs are standard technologies of mastery, which have served through the millennia as justification for holy war and violence of every kind.

Suppose, however, that we were to take beauty as central. (For present purposes I shall attend only to the beauty of nature, in keeping with organic models, though much of what I say would apply also to the more complicated beauties of human making, such as art, music, and architecture.) Deepening sensibility to beauty is, I suggest, an unexplored resource against violence, including violence against women. I can do no more in this chapter than indicate some of the avenues to be investigated if we take beauty as central—if the representation of God as the creator of a beautiful garden is given as much weight as God the giver of the covenant, and the organic metaphors of flourishing as much as the forensic metaphors of the courtroom and salvation.

First, sensitivity to beauty engenders attitudes of attentiveness, preservation, and protection. If I take delight in roses and oak trees, hills and streams, I will want to enjoy them often and do what I can to see that they are protected. It makes no sense to assert that I delight in roses if I then carelessly pour herbicide over them, or to say that I love the hills and streams if it is all the same to me if the streams are polluted and a road or housing estate is built across the hillside. Similarly, if we are attentive to the beauty and flourishing of one another, we will seek to nurture and preserve one another and stand against all forms of violence and violation. Christian theology has had little to say about how beautiful we are, body and soul, and worried much more about the (possibly erotic) attractions of beauty, taking that as a cause of anxiety rather than joy. If instead we were to encourage delight in one another's beauty as each of us is formed by the creator God, like plants in the divine garden in diversity, then destruction, careless or deliberate, is not just ruled out by some kind of law or command, but is contrary to instinctive response to beauty.

Secondly, increased sensibility to beauty encourages empathy and understanding, in which we appreciate things not for their function or utility but for their uniqueness. The intricacy of light through autumn leaves, the darting flight of a dipper over a brook, the rainbow arching over the valley give me pleasure and gladness that has nothing to do with their use value. Moreover, as I develop in delight of these things, sometimes delicate and fragile as alpine flowers, sometimes as steady as the stars, I enter more fully into each unique beauty, not requiring one to be like another but valuing the diversity. I try to understand them better: learn to know where to look for the dipper or how to identify the lichen around a stream. Such increasing sensitivity and appreciation leave no space for violence. If Christian theology were to encourage development of sensitivity to beauty with the same vigor that it has promoted adherence to moral rules, the ethos that tolerates violence would be radically converted.

Finally, beauty prompts generosity. When we experience something especially delightful, we like to share it with those we feel would enjoy it too. We tell them about it, take photographs, send postcards that say "Wish you were here!" There is no need for exclusive possession: indeed most of the time it makes no sense. Who owns a rainbow? Courtroom metaphors have helped to foster ideas that women are in some sense property of men, theirs to be mastered so that they will serve men's needs, and subject to violent discipline if they do not. Organic metaphors that are open to beauty subvert all that, opening the hands to one another instead of closing them in a possessive grip that turns easily into a fist.

Christendom has made much of covenant, holy war, and sacrifice. From the slaughter of animals to the holocaust of Auschwitz and Hiroshima, to the killing fields of Iraq, the world is strewn with the ashes of violence in the name of a jealous God or his self-appointed secular surrogates. Women are disproportionately the victims. But in the Christian tradition, too, is the insistence that God desires mercy, not sacrifice; that God is a gardener who delights in the flourishing of his creation; that God will give

> a garland instead of ashes,
> the oil of gladness instead of mourning . . .
> that they may be called oaks of righteousness,
> the planting of the Lord . . . (Isa. 61:3)

Progressive Christians would do well to appropriate these organic metaphors and develop their resources for change. The beauty of a garden, the flourishing of its plants, bring joy and delight rather than the ashes of sacrifice. Unless we learn to value this beauty, only ashes will be left.

3

The Karma of Women

DAVID R. LOY

What does Buddhism have to say about the social situation of women? Needless to say, there is no simple answer to such a question. True to its own emphasis on impermanence, Buddhism became quite different in different cultures. If Buddhism is not what the Buddha taught, but what he started, we are presented with a complicated set of teachings, practices, and historical traditions, which are not always consistent with each other. To impose a helpful pattern upon this collection of "Buddhisms," one needs to distinguish (1) the original teachings and life story of Shakyamuni Buddha, as recorded in the Pali Canon, the oldest texts we have, from (2) later Buddhist teachings and practices, and also from (3) the actual role of Buddhism today in maintaining or challenging the situation of women in contemporary Buddhist cultures.

Since there are too many Buddhist societies to discuss in any meaningful way, this chapter—like the chapter in this book by Ouyporn Khuankaew—focuses mainly but not exclusively on Thailand, one of the most devoutly Buddhist nations in the world.[1] It also has what is probably the largest and best organized sex trade in the world: up to a million sex workers (out of a total population of about seventy million people), easily dwarfing the declining number of Buddhist monks (less than three hundred thousand *bhikkhu*). One of the main concerns of this chapter is to understand the relationship between Thai Buddhism and its extraordinary sex industry, a major source of Thailand's gross national product. Religions serve a double function in society: they help to mold our most important values,

---

1. There are good reasons for this emphasis on Thai Buddhism. Thailand is the only Buddhist nation never colonized or conquered by the West, which means that Thai Buddhism has been less affected by external religious traditions, and Buddhism continues to play a major role in Thai society.

attitudes, and behaviors, but they also absorb and reflect preexisting values, attitudes, and behaviors. So what role does Buddhism presently play in encouraging or rationalizing the Thai sex business? What role might it play in discouraging prostitution and empowering women generally?

How might antiwoman problems in Buddhism illustrate problems found in the other religions studied in this book?

THE LIBERATION OF WOMEN

The earliest Buddhist texts reveal a curious ambivalence about women, which reminds us to place the Buddha's transformative message in its original social context. Although revered as the original words of Shakyamuni Buddha, these teachings were preserved orally for about four hundred years before being written down, providing many opportunities for some passages to be intentionally or unintentionally "corrected" by monks less enlightened than the Buddha. Just as important, however, we need to remember that the historical Buddha was raised in a very patriarchal culture. His teachings as they have come down to us perhaps reveal a struggle against that sexist conditioning.

Buddhism arose largely in response to the Brahmanical culture developing in India in the middle of the first millennium BCE. Brahmanism emphasized caste and the inferiority of women. As later codified in the Laws of Manu, women were fettered to men for life: first as obedient daughters, then as subservient wives, and finally as aging mothers dependent on their sons. A wife's main duty was to produce sons. She was usually confined to the home and had no rights of her own—certainly no opportunity to study the Vedas (reserved for male Brahmins) or engage in other spiritual practices.

Religiously, a large part of the problem was that women are believed to be polluted and polluting. This refers not only to their association with blood (the messiness of menstruation and childbirth), but especially to their role as temptress and seducer, an uncontrollable threat to the chastity of ascetic men trying to follow a spiritual path. Women were chastised for their stronger sex drive, which today seems like a classic example of psychological projection: ascetics blaming their own problems with celibacy on women, the objects of their lust.

Early Buddhism did not completely escape this misogyny, for there are many such passages in the Pali Canon, some of them attributed to the Buddha, who warned his monks about the impurity of sexuality generally, and the snares of women in particular. A prime symbol of this is the three daughters of Mara, the Buddhist symbol of evil (although a rather bland symbol compared to the malevolent Satan of Christianity), who tempted him just before his final enlightenment: although Mara himself is male, his offspring *Raga* (lust), *Arati* (ill-will), and *Thana* (craving) are always depicted as feminine.

In contrast to reinforcing such patriarchal stereotypes, however, the Buddha's main teaching to householders was almost revolutionary in its historical context. In the *Sigalovada Sutta*, he instructs a husband to minister to his wife in five ways: by being courteous to her, not despising her, being faithful to her, giving her authority (presumably at home), and providing her with ornaments. From the other side, a wife should show compassion to her husband also in five ways: by performing her duties well, being hospitable to relations and attendants, being faithful, protecting what he brings home, and being skilled and industrious in discharging her duties.[2] Such injunctions may seem unremarkable to us today, but what is extraordinary for his time is that the marital relationship is understood to be reciprocal, with both sides having rights and responsibilities—making marriage, in effect, a contract between equals, a momentous step in the male-dominated Iron Age culture of sixth-century BCE India.

But what about the spiritual potential of women? That is the acid test for religious patriarchy, and one that the Buddha passed—but evidently it took him a while. Again, the texts suggest some ambivalence. It wasn't until five or six years after his enlightenment that he agreed to meet with a delegation of women, led by his aunt and foster mother Mahapajapati Gotami. They asked for an order of *bhikkhuni* nuns to be established, to join the male *sangha* of *bhikkhu* monks. Several times the Buddha refused, but when his attendant Ananda asked him if women were equal in their capacity for enlightenment, he admitted that they were as capable of following the contemplative life. He then yielded to their repeated request—but with special conditions, eight additional rules of conduct, that made nuns forever subordinate to the monks.[3] Unsurprisingly, internal textual evidence strongly suggests that those rules were added to the passage later. The text then goes on to have the Buddha confide in Ananda that had

---

2. *Digha Nikaya*, sutta 31.
3. The eight additional rules are: (1) any *bhikkhuni*, no matter how senior, must respectfully salute any *bhikkhu*, no matter how junior; (2) aspiring *bhikkhuni* must undergo a two-year training period and then be ordained by both the *bhikkhu sangha* and the *bhikkhuni sangha*; (3) *bhikkhuni* must not criticize *bhikkhu*; (4) *bhikkhuni* must not receive alms before *bhikkhu*; (5) *bhikkhuni* who violate rules are subject to disciplinary action and then must ask to be reinstated by both the *bhikkhu sangha* and the *bhikkhuni sangha*; (6) every fortnight *bhikkhuni* should ask *bhikkhu* for instruction; (7) *bhikkhuni* must not spend the rainy season retreat in the company of *bhikkhu*; (8) *bhikkhuni* should request the ceremony marking the end of the rainy season retreat from both the *bhikkhu sangha* and the *bhikkhuni sangha*. The *Bhikkhuni vibhanga* commentary on the *Bhikkhuni-patimokkha* includes other sets of lesser rules for women monastics.

women not been admitted as monastics his teaching would have survived more than a thousand years; now due to the admission of women, it would only last five hundred years.[4] Whether or not this prediction was actually made by the Buddha himself, it turned out to be wrong: the Buddhist teachings continue to exist, and in some ways they are thriving more than ever. For devout Buddhists, this is not a trivial point: either the text is corrupt, which implies that other passages may also have been altered, or even the Buddha was capable of significant mistakes—or both. We shall have occasion to return to this dilemma later, but in either case there are important implications for how we should approach the canonical teachings.

The *bhikkhuni*—the first order of female monastics in human history—initially thrived, although their contributions to Buddhism have been neglected by the male monastics who compiled its history. Many of the *bhikkhuni* attained liberation, and the Buddha had occasion to praise at least thirteen of them. Some of their enlightenment verses are included in the Pali Canon, and some of those *Therigatha* suggest a Buddhist protofeminism. For example, Soma Theri wrote:

What harm is it
To be a woman
When the mind is concentrated
And the insight is clear?

If I asked myself
"Am I a woman
or a man in this?"
then I would be speaking
Mara's language.[5]

In other words, when it comes to the spiritual path, discriminating according to gender is a delusion.

So far, so good . . . for a while. But once the Buddha was no longer around to keep an eye on things, patriarchy began to reassert itself, and the situation of Buddhist women began to deteriorate, for both nuns and laywomen. In Theravada countries the *bhikkhuni* order shrank and disappeared—in Thailand, only about three hundred years after it had been established.[6] Some Mahayana sutras claimed that women must first be reborn (or magically transformed) into men before they could become fully enlight-

---

4. See *Anguttara Nikaya* 6.01ff.

5. In Susan Murcott, *The First Buddhist Women: Translations and Commentaries on the Therigatha* (Berkeley, Calif.: Parallax, 1991), 158–59.

6. This claim is controversial: the evidence is limited, and some Thai scholars claim that the *bhikkhuni sangha* was never fully established in Thailand.

ened Buddhas, and this belief became widespread in Asian Buddhism. Other Mahayana scriptures, however, continued to present more positive images of women that are more consistent with the central Mahayana concept of *shunyata* "emptiness": if men and women are equally *shunya*—both lacking any self-essence—then there is no ground for any gender discrimination. In the Chan/Son/Zen Buddhism of China, Korea, and Japan, for example, the enlightened mind is neither male nor female, and there are notable examples of female Zen adepts. But such spiritual subtleties did not serve to check the revalidation of male superiority in Buddhist cultures. With the partial exception of Taiwan, where the Mahayana *bhikkhuni* order is thriving today, women are perceived as inferior to men in Asian Buddhist societies. And there is a Buddhist explanation for that: those unfortunate enough to be born as women are reaping the fruits of their inferior karma.

THE KARMA OF WOMEN'S SUFFERING

In Buddhist societies where women are not allowed to be fully ordained as monks, women are often told by monks that having been born a woman is a result of bad karma. In order to redress this problem, the only thing that women can do is to accumulate a lot of merit in this life, so that in their next life they will be born men, and then they can become monks if they choose to. This way of thinking makes women feel inferior and that they are to blame for the outcome of their lives. It makes them more willing to accept whatever gender-based violence they experience, since it is seen as a direct result of their unlucky fate in having been born a woman.

> When a woman asks for guidance from a monk when the husband is the cause of her suffering (such as instances where he has another woman, is physically or mentally abusive to her, gambles their money away, drinks alcohol, etc.), the monk's main advice is for her to be patient and compassionate. Often times, the monk will say that karma is the cause of her suffering, so she has no choice but to accept and deal with the situation, and continue to be kind to her husband so that one day the karmic force will subside and everything will be fine. We found that this kind of thinking is not only the belief of the monks themselves but that it is also prominent among the followers of Buddhism in Southeast Asia, including women. . . . It is one of the factors that keeps a woman in a marriage even though her life may be in danger, and it explains why neighbors and community leaders choose not to intervene.[7]

---

7. Ouyporn Khuankaew, "Buddhism and Domestic Violence," in *WFB Review: Journal of the World Federation of Buddhists* vol. 39, nos. 3–4 (July–December 2002): 22–26, at 23–24. See also Khuankaew's chapter in this volume.

In this passage Ouyporn Khuankaew shows the relationship between the subordination of women (including the violence they suffer) and the popular Buddhist understanding of karma. Examining this conception and application of karma will be the main focus of the rest of this chapter, especially the implications of this relationship for prostitution and the Thai sex industry.[8]

To begin, it is important to realize that the earliest Buddhist texts do not reflect a disparaging, strongly negative attitude toward women who sell their sexual favors. Unlike the moralism of Western Christendom (but perhaps not unlike the attitude of Jesus himself?), sex workers were not condemned as sinful. Prostitution was widespread in the India of his time and the Buddha did not discriminate against prostitutes. Instead, he provided them with the opportunity to join the *bhikkhuni* order (which required them to reform and become celibate, of course) in order to pursue the path to liberation. These early texts even include positive references to some courtesans, such as the wealthy Ambapali, who is well-known in Buddhist literature for her gift of a mango grove to the Buddha and *sangha*. She later renounced her profession, gave away her possessions, and became a *bhikkhuni* whose diligent practice soon led to enlightenment and a new role as a skilled Dharma teacher. Like some other sex workers, she may have progressed so rapidly on the spiritual path because she had experienced the chaotic extremes of those pursuing sensual pleasure and realized the frustration of a life devoted to satisfying such cravings. Or is the problem better understood as the commodification of sexual pleasure, and the degradation of those expected to provide it?

Her midlife career change points to an imbalance that still persists between the Buddhist *sangha* and the position of women in Buddhist cultures: there is a sharp contrast between the high social status of monks and the inferior status of women, who typically suffer from low self-esteem and feelings of worthlessness. Somewhat similar to the Catholic mother whose son becomes a priest, Buddhist mothers whose sons become *bhikkhus* gain lots of merit, as well as an enhanced status in society; but the *sangha* is no longer an option for their daughters, who therefore may be called upon to serve their families in other ways. This makes the less judgmental attitude of Buddhism toward prostitution a mixed blessing in practice. Most Thai sex workers, like most of those in other

---

8. The role of Buddhism should not be overemphasized. The main causes of the Thai sex industry are economic and political: the poverty of most Thai families, the increasing role of consumerism (including the desire for a higher income), along with the new business opportunities opened up in the 1960s and '70s by the "rest and recreation" of a large number of American G.I.s fighting in Vietnam.

Asian nations, work to send money to their families, which are often large and impoverished. They are trying to fulfill their sense of duty to their parents by sharing the economic burden in the only way they can (although hardly lucrative for the girls themselves, sex work is still much better paid than factory work). The recurring problems of rural agriculture, sometimes aggravated by the father's or sons' gambling debts, not infrequently lead to parents asking a daughter to "sacrifice" for the sake of the family.[9]

One part of a solution to this situation, therefore, might involve reintroducing the *bhikkhuni sangha*.[10] This would not resolve the economic woes of rural families, but it would raise the status (and therefore the self-esteem) of women whose capacity for enlightenment is thereby acknowledged. Not only would parents also gain merit when their daughter became a nun, but respected *bhikkhuni* would be in a better position to advise other women and offer spiritual guidance.

There have been some recent attempts to reintroduce the *bhikkhuni* order in Sri Lanka, Thailand, and Myanmar, but they continue to be resisted by the established *bhikkhu* hierarchy, and it is too early to know how well they will succeed. Up to now, at least, the response of the Thai Buddhist authorities to the sex industry has also not been helpful. The official *sangha* establishment tends to be quite reserved, which is to say conservative, toward all social issues, while individual monks and temples often profit from emphasizing the inferiority of women in general and the bad karma accumulated by sex workers in particular. Women and prostitutes are encouraged to offer *dana* (money and other valuables) to the temple in order to make more merit and guarantee a better rebirth next time. As a result, some temples, especially in northern Thailand, have become wealthy and well adorned as an indirect result of the sex industry.[11]

---

9. Chatsumaarn Kabilsingh, *Thai Women in Buddhism* (Berkeley, Calif.: Parallax, 1991), 78.

10. See Tavivat Puntarigvivat, "A Thai Buddhist Perspective," in John C. Raines and Daniel C. Maguire, eds., *What Men Owe to Women: Men's Voices from World Religions* (Albany: State University of New York Press, 2001), 211–38.

11. Chatsumaarn Kabilsingh, "Prostitution and Buddhism," in *WFB Review: Journal of the World Federation of Buddhists* vol. 39, nos. 3–4 (July–December 2002): 94–98 at 97. There have also been accusations of widespread pedophilia (mainly sexual abuse of boys) within the Thai *sangha*, especially among those in positions of authority, but these are difficult to confirm: those with the power to investigate this evidently do not want to do so (see *WFB Review*, op. cit., 30). If true, the similarity with recent problems in the Catholic Church, especially in the United States, reinforces questions that have been raised about the viability of required celibacy in religious institutions—and, perhaps more fundamentally, about the tendency to identify the spiritual life with celibacy, "the strangest of the sexual perversions" (Jacques Thibault).

The basic presupposition of this behavior, or social trap, is that one's present life situation, whether good or bad, enjoyable or painful, is a consequence of one's moral behavior in previous lifetimes. Ambapali escaped this bind by joining the *bhikkhuni* order and following the path to enlightenment, which puts an end to the cycle of rebirths. Since the *bhikkhuni* order has disappeared, contemporary Thai women must try to counteract the negative consequences of their bad karma in other ways. One can gain merit by reciting sutras and other devotions, but the main way is by making *dana* to the monks and temples. With enough merit, one will be reborn into more favorable circumstances—perhaps even as a man.

Unfortunately, the male Thai *sangha* benefits enormously from this understanding, or rather misunderstanding, of Buddhist teachings about karma and rebirth. Obviously, so do all those who organize and profit from the sex industry, who are relieved of any fleeting guilt feelings they might otherwise have, and also spared any resistance on the part of their sex workers, who have no one else to blame but themselves (in a past life) for their present situation. The responsibility for their own abuse is really in their own hands, not in those of the powerful men and patriarchal social structures that seem to exploit them. It is a classic case of "blame the victim," protecting the perpetrators and wrapping the structures of exploitation in invisibility and inevitability.[12] Moreover, if some women want to get uppity and rebel against this system, they are only creating more bad karma for themselves.[13]

Obviously, this understanding of karma and rebirth has important implications for much more than the Thai sex industry. The connections with other types of physical and structural violence against women could also be discussed, as well as many other nongendered consequences regarding the rationalization of racism, economic oppression, birth handicaps, and so forth. Karma is used to justify both the authority of political elites, who therefore deserve their wealth and power, and the subordination of those who have neither. It provides the perfect theodicy: there is an infallible cause-and-effect relationship between one's moral actions and one's fate, so there is no need to work toward social justice, which is already built into the moral fabric of the universe. In fact, if there is no undeserved suffering, there is really no evil that we need to struggle against.

---

12. Rita Nakashima Brock and Susan Brooks Thistlewaite, *Casting Stones: Prostitution and Liberation in Asia and the United States* (Minneapolis: Fortress Press, 1996), 237.
13. Rita M. Gross, *Buddhism after Patriarchy: A Feminist History, Analysis, and Reconstruction of Buddhism* (Albany: State University of New York Press, 1993), 143.

For these reasons, karma is probably the most critical issue for contemporary Buddhist societies. That brings us to our main concern: Has it been misunderstood? Is it a fatalistic doctrine, or is it an empowering one?

UNDERSTANDINGS OF KARMA

"By the power of my merit, may I be reborn a male . . ." (fifteenth-century inscription of a queen mother).

The previous sections imply that karma (along with its correlative, rebirth) has become a problem for modern Buddhists that can no longer be evaded. To accept the popular, now "traditional" Buddhist understanding about them as literal truth—that karmic determinism is a "moral law" of the universe, with an inevitable and precise calculus of cause and effect comparable to Newton's laws of physics—leads to a severe case of cognitive dissonance for contemporary Buddhism, since the physical causality that modern science has discovered about the world seems to allow for no mechanism for karma or rebirth to operate. How should modern Buddhists respond to this situation?

In the *Kalama Sutta*, sometimes called "the Buddhist charter of free inquiry," the Buddha emphasized the importance of intelligent, probing doubt: we should not believe in something until we have established its truth for ourselves. To accept karmic rebirth in a literal way, simply because it has long been accepted as part of the Buddha's teaching, may thus be unfaithful to the best of the tradition. Given a healthy skepticism about the Iron Age belief systems of the Buddha's time, one should hesitate before making such an enormous leap of faith. Instead of tying one's spiritual path, and social role, to belief in such a doctrine, is it wiser for contemporary Buddhists to be agnostic about it? Consider the way the *Kalama Sutta* concludes. After emphasizing the importance of evaluating for oneself the spiritual claims of others, the Buddha finishes his talk by describing someone who has a truly purified mind:

> "'Suppose there is a hereafter and there is a fruit, result, of deeds done well or ill. Then it is possible that at the dissolution of the body after death, I shall arise in the heavenly world, which is possessed of the state of bliss.' This is the first solace found by him.
>
> "'Suppose there is no hereafter and there is no fruit, no result, of deeds done well or ill. Yet in this world, here and now, free from hatred, free from malice, safe and sound, and happy, I keep myself.' This is the second solace found by him.
>
> "'Suppose evil (results) befall an evil-doer. I, however, think of doing evil to no one. Then, how can ill (results) affect me who do no evil deed?' This is the third solace found by him.

"'Suppose evil (results) do not befall an evil-doer. Then I see my-self purified in any case.' This is the fourth solace found by him."[14]

These intriguing verses can be understood in different ways. The Buddha is speaking to non-Buddhists, so he does not presuppose a Buddhist worldview in describing the fruits of a purified mind. Yet there is another way to take this passage, which is more relevant for twenty-first-century Buddhists. Do our actions bear fruit in a hereafter? For the sake of argument, at least, the Buddha adopts an agnostic view in this important sutta. Maybe they do, maybe they don't. In either case, a purified mind finds solace by cherishing good deeds and avoiding bad ones.

In this sutra, the Buddha's lack of dogmatism shines forth. We can understand his tactful words as a skillful means for speaking with the Kalamas, who are weary of doctrinaire spiritual assertions. But we can also focus on the agnosticism about rebirth, which also implies a different understanding of karma and its consequences. If those of us who are Buddhists are honest with ourselves, we really do not know what to think about karma and rebirth. We wonder if testimony about near-death experiences supports a literal view. At the same time, a literal understanding hardly seems compatible with what modern science has discovered about the physical world. So are karma and rebirth fact or myth? If I consider myself a Buddhist, do I have to take them literally? Here the Buddha speaks directly to our skeptical age: in the most important sense, it does not matter which is true, because if we know what is good for us (and those around us) we will endeavor to live the same way in either case.

Challenging the usual literal understanding is not to dismiss or disparage Buddhist teachings about karma and rebirth. Rather, it highlights the need for modern Buddhism to *interrogate* them. Given what is now known about human psychology, including the social construction of the self, how might they be understood today?

One of the most basic principles of Buddhism is interdependence, but Buddhists do not usually realize what that implies about the original teachings of the Buddha. Interdependence means that nothing has any "self-existence," because everything is part of everything else. Nothing is self-originated, because everything arises according to causes and conditions. Yet Buddhism, it is believed, originates in and remains grounded in the unmediated experience of Shakyamuni, who became "the Buddha"— that is, "the awakened one" —upon his attainment of nirvana under the Bodhi tree. Different Buddhist scriptures describe that experience in dif-

---

14. *Anguttara Nikaya* 3.65. This translation by Soma Thera was found at http://buddhism .kala chakranet.org/resources/kalama_sutra.html (accessed July 8, 2005).

ferent ways, but for all Buddhist traditions his awakening is the source of Buddhism, which unlike Hinduism does not rely upon ancient revealed texts such as the Vedas.

Buddhists usually take the above for granted, yet there is a problem with it: the Buddha's enlightenment story, as usually told, is a myth of self-origination. If the interdependence of everything is true, the truth of Buddhism could not have sprung up independently from all the other spiritual beliefs of the Buddha's time and place (Iron Age India), without any relationship to them. Instead, the teachings of Shakyamuni must be understood as a *response* to those other teachings, but a response that, inevitably, also *presupposed* many of the spiritual beliefs current in that cultural milieu—that took for granted, for example, popular notions of karma and rebirth, which were widespread at that time in India. In some of the Pali sutras, the Buddha mentions remembering his past lifetimes. We should ourselves remember that the reality of past lives was widely accepted then, and that an ability to remember them was not unique to Buddha or Buddhists. Perhaps a contemporary equivalent is the adult recovery of childhood memories—some of which are later discovered to be false.

Consider the following insightful comment that Erich Fromm made about another (although very different!) revolutionary, Sigmund Freud:

> The attempt to understand Freud's theoretical system, or that of any creative systematic thinker, cannot be successful unless we recognize that, and why, every system as it is developed and presented by its author is necessarily erroneous . . . the creative thinker must think in the terms of the logic, the thought patterns, the expressible concepts of his culture. That means he has not yet the proper words to express the creative, the new, the liberating idea. He is forced to solve an insoluble problem: to express the new thought in concepts and words that do not yet exist in his language. . . . The consequence is that the new thought as he formulated it is a blend of what is truly new and the conventional thought which it transcends. The thinker, however, is not conscious of this contradiction.[15]

Fromm's point is that even the most revolutionary thinkers cannot stand on their own shoulders. They too remain dependent upon their context, whether intellectual or spiritual—which, to say it again, is precisely what Buddhist emphasis on impermanence and causal interdependence implies.

---

15. Erich Fromm, *The Greatness and Limitations of Freud's Thought* (London: Sphere Books, 1982), 1, 3.

Of course, there are many important differences between Freud and Shakyamuni, but the parallel is nevertheless very revealing: the Buddha too expressed his new, liberating insight in the only way he could, in the religious categories that his culture could understand and that he himself was a product of. Inevitably, then, his way of expressing the Dharma was a blend of the truly new (for example, teachings about *anatta,* "nonself" and *paticca-samuppada,* "interdependent origination") and the conventional religious thought of his time (karma and rebirth) "which it transcends." That there is always tension between what is new and what is conventional speaks directly to a possible inconsistency that has puzzled many Buddhists over the centuries: is *anatta* nonself really compatible with the older, more traditional beliefs in karma and literal rebirth?

Earlier Indian teachings such as the Vedas tended to understand karma more mechanically and ritualistically. To perform a sacrifice in the proper fashion would invariably lead to the desired consequences. If those consequences were not forthcoming, then either there had been an error in procedure or the causal effects were delayed, perhaps until one's next lifetime (a reason for believing in reincarnation). The Buddha's spiritual revolution transformed this ritualistic approach to controlling one's life into an ethical principle by focusing on *cetana* "motivations," and *cetana* is the key to understanding how he ethicized karma. Probably the most popular early Buddhist text, the *Dhammapada,* begins by emphasizing the preeminent importance of our mental attitude:

> Experiences are preceded by mind, led by mind, and produced by mind. If one speaks or acts with an impure mind, suffering follows even as the cart-wheel follows the hoof of the ox.
>
> Experiences are preceded by mind, led by mind, and produced by mind. If one speaks or acts with a pure mind, happiness follows like a shadow that never departs.[16]

To understand the Buddhist innovation, it is helpful to distinguish a moral act into its three aspects: the *results* that I seek; the *moral rule or regulation* I am following (for example, a Buddhist precept or Christian commandment, but this also includes ritualistic procedures); and my mental attitude or *motivation* when I do something. These aspects cannot be separated from each other, but we can emphasize one more than the others—in fact, that is what we usually do. In modern moral theory, for example, utilitarian theories focus on consequences, deontological theories focus on moral principles such as the Decalogue, and "virtue theories" focus on

---

16. *The Dhammapada,* trans. Juan Mascaro (Harmondsworth: Penguin Classic, 1973), 35, verses 1–2.

one's character and motivations. In the Buddha's time, the Brahmanical understanding of karma emphasized the importance of following the detailed procedures (rules) regulating each ritual; naturally, however, the people who paid for the rituals were more interested in the outcome (results). Arguably, the situation in some Theravada Buddhist countries, including Thailand, is not much different today: male monastics are preoccupied with following the complicated rules regulating their lives (which according to the popular view is what makes them "good" monks), while laypeople (most of them women) are preoccupied with accumulating merit by giving gifts to them (which makes them second-class Buddhists, focused on the future karmic consequences of their commodified relationship with monks). Both of these attitudes miss the point of the Buddha's spiritual innovation.

Earlier, I cited evidence of error and/or alteration in some passages of the Pali Canon, the earliest Buddhist texts we have. What does this imply about apparent inconsistencies in what the Buddha said about karma? Some of his statements—and perhaps it is no coincidence that these tend to favor the material benefit of the *bhikkhu*—support a more deterministic view (for example, the *Culakammavibhanga Sutta*,[17] where karma is used to explain various differences between people, including physical appearance and economic inequality). However, there are several other texts where the Buddha clearly denies moral determinism, for example the *Tittha Sutta* in which the Buddha argues that such a view denies the possibility of following a spiritual path:

> There are priests and contemplatives who hold this teaching, hold this view: "Whatever a person experiences—pleasant, painful, or neither pleasant nor painful—that is all caused by what was done in the past." . . . Then I said to them, "Then in that case, a person is a killer of living beings because of what was done in the past. A person is a thief . . . unchaste . . . a liar . . . a divisive speaker . . . a harsh speaker . . . an idle chatterer . . . greedy . . . malicious . . . a holder of wrong views because of what was done in the past." When one falls back on what was done in the past as being essential, monks, there is no desire, no effort [at the thought], "This should be done. This shouldn't be done." When one can't pin down as a truth or reality what should and shouldn't be done, one dwells bewildered and unprotected. One cannot righteously refer to oneself as a contemplative.[18]

---

17. *Majjhima Nikaya*, sutta 135.
18. *Tittha Sutta, Anguttara Nikaya* 3.61. This translation by Thanissaro Bhikkhu is at http://www.buddhistinformation.com/ida_b_wells_memorial_sutra_library/tittha_sutta.htm (accessed July 8, 2005).

In another short sutta, an ascetic named Sivaka asked the Buddha about a view held by some ascetics and Brahmins that "'whatever a person experiences, be it pleasure, pain or neither-pain-nor-pleasure, all that is caused by previous action.' Now, what does the revered Gotama [Buddha] say about this?"

> Produced by (disorders of the) bile, there arise, Sivaka, certain kinds of feelings. That this happens, can be known by oneself; also in the world it is accepted as true. Produced by (disorders of the) phlegm . . . of wind . . . of (the three) combined . . . by change of climate . . . by adverse behavior . . . by injuries . . . by the results of Karma—(through all that), Sivaka, there arise certain kinds of feelings. That this happens can be known by oneself; also in the world it is accepted as true. Now when these ascetics and Brahmins have such a doctrine and view that "whatever a person experiences, be it pleasure, pain or neither-pain-nor-pleasure, all that is caused by previous action," then they go beyond what they know by themselves and what is accepted as true by the world. Therefore, I say that this is wrong on the part of these ascetics and Brahmins.[19]

Other texts could be cited, but this is not the place for a close textual analysis of all the relevant passages.[20] The point to be gleaned from the preceding references is that the earliest Buddhist teachings about karma are not only sometimes humorous ("produced by wind . . .") but also ambiguous, and therefore insufficient by themselves as a guide for understanding karma today. That brings us back to the Buddha's great insight into the moral preeminence of the motivations of our actions. How should we today understand the originality of his approach?

The most important point about karma is not whether it is a moral law involving some inevitable and precise calculus of cause and effect. The original Sanskrit term *karma* literally means "action" (*phala* is the "fruit" of action), and as this suggests the basic point is that our actions have consequences—and, more precisely, that our morally relevant actions have morally relevant consequences that extend beyond their immediate physical effects. In the popular Buddhist understanding, the law of karma and rebirth is a way to manipulate how the world treats us, which also implies, more immediately, that we must accept our own

19. *Moliyasivaka Sutta, Samyutta Nikaya* 36.21. This translation by Nyanaponika Thera is at http://www.buddhistinformation.com/ida_b_wells_memorial_sutra_library/tittha_sutta .htm (accessed July 8, 2005).
20. See Nagapriya, *Exploring Karma & Rebirth* (Birmingham: Windhorse, 2004).

causal responsibility for whatever is happening to us now. This misses the revolutionary significance of the Buddha's reinterpretation: karma is better understood as the key to spiritual development: *how our life-situation can be transformed by transforming the motivations of our actions right now*. When we add the Buddhist teaching about nonself—the claim, consistent with modern psychology, that one's sense of self is a mental construct—we can see that karma is not something I *have*, it is what "I" *am*, and what I am changes according to my conscious choices. "I" (re)construct myself by what "I" intentionally do, because "my" sense of self is a precipitate of my habitual ways of thinking, feeling, and acting. Just as my body is composed of the food I eat, so my character is composed of my conscious choices, constructed by my consistent, repeated mental attitudes. People are "punished" or "rewarded" not for what they have done but for what they have become, and what we intentionally do is what makes us what we are. An anonymous verse expresses this well:

Sow a thought and reap a deed.
Sow a deed and reap a habit.
Sow a habit and reap a character.
Sow a character and reap a destiny.

What kinds of thoughts and deeds do we need to sow? Buddhism does not have much to say about evil per se, but our *dukkha* (unhappiness) is attributed to the three "unwholesome roots" (*akusala-mula*) of action: greed, ill will, and delusion.[21] These need to be transformed into their positive counterparts: greed into nonattached generosity, ill will into loving-kindness, and the delusion of separate self into the wisdom that realizes our interdependence with others.

Such an understanding of karma does not necessarily involve another life after we physically die. As Spinoza expressed it, happiness is not the reward for virtue; happiness is virtue itself. Likewise, we are punished not for our sins but by them. To become a different kind of person is to experience the world in a different way. When your mind changes, the world changes. And when we respond differently to the world, the world responds differently to us. Since we are actually nondual with the world—our sense of separation from it being a delusion—our ways of acting in it tend to involve reinforcing feedback systems that incorporate

---

21. "There are, O monks, three causes for the origination of action. What three? Greed (*lobha*), hatred (*dosa*) and delusion (*moha*)." *Anguttara Nikaya* III, in *Numerical Discourses of the Buddha: An Anthology of Suttas from the Anguttara Nikaya*, trans. and ed. Nyanaponika Thera and Bhikkhu Bodhi (New York: Altamira, 1999), 49–50.

other people. People not only notice what we do, they notice why we do it. I may fool people sometimes, but over time my character becomes revealed through the intentions behind my deeds. The more I am motivated by greed, ill will, and delusion, the more I must manipulate the world to get what I want, and consequently the more alienated I feel and the more alienated others feel when they see they have been manipulated. This mutual distrust encourages both sides to manipulate more. On the other side, the more my actions are motivated by generosity, loving-kindness, and the wisdom of interdependence, the more I can relax and open up to the world. The more I feel part of the world and nondual with others, the less I am inclined to use others, and consequently the more inclined they will be to trust and open up to me. In such ways, transforming my own motivations does not only transform my own life; it also affects those around me, since I am not separate from them.

This more naturalistic understanding of karma does not mean we must necessarily exclude other, perhaps more mysterious possibilities regarding the consequences of our motivations for the world we live in; there may well be other aspects of karmic cause and effect that are not so readily understood. What is clear in either case, however, is that karma-as-how-to-transform-my-life-situation-by-transforming-my-motivations-right-now is not a fatalistic doctrine. Quite the contrary: it is difficult to imagine a more empowering spiritual teaching. We are not enjoined to accept the oppressive circumstances of our lives; rather, we are encouraged to improve our spiritual lives and social situation by addressing those circumstances with generosity, loving-kindness, and wisdom. With regard to women, patriarchal institutions are not inevitable, for this "new" understanding of karma implies that our social analysis should highlight and expose the selfish (and deluded) motivations of those who benefit from the suffering of women. Rita Gross puts it well: "what causes the negativity of women's existence under patriarchy is not women's karma, but the self-centered, fixated, habitual patterns of those in power, of those who maintain the status quo. . . . This explanation, which locates the cause of women's misery under male-dominated systems in *present* ego-patterns and self-interest, rather than in past karma, also has the advantage of being a thoroughly *Buddhist* analysis, in addition to making sense in feminist terms."[22]

The sex industry in Thailand and elsewhere, like other forms of physical, cultural, and institutional violence against women, should not be accepted by Buddhists but rather challenged as un-Buddhist—indeed as

---

22. Gross, *Buddhism after Patriarchy,* 145.

anti-Buddhist, because incompatible with its liberative message. Properly understood, the karma doctrine does not imply passive acceptance of any type of violence against women, but rather inspires us to challenge the rationalizations that have attempted to naturalize such violence. It teaches us not only how to transform our lives by transforming our own unwholesome motivations, but also that male and female Buddhists must confront the unwholesome motivations of those who maintain patriarchal systems of domination.

4

A *Tafsir* of Praxis: Gender, Marital Violence, and Resistance in a South African Muslim Community

SA'DIYYA SHAIKH

O ye who believe stand out firmly for justice,
as witnesses to Allah,
even as against yourselves, . . . (Q.4:135)

Indeed Allah commands ('adl) justice and (ihsan) the actualization
of goodness, the realization of beauty. (Q.16:90)

For many Muslims in the contemporary world, these Qur'anic verses resonate Islam's deepest spiritual and ethical imperatives for justice. For those who believe justice, God-consciousness, and the perfection of character to be foundational objectives of an Islamic life, the quest for gender equality remains an abiding concern. Muslims committed to gender egalitarianism are troubled by the rampant patriarchy in their communities and in dominant readings of their religious legacy. Qur'anic verses that instead privilege mutuality in male-female relationships provide a corrective that sustains many of us. Verses reflecting such an ethos include the following:

> And the believers, men and women, are protecting friends (*awliya*) one of another; they enjoin the right and forbid the wrong, and they establish worship and they pay the poor-due, and they obey Allah and Allah's messenger. As for these, Allah will have mercy on them. Lo! Allah is Mighty, Wise. (Q.9:71)

Another verse that focuses particularly on marital relations reads:

> And among Allah's signs is this: that Allah created for you mates from among yourselves, that ye may dwell in tranquility with

them, and Allah has put love and mercy between your (hearts): verily in that are Signs for those who reflect. (Q.30:21)

The notions that believing men and women provide friendship and mutual protection for one another, that they equally undertake moral agency in the world, that human beings strive to live in a state of tranquility with their spouses, that marital relationships are to be approached as the embodiment of divine love and mercy, collectively reflect the Islamic ideal of gender relations to many such committed Muslims.

Such Qur'anic verses also support feminist critiques of hierarchical gender power-relations within Muslim societies. Many Islamic feminists approach the Divine Word as an active and dynamic hermeneutical encounter.[1] Revelation speaks to human beings who are constantly striving to reach progressively deeper understandings of God and the nature of human realities. Within this view, *tafsir*, or Qur'anic exegesis, is woven intricately with ever expanding human conceptions of justice and equality that sculpt the living, emerging, social texts of Islam. Tradition and religious knowledge as such are continually created. Religious ethics then unfold in the human engagement with the Divine. Significantly, such an approach also recognizes that Islamic principles, as articulated within the Qur'an, have always been negotiated within the confines of specific social forces, historical norms, and collective consciousness.[2]

A competing approach in some Muslim communities however, interprets Islam to be a handmaiden of patriarchy.[3] Proponents of this approach may invoke other Qur'anic verses that speak to gender hierarchy as the basis for their perspectives. They cite some of the following verses:

Divorced women shall wait concerning themselves for three monthly periods. Nor is it lawful for them to hide what God has created in their wombs, if they have faith in God and the Last Day. And their husbands have the better right to take them back in that period, if they wish for reconciliation. And women shall have rights similar to the rights against them, according to what is equitable; *but men have a degree (of advantage) over them.* And God is Exalted in Power, Wise. (Q. 2:228)

1. See, for example, the exegetical works of Amina Wadud, *Qur'an and Women: Rereading the Sacred Text from a Woman's Perspective* (New York: Oxford University Press, 1999); and Asma Barlas, "Believing Women," in *Islam: Unreading Patriarchal Interpretations of the Quran* (Austin: University of Texas Press, 2002).
2. For a discussion on the relationship between context and Qur'anic revelation see Fazlur Rahman, *Islam* (Chicago: University of Chicago Press, 1979).
3. See, for example, Barbara Daly Metcalf, *Perfecting Women: Maulana Ashraf 'Ali Thanawi's Bihishti Zewar* (Berkeley: University of California Press, 1990).

Some of these individuals may use the following verse to justify polygyny:

> If you fear that you shall not be able to deal justly with the or-
> phans, marry women of your choice, two or three or four; but if
> you fear that you shall not be able to deal justly (with them), then
> only one, or (a captive) that your right hands possess, that will be
> more suitable, to prevent you from doing injustice. (Q.4:3)

The contestations between religious perspectives that espouse gender hierarchy and male power on the one hand, and those that embrace gender equality and justice on the other, are enduring within most religions of the world. Within varying traditions, opponents of patriarchy have challenged the male domination of their official religious canons. Feminist scholars especially have illustrated how much of the normative religious legacy that passes as objective religious knowledge in fact represents the historical product of male subjectivities.[4] Moreover, these are primarily the perspectives of elite scholarly men living in societies pervaded by patriarchal assumptions. Attempting to contest the overwhelming male biases characterizing scholarship, feminist theory has focused on women's experiences as a conceptual category to redress the historical gender imbalance.[5]

I argue that these theoretical insights are particularly valuable for Islamic feminists in relation to Qur'anic *tafsir* (exegesis). Methodologically, contemporary Islamic feminist exegetes have engaged with the varying positions on gender within the Qur'an by arguing that despite a seeming ambiguity, the overall ethos of the Qur'an indicates a movement towards gender equality.[6] In the process, Islamic feminists have argued that verses reflecting patriarchal norms mirror the historical dimensions of the revelatory context.[7] As such the biases in these verses represent a descriptive dimension of the Qur'an that speaks in relation to existing gendered assumptions of seventh century Arabia.

Building on these important hermeneutical insights, I suggest that an additional perspective needs to be developed within the arena of contem-

---

4. See, for example, Rosemary Radford Ruether, *Sexism and God-talk* (Boston: Beacon Press, 1983).
5. For varying feminist discussions on the category of experience and female subjectivities, see, for example, Sandra Kemp and Judith Squires, eds., *Feminisms* (New York: Oxford University Press, 1997); Ursula King, *Religion and Gender* (Oxford: Blackwell, 1995); Judith Plaskow and Carol P. Christ, *Weaving the Visions: New Patterns in Feminist Spirituality* (San Francisco: Harper, 1989).
6. See Amina Wadud, *Qur'an and Women* (New York: Oxford University Press, 1993), and Asma Barlas, "Believing Women" (Austin: University of Texas Press, 2002).
7. Ibid.

porary feminist exegesis of the Qur'an. I propose a Qur'anic hermeneutics that consciously reflects on the real life experiences of Muslim women when understanding gender ethics. This perspective contributes to the growing awareness that intellectual work involved in the formulation of Islamic ethics needs to be informed by, and responsive to, the contextual lived realities of marginalized sectors of the communities.

Given the high levels of spousal violence against women globally, I argue that the Qur'anic verse Q.4:34 particularly demands reconsideraton from the perspective of women's experience. The verse reads as follows:

Men are (*qawwamun*) protectors and maintainers of women,
Because God has given the one more (strength) than the other,
and because they support them from their means.
Therefore the righteous women are devoutly obedient,
and guard in (the husband's absence)
what God would have them guard.

As to those women on whose part you fear
(*nushuz*) disloyalty and ill conduct:
Admonish them (first), refuse to share their beds (next)
and (last) (*wadribuhunna*) beat them (lightly).
But if they return to obedience
seek not against them means (of annoyance)
for God is the most high, Great (above you all).

While this verse clearly reflects the gender mores of the seventh-century Arabian context, it can and has been used in the contemporary era to buttress patriarchal ideologies. When approached in this manner, the verse appears to advocate a general marital hierarchy and can be interpreted as a license for men to beat their wives. Feminist exegetes have argued that such interpretations lack historical and sociological awareness of the Qur'anic context and culture, as well as its methodology of reform.[8] As such, it reflects a decontextualized and simplistic interpretation of the text that results in suffering for women and children, the very reality that the Qur'an tries repeatedly to change.

I examine ways in which ordinary Muslim women who have experienced spousal violence engage the ethical issues surrounding interpretations of Q.4:34. In this process, I engage Qur'anic hermeneutics informed by the full, embodied realities of Muslim women. In effect, I examine the social world of the Qur'anic text in a contemporary South African

---

8. See Barlas, "Believing Women," 184–89.

Muslim context. I focus on how ordinary women engage, interpret, contest, and redefine the dominant understandings of Islam and how their engagement can inform some of the ethical quandaries that emerge from ahistorical interpretations of the Qur'anic text. I argue that this often invisible community of the text, through its explicitly experiential grappling with Qur'anic ethics, offers us a *"tafsir* through praxis."

My approach presents a departure from the standard conceptions of *tafsir* or exegesis characterized by men's cerebral and dispassionate engagement with scripture. I contend that such conceptions mask the reality that hegemonic interpretations are saturated by male experiences of reality. Instead, my approach explicitly foregrounds how a group of Muslim women think and speak in relation to the text and engage God, ethics, and religion through the realities of their suffering and oppression. What they often emerge with is an understanding of Islam that provides a very different ethical and existential vision than that of traditional male scholars, their husbands, and clerics around them. By suggesting that their experiences constitute a mode of *"tafsir,"* I argue for a transformation and redefinition of traditional boundaries of what counts as Qur'anic exegesis. I maintain that this more expansive approach to *tafsir* will allow contemporary Muslims to engage dynamically with Islamic ethics, Qur'anic texts, and their embodied realities.

LITERATURE REVIEW

I provide a selective review of exegetical approaches to verse Q.4:34 ranging from the interpretations of classical male scholars to those of contemporary women exegetes. While these approaches have varying understandings of gender, they share the methodological assumption that *tafsir,* or Qur'anic exegesis, is essentially a scholarly, intellectual hermeneutical enterprise. My review provides a broader historical context for understanding the different ways that Muslims have interpreted the ethical realities of Q.4:34.[9]

In the classical tradition the *tafasir* Abu Jafar al-Tabari (839–922), Abu Qasim al-Zamakshari (1075–1144), and Fakhr al-Din al-Razi (1149–1210) are highly regarded.[10] Despite the great richness, diversity,

---

9. In a previous work I examined in depth some of the *tafasir* of the authoritative classical exegetes on Q. 4:34. See Sa'diyya Shaikh, "Battered Women in Muslim Communities in the Western Cape: Religious Constructions of Gender, Marriage, Sexuality and Violence," master's thesis, University of Cape Town, 1996.

10. For a more detailed analysis of their positions on Q.4:34, see also Sa'diyya Shaikh "Exegetical Violence: *Nushuz* in Qur'anic Gender," *Journal for Islamic Studies* 17 (1997): 49–73.

and sophistication of their discourses, their interpretations of Q.4:34 were heavily influenced by the normative gender assumptions of their cultural and historical contexts. I illustrate this point by reflecting on how each of these scholars interprets two particular concepts in this verse, namely *qawwamun* and *wadribuhunna,* respectively.

The first part of the verse that makes a broad statement about the nature of marital relations states: "Men are protectors and maintainers (*qawwamun*) of women, / Because God has given the one more strength than the other . . ."

For Al-Tabari, the relationship of *qiwama* reflected a material preference that God has given to men in relation to their wives.[11] He suggested that this preference implied the financial responsibility of men to provide their wives with marriage dowers (*mahr*), and with financial maintenance (*nafaqa*).[12] Thus al-Tabari conceptualized the relationship of *qiwama* as contingent on a socioeconomic phenomenon rather than some inherent quality of man or woman per se.

Two centuries later, also during Abbassid rule, al-Zamakshari interpreted *qiwama* as the unambiguous and categorical rulership (*musaytirun*) of men over women.[13] He suggested that the male-female relationship paralleled the relationship between sovereign political leader and a male citizen. Al-Zamakshari stated that in the same way that a political leader instructs his subjects to perform or abstain from particular acts, so also do men command and forbid their women.[14] His analogy drew heavily on his twelfth-century realities of Muslim polity where autocratic sovereigns wielded extensive power and authority over ordinary male citizens. Clearly his *tafsir* reflects the particularities of his own political and social experiences.

In addition, al-Zamakshari stated that the relationship of *qiwama* was based on natural preferences that God had granted to men over women.[15] Writing a generation after al-Zamakshari, al-Razi, the Asharite, concurs with this view.[16] Both al-Zamakshari and al-Razi regarded men as naturally gifted with a number of superior attributes that ranged from intellect and determination to literacy and horsemanship.[17] Due to this notion of a qualitatively superior male constitution, they argued that men

---

11. Abu Jafar al-Tabari, *Jami' al-Bayan 'an ta'wil ay al-Qur'an*, 30 vols. (Beirut: Dar al Fikr, 1948), 57–59.
12. Ibid., 57.
13. Abu Qasim al-Zamakshari, *al-Kashshaf 'an haqa'iq ghawamid al-tanzil wa-'uyun al-aqawil fi wujuh al-ta'wil*, 4 vols. (Beirut: Dar al-Haqq, n.d.), 505.
14. Ibid.
15. Ibid.
16. Fakhr al-Din al-Razi, *al-Tafsir al-Kabir*, 32 vols. (Makkah: Dar ul-Fikr, n.d.), 90.
17. Ibid., 91; al-Zamakshari, *al-Kashshaf*, 505.

are natural leaders in the spheres of religion, politics, the judiciary, and marriage.[18] In presenting a set of criteria for difference between men and women, al-Zamakshari and al-Razi conflated biological and socially constructed potentials. For these men, the notion of intrinsic, natural differences between men and women constitute part of their core assumptions on human nature. This religious discourse of intrinsic gender difference reflects the normative gender ideology and gender roles characterizing the social, cultural, and historical realties and experiences of these exegetes.

The second element of the verse relating to a husband physically striking his wife reads: "As to those women on whose part you fear (*nushuz*) disloyalty or ill-conduct, admonish them (first), refuse to share their beds (next), and (last) beat them (*wadribuhunna*)."

Al-Tabari interpreted *wadribuhunna* as a last resort toward a disobedient wife and stated that it involved striking her "without hurting her (*gayr mubara*)."[19] Al-Razi appears the least prone to offer an endorsement of violence. His interpretation of this part of the verse stated that while hitting is permissible, to desist from it is better.[20] This pronouncement from al-Razi is accompanied by a quote from the *hadith* where the Prophet said that men who beat their wives are "not among the better men."[21] Al-Razi suggested that this was a clear indication that it was preferable not to hit women. He suggested that the rationale for the three-step conflict resolution (first to admonish, then to separate beds, and finally to strike) was not a license but rather a restriction on prevalent male violence.[22] Even when al-Razi conceded that men may ultimately resort to the *darb*, he attempted to practically abrogate its potentially violent component by stating that only a folded handkerchief or *miswak* (a small twig used as a toothbrush) could be used for such purposes.[23] This recommendation implies that the *darb* was a token or symbol of male authority, which al-Razi appeared quite willing to maintain. However, it was the substantively violent potential of the *darb* that he tried to reduce through interpretation.

---

18. Ibid.
19. Al-Tabari, *Jami' al-Bayan*, 68.
20. Al-Razi, *al-Tafsir*, 93.
21. Ibid.
22. Ibid. Indicative of the "normality" of violence against wives is a *hadith* quoted in the exegesis of al-Zamakshari. Asma bint Abu Bakr is reported to have said, "I was one of four wives of Zubair ibn al-Awwam. If he got angry he would hit us with a stick, on which clothes are hung, until he broke it." Her husband is reported to have responded by saying that "if her sons were not around then I would hit her more" (al-Zamakshari, *al-Kashshaf*, 507). Hence it appears that violence against wives was prevalent in sectors among the Prophet's society.
23. Al-Razi, *al-Tafsir*, 93.

Al-Zamakshari, unlike al-Razi, was unapologetic about condoning violence in his interpretation of the *darb*. He quoted a *hadith* where the Prophet is reported to have told a husband to "hang your whip in such a place that the family can see it."[24] However, Zamakshari conceded that this *hadith* has a weak chain of narration, implying that it is possibly spurious. This type of interpretation and narrative provides religious legitimacy for a worldview that sanctions violence against women. For example, even al-Razi, who made constant practical recommendations to men to be restrained and prudent, still affirmed, even if only symbolically, men's rights to physically discipline women who disobey their husbands. Despite their clear differences on the acceptability of male violence, these exegetes' interpretations of the Qur'an are premised on a hierarchical gender ideology. The classical *tafasir* evidently reflects premodern, patriarchal assumptions that systematically silenced and excluded women's voices.

In the present era, women scholars such as Amina Wadud, Asma Barlas, Maysum Faruqi, Riffat Hassan, and Azizah al-Hibri have also engaged in Qur'anic exegesis.[25] They interpret Q.4:34 in ways that both draw on the classical *tafasir* while simultaneously contesting much of the premodern gender ideology. Despite rich differences in their methods and perspectives, these contemporary female exegetes each foreground visions of gender justice and universal human dignity in their readings of the Qur'an.

Within the genre of contemporary feminist-oriented *tafasir*, Q.4:34 is generally interpreted in relation to other Qur'anic verses that address gender and interpersonal relations. In particular, many of these scholars argue that Q.4:34 reflects an ameliorative Qur'anic response to very particular and contextually based seventh-century gender norms that are not universally applicable. In fact, echoing al-Tabari's position, many of these scholars limit *qiwamah* to the financial roles that men have occupied in relation to women, given the latter's role in childbearing. At the same time, they argue that such gender relations are not static but reflect one of many possible ways to establish equitable roles and responsibilities.

In terms of the recourse to striking one's wife in Q.4:34, these scholars argue that the verse represents the introduction of a pragmatic three-step solution to discourage spousal violence in a society where such vio-

---

24. Al-Zamakshari, *al-Kashshaf*, 507.
25. Barlas, "Believing Women"; Maysum al-Faruqi, "Women's Self-Identity in the Qur'an and Islamic Law," in *Windows of Faith*, ed. Gisela Webb (New York: Syracuse University Press, 2000), 72–101; Azizah al-Hibri, "An Introduction to Muslim Women's Rights," in *Windows of Faith*, 51–71; Riffat Hassan, "An Islamic Perspective," in *Women, Religion and Sexuality*, ed. Jeanne Becher (Philadelphia: WCC Publishers, 1990), 93–128; Amina Wadud, *Qur'an and Women: Rereading the Sacred Text from a Woman's Perspective* (New York: Oxford University Press, 1999).

lence against women was deemed acceptable. As such, they see the verse as descriptive of the gender norms characterizing the context of revelation rather than a prescriptive Qur'anic verse on the nature of gender relations. Incidentally, a descriptive rather than prescriptive interpretation of violence is common to both the contemporary feminist reading and the approach of al-Razi as discussed previously. The contemporary feminist view, however, insists that violence against wives is contrary to the logic of the Qur'an. These women exegetes propose a holistic approach to the Qur'an, arguing that an abiding Qur'anic concern to establish social justice is the hermeneutical center from which to read other verses. In cases of perceived tensions around issues of gender, they argue that the Qur'anic themes of justice, moral agency, and human equality are to be unconditionally prioritized. Wadud, for example, argues that the Qur'an, through many of the gender reforms it initiated in seventh-century Arab society, starts a trajectory of gender transformation that Muslims are to continually develop.[26] Similarly, Barlas states that the Qur'an offers possibilities to imagine gender equality in progressive and expansive ways for the future.[27]

Despite the variety of scholarly perspectives reflected in both premodern male and contemporary feminist exegeses, it is clear that all exegetes bring their experiential realities, including the dominant gender ideology of their respective sociohistorical contexts, to their interpretations of the Qur'an. Thus my focus on perspectives of women who have survived violent marriages allows me to expand the types of experiential perspectives informing understandings of Qur'anic ethics as it relates to marital relations. Moreover, their unique positioning brings to the *tafsir* discourse a contemporary social world of the text and the real-life urgency of engaging gender ethics in Islam.

METHOD

Using a feminist qualitative research approach, I conducted in-depth, lengthy interviews with eight Muslim women between twenty-eight and forty-three years of age in the greater Cape Town area in South Africa during 1994 and 1995. I made contact with these women through local community social service centers. All participants were survivors of violent physical abuse by their husbands or ex-husbands and lived in Indian or Malay communities. Seven of the eight participants were either separated or divorced and one was still married at the time of the interviews.

---

26. Wadud, *Qur'an and Women*, xiii.
27. Barlas, "Believing Women," 133.

Respondents were asked open-ended questions from a semistructured interview schedule that I had jointly constructed with two counselors who had worked extensively with battered women. One of these counselors was also a survivor of a violent previous marriage.

RESULTS

Participant's responses indicated that their socialization and education presented traditional gender roles and marital hierarchy as religiously ordained. Moreover, during their abusive marriages, their families, the community, and religious leaders to a large extent did not actively support them in resisting their husbands' violence or in being explicitly critical of such behavior. Islam, in their experience, was often presented as the rationale for women to stay in marriages, irrespective of the circumstances. Nonetheless, my findings show that these women actively asserted their agency and that they contested implicitly and explicitly the dominant patriarchal understandings of Islam. Through experiences of violence the women developed their own sense of religious identity that often challenged gender hierarchy in religious terms. In this sense, their lived responses to violence present a different mode of exegesis and interpretation of Qur'anic ethics. I call this lived response a "*tafsir* through praxis" or an "embodied *tafsir*" that emerged from experiences of pain, marginality, and oppression, realities that the Qur'an itself constantly and consciously seeks to address.[28] I now explore and analyze in more detail some of the themes that emerged from the women's realities.

ANALYSIS

Religious Identity

All the women in the sample were socialized in families in which traditional gender roles and male authority were considered the religious norm. When asked to define a good Muslim woman, the most common themes in their responses related to virginity before marriage and sexual fidelity during marriage, appropriate Islamic dress that involves covering of the hair, being a good mother, and ensuring education of the children. A few of the women also mentioned praying regularly.

A striking common thread running through the women's stories relates to how strongly sexual chastity was connected to their religious identities. As single women, most of them had encountered social forces

---

28. For example, Q.107:1–7 explicitly admonishes worshipers who merely perform outer ritual prayer while being heedless to the suffering of orphans, the hungry, and other marginalized groups of people around them.

that expressed their religious value in relation to the status of their virginity. One interviewee describes how her parent's anxiety around her sexuality caused them to pressure her into an early marriage as opposed to pursuing higher education. Fatima said:

> As a young Muslim girl my parents feared for me. . . . I suppose it's natural for any parent to fear for their daughters. But I still feel that they knew what kind of person I was, and that I could look after myself, like you know, I was never really interested in boys, I was more interested in my studies.

Another interviewee, Shayda, stated:

> There was only one thing I was taught by my mother about sex when I was young. She said that when a man uses you, there's a first time, then he breaks you and he takes your *izzet* (honor) away, so always look after yourself. So I always looked after myself, I never let any boys touch me. . . . You know how strict the Indian community and the Indian culture is, especially where a woman's *izzet* is concerned, where the pride is concerned. My mother brought us up very strict.

Here sexuality, associated with anxiety and danger, is central in defining women's worth. Shayda's mother's description of sexual relations is saturated by images of male aggression where men "use" and "break" women's bodies. In response to such predatory male sexuality, a woman's honor and worth depends on how successfully she managed to preserve her sexual chastity. Significantly, none of the women once mentioned the religious importance of male chastity. On the contrary, in many of these narratives there was an implicit assumption that women needed to be vigilant precisely because men were sexual opportunists who prey on women. In these narratives, men and women are seen to be accountable to very different standards of sexual ethics.[29]

For all the participants the definition of a "good Muslim woman" was consistently associated with modest dressing and chastity. As such, female religiosity is significantly related to sexual propriety. Many respondents also included being a "good mother" and a "good wife" as integral to their religious life, suggesting a relational notion of religious

---

29. As reflected in a study in the United States, these types of sexual double standards are not restricted to Muslim societies but are reflected in varying forms in other societies. See Mary Crawford and Danielle Popp, "Sexual Double Standards: A Review and Methodological Critique of Two Decades of Research," *Journal of Sex Research* 40(1) (February 2003): 13–26.

identity. For these women, religiosity involved the quality of one's inter-personal relationships, particularly as related to the domestic and social spheres. The participants' responses to explicit and formal questions regarding their religious identity tended to elicit gender-stereotypical responses. However, when examining the same participants' responses to real life situations, it appeared that they challenged traditional gender stereotypes, sometimes in explicit religious terms. The urgent need for them to challenge the prevailing gender ideologies becomes clear when examining these women's marital experiences.

Marital Violence, Female Subjectivity, and Family Responses

Participants' descriptions of their marriages reveal extremely hierarchical power dynamics. Women reported extremely controlling behavior by their husbands, such as monitoring their wives' movements, conducting random searches of their bags, restricting their mobility and life choices, and systematically isolating them from friends, family, and other potential support networks.

The interviewees described excessive levels of violence and aggression to which they were subject in their marriages. One respondent described an incident in which her husband pointed a gun at her. Others reported being hit in the face with the butt of a gun, being beaten with lead wires, and being partially strangled. One respondent even reported being attacked with a knife such that she required stitches on her face. The extremely violent nature of these male-female power imbalances was mirrored in the women's common fear of being killed by their spouses. Their experiences bear testimony to the brutality of patriarchy as it manifests in the everyday lives of many women.

A significant number of the interviewees stated that religiously they were taught to stay married irrespective of the circumstances. For them this religious teaching had been a central underlying factor influencing their decision to stay in violent marriages for a long time. Jaynub, a thirty-year-old woman with three children, stated that remaining in an abusive marriage reflected her understanding of the Islamic virtues of patience and female obedience:

> Islamically you are brought up to be obedient as a girl, taught to make "*sabr*," so I took the beatings as much as I could . . . and finally when I couldn't take it anymore I did run to my parents' home. My mother used to tell me to go back and me being the obedient child use to listen and go back . . . as for my father, when I go home he never ever wants to know what's going on in

my marriage. Even now when I go home with a problem he walks past like he doesn't hear me, like he doesn't *want* to hear me and he doesn't *want* to listen.

Like many of the others, Jaynub's social and family contexts facilitated the husband's abusive behavior. She had been taught that as a Muslim woman she was expected to be obedient, submissive, and an emotional minor. Although an adult married woman, she described herself as the "obedient child" listening to a mother who directed her to return to an abusive marriage. The father's unresponsiveness and silence in this situation reflected his complicity with or even indifference to his daughter's plight. It also possibly reflects his powerlessness in a patriarchal power structure where, once authority over a woman is passed from father to husband, the husband can do as he pleases. Both her parents' responses legitimized and normalized the abuse. They ultimately denied their daughter her claim to physical integrity and her complete value as an individual human being.

Many of the other interviewees also pointed out their family's silent complicity with the abuse. This is illustrated in the following excerpts:

> After the abuse when I went back to my family's home, he would come to my mother and apologize for his behavior. She would say to him, "Come and sit here." She said that he is another person's child and she will always listen to him. That was the problem as well. She shouldn't have done that. If that happened to my daughter, I won't say come and sit down here, I'll really give it to him. That's the problem; it was almost like he was encouraged (Jaynub).

Anisa said:

> I used to feel anger inside me when he used to come to my people and they all talked so nicely to him and they forgot what he's done and what he is doing to me. I used to ask them, "Why are you so nice to him and you don't even ask him why he is doing that to your daughter?" They did nothing at all!

For many of the respondents, their families did not hold the batterer accountable for his violence. On the contrary, their "niceness" and empathy towards the aggressive husband translated into complicity with his behavior. In this study, battered women expressed their experiences of acute alienation from their family that stemmed from a lack of social and family support. Religious and cultural constructions that idealize female obedience and submissiveness, premised on assumptions of marital hierarchy, thwarted collective resistance to abusive marital power relations.

Women's Agency and Religious Contestations

Despite the lack of social support, it is remarkable that all but one of the women contested their husband's violence in ethical and religious terms. Often they directly interrogated the batterer. Shayda said: "When he hits me, he doesn't even say, 'I am sorry for the way I hit you.' He just goes on to ask Allah *ma'af* (forgiveness). I say, 'How can you ask Allah *ma'af* when you didn't even ask me *ma'af*? You think Allah will accept your *ma'af*? He won't accept it!'"

Farida said: "When I ask him, 'How can you hit me and then go to the mosque and pray?' then it ends up with him hitting me again for just saying that because it hurts him."

Fatima said: "As the years went by, I could never get myself to make *salat* (prayer) with this man. I couldn't let him stand in front of me (that is, lead me in prayer), knowing that he is not a leader that I could respect, not even as a husband . . . and it's just because he ill-treats me so badly. . . ."

For all the participants in the sample, the realm of closeness to God and religious authenticity are irreconcilable with violent abuse. By saying that God will not accept an abusive husband's petition for forgiveness before the husband has asked his wife for forgiveness, Shayda argued that ethical human relationships are integral to one's relationship to God. Farida pointed to the ethical contradiction and incongruity of her husband's behavior—he hit her and then went to the mosque to pray. Fatima could not bring herself to pray behind her abusive husband. She rejected both the leadership and the religious integrity of a man who was violent with her. For these women, brutalizing other human beings without genuine repentance and accountability could never be justified in the name of Islam. They believed that God took their humanity seriously enough so as not to forgive those who consistently and deliberately violate them. For these women, Islam provided an ethical framework that demanded a social covenant among believers as a prerequisite for a meaningful God-human relationship.

Through these women's voices an "embodied *tafsir*" emerged in which violent male behavior was viewed as inconsistent with practice of Islam and the divine imperatives for human beings. Through articulating their experiences, their understandings of the nature of God emerged—God is just, demanding that human beings account for the injustices they perpetrate on one another. For these women, God is the antithesis of violence and one could not present oneself to God after flagrantly violating another human being.

In their responses an image of God emerges as the witness-bearer of the oppressed, who will not accept the brutality and religious hypocrisy of the violent oppressor. Through very harrowing and painful experiences these women stated that they existentially grappled with notions of God, human behavior, and religious ethics. Their experience of the brutal face of patriarchy caused them to deeply engage and contest notions of their humanity. What emerged as a result was an Islamic ethical and theological framework that challenged misogynist and utilitarian religious views on women and explicitly interrogated the abusive relationships on religious bases. Their interpretations or "*tafsir* through praxis" amount to feminist contestations of patriarchal understandings of Qur'anic teachings—a clear indictment of those who interpret Q4:34 as a license to physically abuse women.

The women also contested more broadly the religious basis for marital hierarchies, and what they perceived as incongruities between beliefs and practices prevalent in their communities. Maryam said:

> I accept Islam and I respect it very much as my religion. So Islam is not the excuse just because these men have got Muslim names and use Islam for their own purposes . . . it's an individual person himself actually that is to blame. But I will think twice before I marry a Muslim man again . . . maybe it's the way we are brought up in an Islamic culture. At work I've heard the white girls speak of their husbands, how they work together, how they respect each other and how they help one another, while both are working . . . we don't get that support from our Muslim men, for Muslim men their wives . . . we are like maids, we are like slaves.

Farida said:

> Muslim men, especially religious ones, have the idea that they are above women . . . but it is also the kind of person I am. I am very proud of being Muslim although I am not very religious.

For both these women, Muslim men and the prevalent forms of religious socialization that assumed male superiority were clearly the problem. Maryam attributed the gender power imbalances partially to "Islamic culture." Her exposure to non-Muslims ("whites") and her admiration of their marital relationships as based on mutuality, shared responsibility, and partnership was starkly juxtaposed with her personal experience of male domination in marriage with a Muslim man. By stating that her ethical ideals of relationships were reflected in marriages outside of her religious community, she was clearly critical of the dominant mode of gender relations within the Muslim community.

It was particularly revealing that Farida stated that "especially religious" men assumed that they were "above" women. On the basis of patriarchal male articulations of Islam, hierarchical modes of gender relations were viewed to be religiously normative. When Farida refused to accept these norms she considered herself not to be "very religious." Thus, in her self-understanding, her rejection of patriarchal norms placed her outside the sphere of religiosity. Paradoxically, she indicated feeling proud of her Muslim identity and yet was personally unable to accept hierarchical religiously gendered constructs. This dissonance was a consequence of the harmful impact of sexism in her experience of Muslim societal practices. Her ambiguity reflects a broader tension experienced by many Muslim women: on the one hand Islam is about treating human beings in a just, fair, respectful, and egalitarian manner and on the other hand, Islam simultaneously seems to be characterized by underlying hierarchal gender ideology.

Farida's response reflects the urgent need among Muslims for popularizations of feminist articulations of Islam, articulations that contest gender discrimination and prioritize the Islamic impetus for gender justice and women's equality.

The only woman in the group of interviewees whose engagement with Islam reflected a more singular and problematic internalization of patriarchy was Shamima. She said:

> I must try and adapt to him, start living like a proper Muslim . . . he lives like a good Muslim should, and if I live like that too there will be less hassles because I will be praying five times a day, and if you do it every day it will be on your mind, and I'll be a different person . . . then you say to yourself I shouldn't get angry because I just prayed five minutes ago . . . before I said what I wanted to say and did what I wanted to do, I'll be more careful now, communication will be better and there will be less violence, but it has got to also come from inside of me.

While Shamima was considering divorce, she was the only one of the participants who had remained in her marriage despite severe conflict and violence. Although her husband was violent, she maintained that "he is a good Muslim" because he performed his ritual prayer regularly. She saw no contradiction between his violence and the legitimacy of his supposed religiosity. Unlike the other participants, for her being "a good Muslim" did not extend to fair and egalitarian human interactions. In fact, she assumed responsibility for the abuse by saying that if she changed her behavior and became a better Muslim, there would be less violence. In the view of Islam espoused by Shamima, women were ideally acquiescent, tolerant, and nonexpressive in terms of their needs. Women's internalization of such religious constructs undermines resistance against male violence and supports conditions under which an abusive patriarchal ideology may flourish.

Community, Imams, and Religious Authority

All the women in the sample reported that they had consulted with Muslim clerics (*ulama*) who mediated in situations of marital conflict within their community. Two themes recurred in these women's experiences with these clerics. Firstly, and most commonly, these *ulama* consistently tried to keep the marriage together at the expense of the women's well-being. Such attempts were in keeping with a "reconciliation at all cost" approach and was encapsulated in Shayda's comment:

> They (the imams) don't care about the pain and abuse that the women are experiencing because even now, even after all this abuse, this imam said, "I am not performing any *talaq*, I'm not doing anything, because I believe in reconciliation." Even after what I told him, even after what he knows I'm going through, what my children are going through, that's the answer I got.

Secondly, a pervading theme in their interactions with the clerics was that the women were made to feel responsible for the violence. For example, Maryam described how she visited the local *ulama* offices many times:

> I use to sit there for hours waiting to see one of them. Finally when they did see me all of those imams say the same thing: "What do you do to make him so angry?" . . . They always said, "You and your husband must come together and you must talk."

Farida noted, "The imam's attitude is like I am the one at fault. At the end of the day it was my husband. It's like the violence and abuse meant nothing to them. And it *was* a big thing."

The type of clerical response reflected in the preceding quotations abets male violence. By not criticizing, challenging, or explicitly condemning the husband's behavior, these religious authorities in fact enabled, legitimized, and perpetuated the systems of male violence. Maryam attributed this clerical bias to their male subjectivity, stating "the problem with these *shaykhs* is that because they are men, they often side with the husband." Anisa described the cleric's incapacity to empathize with her experience in the following manner:

To tell you honestly, because of all the beating, there's something inside that happened to me . . . even though there was love originally, that love turns to hatred and disgust and all these horrible feelings towards that person. You just can't help it but when I speak to the imam and I tell him how I feel, he says, "Oh, but you mustn't say these things, it is not Muslim and it's not Islamically right." Then I tell him, "But I'm telling you how I feel. This is how I feel, it's the truth, why must I lie, because that's how I feel and it's this man that's caused this feeling inside." It's just natural I suppose, because of the way I've been ill-treated. That's another thing about these imams, I don't know, because I think they are not also trained in that way to really help the people.

In fact, Anisa very astutely pointed out an important systemic gap in the education of the clerics. In the process of becoming religious scholars or leaders, they were typically not trained in counseling, mediation, or communication skills. It was assumed that since many of them studied Arabic language and the premodern Islamic legal and exegetical canon, they were somehow equipped to administer pastoral care. However, in reality the opposite was true. Their intensive focus on an intellectual legacy formulated in the context of premodern gender norms tended to entrench arcane assumptions of gender relations as intrinsic to Islam. Often what was missing in their training was an active engagement with Islamic gender ethics as a living, dynamic, and contextually unfolding phenomenon. Not only was this omission a serious aporia in their discourse, its lack served to present "official" Islam as embodying a stagnant, ahistorical perspective of gender born from patriarchal readings of the text. This static and masculinist lens is reflected in Anisa's interview where the cleric lacked any sensitivity to her pain, condemning her negative feelings towards the batterer as "unIslamic." Nowhere in his response did he denounce the husband's violence as "unIslamic." As such, Islam was instrumentalized to silence the woman's emotional rebellion to male violence.

A particular situation that warrants more detailed discussion is that of Fatima, whose marriage was performed only in accordance with Muslim rites. At the time, South African law did not legally recognize Muslim marriages, and children born from such unions were legally considered illegitimate. The law at the time also stipulated that the mother had sole custody of children born out of wedlock.[30] So after the divorce, in terms

---

30. South African law has changed since that time. In 1997 the "Natural Fathers of Children Born Out of Wedlock Act" was passed whereby unmarried fathers were granted legal rights regarding custody and access to their children.

of Muslim legal rites, Fatima, in terms of South African law, had full custody of her children. Her ex-husband had a history of physical abuse towards her and their children. She was therefore intent on denying him access to them. In response, the ex-husband, together with the imam, drew up supposed legal documents to attempt the father's visitation and access rights to the children. In pursuit of the husband's cause, the imam visited Fatima and told her that it was Islamically incumbent on her to sign these papers. The following interchange was reported to have taken place:

> I told the imam that I don't have to sign that document, which also included property rights. He told me, "*Shari'ah* says that the father has rights over the children," and "*Shari'ah* says this . . . and *Shari'ah* says that. . . ." I said, "*Shari'ah* is fine, I'm not arguing with *Shari'ah*, but I have a valid reason for not wanting to allow him rights to the children. He's the father but he is violent. I'll never sign something like that." This imam just wanted me to sign so then he says to me, "*Ja jou kop is deurmekaar* (your head is confused), *kom maak istikhara* (perform your *istikhara* prayer)." I said, "Fine, I'll go make *istikhara*." The next day I phoned him back. I said, "Please, throw that document in the dirt-bin, because I didn't sign it." He said, "No, but you don't have to sign because your husband signed already and it's legal." How can one partner only have the rights to sign concerning properties and maintenance and custody?! I don't have any rights??! As for the imam, how can he, who is supposed to be Islamically inclined, how can he help my husband to take away my rights just like that. . . . When I took the document to Lawyers for Human Rights, they said to me that the document was not legal; even if I had signed, it was not legal.

I am not going to comment on the self-evident manipulation and dishonesty that this cleric resorted to (except perhaps to pray that God shows him full justice in this life and the next!). However, Fatima's response to the cleric's attempted manipulation was extremely powerful. She remained undaunted at the cleric's efforts at psychological and emotional blackmail or at his purported religious authority. By claiming that she had no problems with the *Shari'ah*, she indicated that an ethical interpretation of religious law would not jeopardize her claims. In this manner, she contested the cleric's unjust and expedient invocation of the *Shari'ah*. She also challenged the religious authenticity of an imam who purported to represent an ethical Islamic position but actually acted unjustly and connived to disempower her.

The counterproductive role of the clerics who ministered to the women in the sample was also reflected in their transmissions of Qur'anic teachings in the context of marital violence. In most cases it was noteworthy that the invocation of Q.4:34, either directly or indirectly in their experiences, occurred only *after* the clerics had mediated in the marital conflict. Jaynub stated:

> In times of problems I have told the imam about the way my husband beats me up. He (the imam) spoke to him and after that he (the husband) told me that the Qur'an states that he should not lift his hands on his wife, but if his wife doesn't want to listen to him then he is allowed to hit her. Where in the Qur'an does it state that? I don't believe that it can say that in the Qur'an, but my husband, after talking to the imam, tells me that.

Anisa said:

> They (the clerics) say that the Qur'an says that the husband can hit his wife with the *miswak*. . . but I don't accept that. You can't hit your wife with the broom the way he does. He really whips me. That man is cruel, really cruel.

In these women's experiences, male religious leaders have understood and invoked Q.4:34 as a justification for male violence against women. It is striking that in all but one of the interviews, the batterers had not invoked Islam or the Qur'an as a rationale for their behavior by themselves. Instead, in the above two cases, it was the clerics who had been ministering to the batterers and who, perhaps inadvertently, provided them with scriptural justification for their behavior. The religious leaders in the community thus exacerbated the problem rather than alleviated it. Moreover, these problematic interpretations of Q.4:34 also raise the thorny issue of how to interpret Qur'anic texts that describe aspects of a seventh-century patriarchal gender ideology.

A salient feature emerging from the interviews was that the women refused to accept that the Qur'an intended to condone cruelty and violence against them. One of the women whom I had initially consulted when drawing up the interview schedule was a lay counselor, herself the survivor of a violent previous marriage. Her response to the problematic Qur'anic verse was quite poignant. She stated:

> Recently I gave the Qur'an as a present to an agnostic friend who was interested in Islam. Before I gave it to her I struck out that verse (Q.4:34). I did this because I think that this verse is open to

misinterpretation. After my experiences I just refuse to accept
that Allah allows or condones violence against women.

Her comment reflected her deep pain and sense of betrayal that the
Qur'an could be interpreted in a way that legitimated violence against
women. This woman continued to have a deep commitment to Islam and
the Qur'an. For her, any interpretation of Q.4:34 that condoned violence
against women represents a misunderstanding of Islam's ethical imperatives. She, like some of the other participants, refused to accept that the
Qur'an intended harm or condoned violence against them. Through their
experiences of violence, their encounter with Q.4:34 resulted in an active
contestation of violence against women and as such, they constitute an
alternative interpretive community of the text. Similar to the contemporary women exegetes of the Qur'an, this group of women subjected
Q.4:34 to a broader Islamic framework where an ethics of justice and fair
treatment is seen to be integral to the revelatory message. Hence their experiential "*tafsir*" abrogated the literal and patriarchal readings of
Q.4:34 that were reflected in the approach of some of the clerics.

Finally, two interviewees found alternative voices among the traditional
clerics. These unusual clerics, after unsuccessfully intervening with the batterers, advised the women that their marriages were damaging them and
that Islam did not require them to tolerate such abuse. Shayda reported:

He (the *shaykh*) said that because my husband is beating me
and then he was messing around with other woman, in the end
I am going to sit with AIDS. He told me straight to leave the
marriage . . .

While clerics concerned with the health and well-being of battered
women constituted a minority voice among the Cape *ulama* at the time,
it was nonetheless noteworthy that these women-friendly perspectives
were articulated. Such perspectives illustrated the potential for egalitarian voices to emerge from traditional religious authorities. There is
clearly a dire need for broader clerical bodies to transform their gender
lenses and embrace more gender-egalitarian approaches. This is particularly urgent given their pivotal roles in the community as mediators in
marital conflict, as well as the fact that they are seen to be the purveyors
of religious authority more generally.

Women as Transformers

Despite the odds being stacked against them, the women interviewed in
this study embodied a remarkable resilience and resistance to dominant
stereotypes of female passivity. In fact, they often acted as agents of trans-

formation. In one particular case, a participant displayed extraordinary courage and uncanny survival skills within life-threatening situations. Anisa stated:

> You know, the first time I retaliated physically was after fifteen years of marriage. When he was hitting me with the stick, I grabbed it from his hand and hit him. . . . I was so scared that I had hit him but I realized that when I pulled back and defended myself, he actually backed off, and then I was shocked at myself. I thought, "Why didn't I do it long ago, because he got scared." After that I thought to myself, "Now I'm going to put my foot down." I was nervous and I was scared, and I tried not to show it, and I said to him, "Don't ever lift a finger on me again or I'm going to kill you!" I said, "Don't ever do it again." And since then he has not done it. Sometimes when I thought he wanted to hit me, I went right up to him and I said, "Don't! Don't ever try to do it! I'm going to kill you. Don't try it with me again, you are not going to start that nonsense again, I'll kill you." I just say that all the time.

In this situation, the continuous experience of being physically violated by her husband caused Anisa to contravene religious and other socialization that positioned her as a submissive wife. She broke out of the traditional model of femininity by physically defending her bodily integrity. Finding herself unexpectedly successful, she maintained a rigorous psychological and physical vigilance against her husband by preempting him with death threats whenever she suspected he might veer in the direction of violence. Her response was unique; the same type of response to another abusive husband might result in the wife's death. While Anisa did not articulate her transgression of traditional gender roles in religious terms, her response functioned to critique normative assumptions of femininity presented by her religious socialization.

Other women's agency is reflected in their active search for alternative understandings of Islam and gender relations. Fatima stated:

> I went to the library and took out these cassettes by Jamal Badawi, and he spoke in general about all the rights of Muslim women. I thought, "Gosh! I do have rights as a Muslim woman," and that also helped in slowly changing my approach and I stopped accepting this relationship.

Here the woman actively educated and empowered herself in relation to Islam, rejected a "victim" status and embraced teachings that focused on the tradition's heritage of gender justice. Another interviewee stated that alternative types of religious socialization and education were necessary to transform society. Here Shayda stated:

> We need to teach our children to behave differently. My son does domestic chores. When he started to bully my daughter, I stopped him and told him that just because he is a boy does not mean he can treat his sister badly. I always tell the boys that one day when they get married they must never do what their father does to me, it's wrong and very unIslamic.

Defying oppressive and sexist stereotypes, Shayda stated that she taught her children very different modes of gender relationships. She embodied the potential for transformation in societal and religious constructs. In these instances empowering and liberating Islamic constructs provided resources for female agency and transformation.

DISCUSSION AND CONCLUSION

In this study, it was clear that a multiplicity of factors informed the women's understandings of Islam. These factors included their religious socialization in the family and community where traditional gender roles and male religious authority were considered normative. Until these women had entered marriages with violent spouses, none of them appeared to have actively contested the pervasive views of male power and authority within their communities. However, the experiences of violence from their spouses presented a situation of crisis when they became subject to one of the most negative faces of patriarchal ideology. For most of these women their violent realities initiated an experiential confrontation with the destructive possibilities of the dominant gender ideology. I contend that these experiences triggered a type of ideological rupture with the dominant patriarchal power structure that the women had hitherto tacitly accepted. This rupture or dissonance between the women's inherited notions and their experiences brought the dominant ideology into question. Here the Gramscian theory of hegemony is illuminating. For an ideology to effectively maintain its hegemony, both the oppressed and the oppressor need to accept the given power structure as natural. As such, the hegemonic ideology presents itself as providing the highest good to all concerned. In the present study, the dominant ideology of male authority and power, articulated in religious terms, was based on the unstated claim that it benefited all members of the society. The women's experiences of violence gave the lie to these claims. Spousal abuse presented an explicit contravention of the women's sense of well-being, protection, and value that the status quo purported to provide.

Significantly, these women did not ultimately bow down defeated by this experience of dissonance and rupture and neither did they reject Islam. Instead, they actively engaged in reconstructing their sense of self, of Islam, and of Islamic ethics. This reconstitution involved, inter alia, a contestation of the dominant ideology that promoted their docility and submissiveness in the face of violence. Through their experience of crisis, the women in the sample highlighted the contradictions between patriarchal Islamic ideologies that claim to speak for all humanity's higher good on one hand, and the real brutality symptomatic of patriarchal religious ideologies on the other. By instead practicing Islam in empowering ways, they destabilized male-centered religious perspectives. Assuming the capacity and the authority to act in their own best interests, they spoke to Islamic ethics and gender relationships in very different ways from the dominant power structures. Through their struggles they engaged in a performative encounter with Qur'anic revelation. Their embodied understandings of Q.4:34 constituted a "*tafsir* through praxis" that contested violence against women and asserted women's full humanity in religious terms.

Through their mode of *tafsir* it is apparent that the contemporary social world of the Qur'anic text is an arena of engaged, dynamic, and polysemic encounters. This chapter critically reflects on fundamental theoretical questions of religious authority and interpretation. I have illustrated how Islamic ethics and Qur'anic exegesis are not simply practiced by those considered authoritative in the traditional power structures, such as al-Tabari in the ninth century, or even in the burgeoning erudite scholarship of Islamic feminists such as Amina Wadud and Asma Barlas in the twenty-first century. As such, I challenge dominant perspectives that limit the creation of religious meaning and knowledge production to a scholarly elite. Instead, I have focused on the perspective of those outside the centers of social power whose very lives embody meaning-making in relation to religion, gender ethics, and the Qur'an as social text. Qur'anic *tafsir*, as an embodied praxis, is engaged in by women in their private and domestic spaces. It may be practiced by rejecting their husbands' violent behavior as contrary to real Islam, or by teaching their sons or daughters to become different kinds of Muslim men and women. In this study I have offered an exemplification of feminist theory that posits women's experience as a source of understanding and knowledge production within religious traditions.

5

The Mother of Life
and the God of Death:
Religious Roots of Violence
against Women in Christianity

JOHN RAINES

When struggling to understand how violence against women is rooted in religion, one comes again and again upon the issue of control. Male control over females and especially control over their sexuality is a theme that haunts sacred texts and legitimates coercive and even violent means of maintaining that control. But why control? What is it that needs controlling?

The ultimate "out of control" for humans is death. Before death we are utterly defenseless. All animals die, but we humans die in a different way. We are *conscious* of our mortality. Of all living beings on planet Earth we alone seem to live our life *in the face of death*, and that powerfully influences religion. Sometimes we have written fear and anger about that mortality into our religious traditions. I deal here only with the Western, and more specifically the Christian, tradition. But the same issue infects other religions as well.

This "out of control" haunts the male gender in a peculiar way because we have defined masculinity in terms of control. That is also how we [men] have written God, God's character and actions, into our sacred texts. In picturing God in terms of control we also picture to ourselves the "ideal" male. If control is a key determinate in violence against women, and if death symbolizes [to males] our ultimate out-of-control, our first task in detoxifying that male fear and anger is to examine how men write the story of death into sacred texts and the place we assign to women within those texts. That task begins with examining how those foundational cultural stories first get told.

POWER, INTERESTS, AND SACRED TEXTS

It may sound strange to say that males write sacred texts, but that is in fact the case. And it is not just any males who write those texts but males who enjoy prestige and recognition within their social contexts. That is to say, the authors of those texts and the commentaries and theologies that follow enjoy power and employ power and thus have a fundamental interest in *control*.[1] The history of the obsessive interest that religious texts display toward the idea of control begins with the interests of the authors. To claim this author is an abstract "he," a nongendered "he," or a "he" without this-worldly interests is to sidestep an uncomfortable but revealing truth.

Still more, it is my view that texts do not become *sacred* when they are written but only when they are received by those who hear in those texts their very own sacred voice speaking. Those who recognize a text as authoritative for them, and authorize that text as their very own authority— it is in that process of delegation that a text becomes a sacred text.[2] And this raises a still further question of gender, not just the gender of the author but the gender of the audience the author had in mind when writing. When it comes to texts that are received as sacred, both the author and the intended audience are male. Sacred texts are doubly gendered. When women listen to such texts they almost always are listening *off-stage* to an intramale discourse, to a male "we" talking about a female "them."

But why would nonelite males, who suffer oppression and exploitation at the hands of the socially powerful, find in the voice of those texts their very own sacred voice speaking? It is because nonelite males find le-

---

1. When speaking about "the author" of a sacred text I do not refer to the founders of the religious movement, whether Jesus of Nazareth or Muhammad or Siddartha Gotama (the Buddha). The founder's teachings and practices were first remembered and passed on orally, often for many generations, before being written down. Those who decided what to write down out of this oral tradition, and even more those who had the power to decide which texts would or would not be included in the orthodox canon—all these were males who held positions of power within their religious communities and were, therefore, interested in control.

2. Pierre Bourdieu makes this case in arguing, partially against Weber's idea of charisma, that authoritative language is the product of what he calls "symbolic power"—a "social magic" displayed most powerfully in religious rituals. But the irony is that those who authorize that language as authoritative for them cannot recognize what they are doing if the "ritual magic" is to work. It is "misrecognition" that makes the recognition work. Bourdieu puts it this way: "the language of authority never governs without the collaboration of those it governs, without the help of the social mechanisms capable of producing this complicity, based on misrecognition, which is the basis of all authority." *Language and Symbolic Power* (Cambridge: Harvard University Press, 1991), 113.

gitimated in those texts the few areas of control in their everyday lives they still possess and enjoy—control over their wives and daughters, and even their mothers. Having lost control over political-economy they get in return the façade of control in matters of "family values." The texts, and the commentaries and theologies that follow, tell them they can and should enjoy the rights of the patriarchal household and are obliged to enforce those rights.[3]

The Bible is a book where *men talk to men* about taking control. And when that talk begins to talk about women the voice often becomes angry and even violent. That worried male voice begins speaking in the very first pages of the Bible.

A MISBEGOTTEN BIRTH

In the creation story, the story of women and their bodies and the need to control those bodies is written as the story of Eve. It quickly becomes a story of disobedience and disorder requiring punishment and the forceful reinstating of order and control. In the West, the story of religiously legitimated violence against women begins in the beginning![4]

Some of the most violent words against women in the Bible are found in the words of God's punishment directed at Eve after she eats the forbidden fruit and induces Adam to do the same. In that passage we hear a very worried and very angry male voice proclaim (and it is a *male* voice!): "in pain you shall bring forth your children . . . yet your desire shall be for your husband . . . and he will rule over you."[5] Expressed here is a complex set of male fears having to do with desire, fertility, and dependency, and the determination to appropriate that generative and dangerous

---

3. This ancient drama seems to be playing again in contemporary American politics. Beginning with de-industrialization in the 1970s and extending into the off-shoring of white collar jobs in the 1990s, working- and middle-class males have lost control over their traditionally defined social role as family providers. Displaced from this core of their former identity they have sought out other domains of control. Concern for "family values" lets them gain the impression of control in what remains a larger picture of abandonment by an elite whose economic interests have become international. On this issue see Gloria Albrecht, *Hitting Home: Feminist Ethics, Women's Work, and the Betrayal of "Family Values"* (New York: Continuum, 2002). See also Barbara Hilkert Andolsen, *The New Job Contract: Economic Justice in an Age of Insecurity* (Cleveland: Pilgrim Press, 1998), and Mary Hobgood, *Dismantling Privilege: An Ethics of Accountability* (Cleveland: Pilgrim Press, 2000).

4. Adam and Eve and the story of creation have proved a rich source of commentary through the ages by Jewish, Christian, and Muslim scholars. An excellent source book for the diversity of views expressed is *Eve and Adam: Jewish, Christian, and Muslim Readings on Genesis and Gender*, ed. Kristen E. Kvam, Linda S. Schearing, and Valarie H. Ziegler (Bloomington: Indiana University Press, 1999).

5. All quotes are from Genesis, chapters 1–3, Revised Standard Version.

territory to male control by inscribing it for women as self-induced punishment ("in pain you shall . . .") and an area requiring male supervision
and discipline ("and he will rule over you"). It is a male story told out of
fear and suspicion and does violence to female sexual desire and fertility
by using those as weapons to humiliate and thereby control these powerful feminine agencies.[6]

What is the source of all this fear and anger? What is it that we men
need and want so desperately to control? We move now to the very core,
to the religious taproot of religiously legitimated violence against women.

In Genesis Eve receives her name because she is "mother of the living." But the male writers of her story know that she is not so much the
mother of life as the mother of a life-destined-to-die. Yes, Eve gives birth
to life, but a life that knows it will end in death. And the male writers of
our sacred texts are anguished and furious about that, and they want to
place blame!

In Genesis Eve is presented as the world's first critical thinker and
questioner.[7] It is she, not Adam, who enters into debate about God's commands. But she debates with the clever snake and ends up with a disas-
trous exegesis. Persuaded by the snake, she bites the forbidden fruit and
gives it to Adam. The story portrays her as a betraying nurturer, one who
feeds Adam dangerous food. Birthing and feeding—the primordial powers of life—are in Genesis inscribed with male fear, with criticism and
anger. But that male anger has not yet reached to the cause of death. And
for Christianity it is death that will come to haunt the work of Eve.

A close reading of the Genesis text shows that it is not our fallen nature but our created nature that accounts for mortality. "Now, lest they

---

6. Rosemary Reuther in her *Sexism and God-Talk: Toward a Feminist Theology* (Boston:
Beacon Press, 1983) speaks again and again about the determination of patriarchy to take
control of female sexuality and the use of scripture to legitimate that expropriation. She
says: "For radical feminism the core issue is women's control over their own persons, their
own bodies as vehicles of autonomous sexual experience, and their own reproduction.
Patriarchy means, above all, the subordination of women's bodies, sexuality, and reproduction to male ownership and control" (228). For a perspective on these issues that addresses other world religions see *Feminism and World Religions,* ed. Arvind Sharma and
Katherine K. Young (Albany: State University of New York Press, 1999). See also Judith
Plaskow, "God: Some Feminist Questions," in *The Coming of Lilith: Essays on Feminism,
Judaism, and Sexual Ethics, 1972–2003,* ed. Donna Berman (Boston: Beacon Press, 2005).
7. Phyllis Trible first made this suggestion in her chapter "Eve and Adam: Genesis 2–3
Reread" in *Womanspirit Rising: A Feminist Reader in Religion,* ed. Carol P. Christ and
Judith Plaskow (San Fransisco: Harper and Row, 1979). I find that Trible's attempt to "rescue" Eve by a feminist reinterpretation fails to deal seriously enough with the angry male
voice of the author. Judith Plaskow in *Standing Again at Sinai: Rethinking Judaism from
a Feminist Perspective* (San Fransisco: Harper and Row, 1990) is closer to my reading in
that she takes with full seriousness the misogyny within the text.

take and eat also of the tree of life . . ." (3:22) tells the story of a creature born to die and prevented by God from escaping the destiny shared by all animal creation, even though as humans and conscious of death we seek such an escape. But in Christian history Saint Paul and the early church will rewrite that story and interpret death not as our natural end but as punishment for our sin. Following from that, Eve in generations to come will be portrayed in innumerable Christian sermons as the seductress by whom through lust we [men] were introduced to death. Male anger against women and preoccupation with control over their bodies grows a deeper and a more bitter root.[8]

This deplorable history finds an early and vivid voice in the Gnostic Gospel of Thomas. Although eventually excluded from the biblical canon, it witnesses to the profound suspicion about women in the early Christian era, a suspicion rooted in the perceived connection of women to death, and the need for males to escape from that. It is a collection of 114 secret teachings allegedly left by Jesus and includes the following exchange: "[The disciple] Simon Peter said to them, 'Let Mary leave us, for women are not worthy of life.' Jesus said, 'I myself shall lead her in order to make her male, so that she too may become a living spirit resembling you males. For every woman who will make herself male will enter the kingdom of heaven.'" And then said even more directly (and put again into the mouth of Jesus): "Whoever does not love his father and his mother *in my way* cannot be my disciple; for my [earthly] mother gave me death but my true [divine] Mother gave me the Life."[9] The life that women offer is a life destined to die, and life eternal requires escape from that misbegotten birth, indeed a "new" birth, a birth not of blood but of water. Desire betrays us [men]. In the end fertility, maternity, and nurturance—the generative powers of life—lead only to that punishment that is death. In the second and third centuries of the church this connection of women to death provided an important legitimating ideology for marginalizing women from their earlier positions of influence and leadership.

---

8. Elisabeth Schüssler Fiorenza has written a brilliant and detailed analysis of how the early Jesus movement of "equal discipleship" drew many women to join only to find themselves in the years to follow more and more marginalized. See parts II and III in *In Memory of Her: A Feminist Reconstruction of Christian Origins* (New York: Crossroad, 1989). However, I locate the problem not simply in the patriarchal culture into which early Christianity had necessarily to insert itself. I locate the root source in male fear and denial of death.

9. Until recently, the only information we had about the Christian Gnostics came from the writings of apologists like Irenaeus (died ca. 200) in his *Exposition and Refutation of Knowledge Falsely So-Called*. As the title indicates it was not an unbiased text. However,

What is the story of women's work told in our Western sacred text and its subsequent commentaries and theologies?

—*bad food, bad birth, bad wife, bad theologian, bad woman*—

This depiction of Eve as one who has an untrustworthy and even betraying relationship to her husband Adam has served to legitimate all sorts of violence against women within the Abrahamic tradition—physical violence, psychological violence, and structural violence. Just look at the history of divorce laws in Judaism, in Christianity, and in Islam. Whether in synagogue, church, or *masjid*, religious practices and ideology privilege male domination in marriage. The psychological attack on women's bodies is equally ubiquitous. Because of her body she is not permitted to be ordained, not permitted to serve as a judge, not permitted to lead in worship or, in many cases, even to be present in worship. That some of this has been changed more recently only proves the larger point. Women appear in sacred texts as faceless and voiceless. Almost always she is the absent "they" of an intramale dialogue, listening to a male divine voice talk to a male human audience discussing what to do "with her." And with few exceptions (almost all of them recent) she is not permitted to study these sacred texts or to interpret them from her own point of view.

All of this is obviously disgraceful, and it is doubly disgraceful because often it is not seen as obvious. But the problem goes deeper. It is not simply the problem of male fear written into the story of Eve. Male fear and its obsession with control writes itself as the myth of creation itself. Creation is a story about control, or, more accurately, a story about the fear of loss of control. It is this idea of creation, our Western myth of the beginning, that we must deconstruct if we are to follow the deep root of violence against women.

The story begins with a Creator standing outside of and before the beginning of material reality. The Creator is presented as a Sovereign Outsider to all that will be inside the created world, who relates to that world by way of command—"let there be . . . and there was." And the creative task itself is fundamentally one not of connecting but of divid-

---

in 1945 an entire library of Coptic writings was found, some four dozen treatises. The gospel cited here is found in those writings. See Frederik Wisse in his chapter "Flee Femininity: Antifeminity in Gnostic Texts and the Question of Social Milieu," in *Images of the Feminine in Gnosticism*, ed. Karen L. King (Philadelphia: Fortress Press, 1988). Elaine Pagels has done much to bring to our attention how in the Gnostic literature the idea of the Divine Mother or the Feminine in the Godhead makes its appearance. She and others find in this literature a powerful source of criticism for the way in which the male hierarchy marginalized the female in orthodox theology and practice. However, before becoming too enthusiastic about Gnosticism, we should recall that the Divine Mother was elevated only by reducing our earthly mother and material birth to the work of death.

ing, of separation, creating order by establishing difference and distinction—"light/dark," "land/waters." Such a binary order requires not only the original ordering activity but also continuous supervision and control. Chaos, the undifferentiated and thus unorganized disorder that preceded the beginning, is never entirely removed from the subsequent picture. Order once achieved must be continuously disciplined to remain orderly. The God who creates order is necessarily the God who continues to give orders and who demands obedience to those orders. Relationships in the creation myth bear the marks of separation, hierarchy, and the demand for obedience, not connectedness and mutuality. It is a male story of power, a story of hierarchical command and control.[10]

In Genesis God is presented as Creator/Commander, the one in ultimate control. And to be human and bear the image of that God is also to have control, but a dominion that is unequally distributed between genders (and social classes). In the Christian appropriation of that story, God, who is both Creator and Law Giver, is portrayed as the exact opposite of our flesh and blood mothers, who can give birth only to selves that die. In the Christian mythos that seeks to supersede Jewish scriptures, we (Christians) have a chance for a second birth, a radically different birth than Eve and her gender can give. The birth that begins with Eve leads only to our ultimate (male) out-of-control. But washed in a different birth fluid (baptism) and fed by a different food (the Eucharist)—both controlled by the male hierarchy of the church—we gain entrance to eternal life. Eden with its tree may be forever lost, but hope is not lost. For God the Creator and Law Maker becomes in Christianity also God Our Savior, who births us (by a male sacrifice!) to a different life than our fleshly mothers can, a life beyond the reach of death.[11]

Now death is written not as the natural end of life, but as the product of a misbegotten birth, a birth destined to sin and with that the punishment that inevitably follows that sin. If we are to defuse the male anger and violence against women which that story of life/death legitimates, we need to think more clearly about our mortal bodies.

---

10. Mary Daley has written eloquently about the need for women to escape this male mythic world. See her *Beyond God the Father: Toward a Philosophy of Women's Liberation* (Boston: Beacon Press, 1973) and also *Gyn/Ecology: The Metaethics of Radical Feminism* (Boston: Beacon Press, 1979).

11. For an important article on the male appropriation through male-dominated ritual practices of traditionally female activities (such as birthing and feeding) see Christine Gudorf, "The Power to Create: Sacraments and Men's Need to Birth," in *Horizons* 14/2 (1987). There she senses what I analyze more fully here, where she says, "The clerical claim to control real life—spiritual life—as opposed to material life, has had dire consequences in our world" (303).

WHERE IS LIFE? WHERE IS DEATH?

Most of us, when we think about life, locate that life inside our own skin. We think that is where life resides as long as we have it. But what if life, all of livingness, is mostly outside our skin, something we have only so long as we remain intimately in touch with the material world around us? That fleshly, material world is not so much "around us" or "outside of us" as necessarily inside of us, and we inside of it. We breathe; we take in oxygen and exhale carbon dioxide. And we do that with all the other animals here on planet Earth who breathe as we breathe. How, then, can there be any oxygen left after these millions of years of animals breathing? Because we do not breathe alone, because of photosynthesis! We and all other animals breathe in unison with all trees and grass and other green things. We breathe only because they breathe with us—taking in our carbon dioxide and giving us back oxygen. So where does that mean life resides? Is it inside each of our skins, is that where we are alive? Or is life in the larger flow of life, and we alive only in that flow? And if life is in that great community of livingness, that intimate and intricate dance around us and inside of us, then what or where is death?

Death, we are told, is what happens when life inside our skin stops living. Western medicine and its arts of healing are all conditioned by this thought—a practice directed toward healthy, ill, or fatally failing organs inside individual bodies. We are taught to view death as the end and destruction of our life here inside. And sometimes we are told to understand that destruction as a deserved punishment, a judgment imposed by a Creator who has the right to take back what he has first given.

But is that an accurate way to understand death, as a catastrophe that happens to us individually, our destined and perhaps deserved end? What if life and death are not opposites, not mutually exclusive, but two parts of the same story, a story of intimate interaction and interdependence? That nondualistic way of reading reality is also a way of reading Darwin's theory of evolution, but a possible reading that was mostly missed.

To read only the surface of *The Origin of Species* (1859) is to be led by Darwin's words to confront a picture of evolving life that is everywhere overwhelmed by death. He speaks of "the battle" or "the war" of life where time and again living species become extinct and disappear from the continuing story of life. It is this reality that is so plainly written into the fossil record. Starvation and death are the driving forces of evolving life! In each generation of living entities many more progeny are born than can survive given the limited food supply. Whenever a random mutation gives to an individual the slightest advantage in this battle it gives that individual a decisive advantage in the struggle to survive, and that advantage will be passed on to its descendants. Left behind in the immense graveyard of life will be the vast majority of the unmodified. But even the few lucky winners in this struggle will, in turn, become victims of the continuing war as random modification and natural selection continue to select.

What disturbed religionists when they first read this theory was not primarily the fact that if Darwin was right then the story of Genesis, with its fixed and finished species, was wrong. Far more disturbing was the bleakness of the tale being told—life everywhere and always assaulted and defeated by death, today's living residents a passing surface resting on top of a vast killing field. Disturbing to the thin-skinned religionists, this story of perpetual struggle received a more favorable reading by social scientists, who wrote that picture into their prescriptions for social policy. Competition for survival, they argued, is the way nature evolves and progresses. Human social policy too should encourage struggle, reward winners, and leave losers behind, for there is no mercy nor should there be in natural selection. A society without a safety net for those who falter or never get into the game advances what nature intends.[12]

The problem with this way of reading Darwin can be stated quite simply. Nature's most perfect and fearsome "battle wagons"—the great dinosaurs—became extinct, unable to adjust to a suddenly transformed external environment (probably a devastating encounter by Earth with an asteroid). But other life forms, less fit it would seem for battle, did adjust and thus continued the story of life. So what is that story? Is it battle and war? Is it power to oppose and to impose and thus to win? Or is it being ready to change and by changing to stay in the ever-changing dance of life—what Darwin himself referred to as a system of "infinite and beautiful co-adaptations?"[13] Co-adaptation sounds more like cooperation than opposition and struggle. Perhaps the "survival of the fittest" is the survival of the "fitting-ness"—those most adept at adapting.

If that is the logic of survival, not opposition and battle, then how are life and death related? Can it be that life is not opposed to but cooper-

---

12. The most famous of these was Herbert Spencer, a nineteenth-century British social theorist who introduced a school of thought that would be called Social Darwinism. That school of social science was to have significant influence on the development of economic and social theory in the United States. See Richard Hofstadter, *Social Darwinism in American Thought* (Boston: Beacon Press, 1955). It was against this kind of Social Darwinism that Emile Durkheim wrote his *The Division of Labor in Society* in 1897, where he argued that such ideas would lead to social anomy and chaos.

13. Darwin was not just a naturalist with a hypothesis but also a writer who had to decide how to write his hypothesis. In that second task, he was also an author writing within a particular social and historical context, an author sharing that context with his anticipated audience. That Darwin privileges the metaphor of "war" and "battle" over the far less aggressive metaphor of "co-adaptation" has much to do with the contemporary British colonial practice, which was established and maintained by force of arms.

ates with death, life using death to evolve itself as life, from a one-celled primordial ooze to more and more complex forms of life? It is possible to read Darwin's theory of evolution not as a story mostly of death but rather the story of life that takes death into itself and by that process evolves itself as life.[14]

As that story unfolds (here on planet Earth), eventually there will evolve a fledgling autobiographer called homo sapiens who will begin to write the story of life, struggling to understand how to write that story accurately and bring that story into consciousness of itself. That would be a different way of understanding "the image of God"—not the right delegated to humans to dominate and by dominating to survive, but an invitation to understand how the dance of life works and a chance thereby to keep on dancing in that dance. This is a fundamentally different way of understanding the relationship of life and death, and the work of men/women within that story. That work could be named "learning how to dance the Dance of Life."

THE RESURRECTION OF THE BODY[15]

One of the great world religions pictures life as life living in the flow of life. It is the religion called Daoism. Daoism provides us with a very different way of imagining the beginning, and thus of conceiving and writing the story of life, from that given to us in Genesis. It serves to remind us that our Western dream of reality is only one of many possible imaginations, and it opens up the possibility of creative reinterpretation.

In Daoism we find "Mother" as Ultimate Reality and her creativity is pictured as the work of gestation and nurture.[16] Here is how Daoism conceives and writes the beginning:

---

14. For a fuller presentation of this idea, see John Haught, *God after Darwin: A Theology of Evolution* (Boulder: Westview Press, 2000).

15. In a chapter entitled "The Redemption of the Body: Post-patriarchal Reconstruction of Inherited Christian Doctrine," Paula Cooey examines many of the issues I have examined here—namely, the connection in Christian doctrine of women to the body, and therefore also to death. Her purpose is to write a constructive theological response within that tradition. See *After Patriarchy*, ed. Paula M. Cooey, William R. Eakin, and Jay B. McDaniel (New York: Orbis, 1991). Moving in a very different direction, and one that parallels my own argument, is Grace Janzen's *Becoming Divine: Towards a Feminist Philosophy of Religion* (Bloomington: Indiana University Press, 1999). Janzen argues that theories of religion should turn from preoccupation with death to a focus on life, turning from *mortality* to assessing the "hope, possibility, and wonder" implicit in *natality*. The "resurrection of the body" begins not with death but with birth.

16. The use of the word "mother" in the text is not a female gendering of Ultimate Reality. Dao is considered to include and incorporate both *yin* and *yang*. Rather Dao is a transgendered vision of the Ultimate Nature of the Life Process, which is the recommended "way" (Dao) for both women and men to imitate and to follow.

> There is something nebulous existing, born before heaven and earth, silent, empty, standing alone, altering in no way. Moving cyclically without becoming exhausted, which may be called *mother* of all under heaven. I know not its name. I give its alias, Dao.[17]

Or again,

> The Great Dao flows everywhere. It may go left or right. All things depend on it for life, and it does not turn away from them. It accomplishes its task, but does not claim credit for it. It clothes and feeds all things but does not claim to be master over them. Always without desires, it may be called The Small. All things come to it, and it does not master them. It may be called the Great.[18]

In Daoism, before there is heaven and earth there is "Mother," whose alias is Dao. She feeds all things and clothes all things *but does not claim credit and does not master*. Dao is ubiquitous and anonymous, conspicuous by its lack of ostentation. Here the story of life is one of generous giving, and then letting be and letting go. There is no demand for obedience; and there is no Fall and no punishment. Most astonishing of all is a birthing that refuses to master, refuses to rule, and seeks instead only to nurture and mature.

> Dao gives birth to all beings but doesn't try to own them. It acts on all beings but doesn't make them dependent, it matures them but doesn't rule them.[19]

The repeated negatives in this and the earlier quote show a self-conscious determination on the part of the original Daoist writers to negate what so many religions present as the Really Real—namely power, authority, obedience, and rule. Indeed, there is a clear intention to subvert hierarchy as the pattern of the divine/human relationships and, therefore, the right pattern of human/human relationships. There is also in Daoism a self-conscious rejection of the usual gender hierarchy.

---

17. Chapter 25 of the *Lao-Tzu*, quoted from the chapter on Daoism by Liu Xiaogan in *What Men Owe to Women: Men's Voices from World Religions,* ed. John Raines and Daniel Maguire (Albany: State University of New York Press, 2001). The *Lao-Tzu* is most likely a product not of a single person, Lao-Tzu, but of a literary genre of wise sayings. Daoism is not to be taken without critical distance. Its classical texts soon fell under the domination of Confucian patriarchy. While many powerful females are remembered in Daoist literature, the religious institutions fell under the domination of monks who sometimes exploited females, especially the young female body. See "Feminism and/in Taoism" by Karen Laughlin and Eva Wong in *Feminism and World Religions,* op. cit., and also the chapter by Hsiao-Lan Hu in this book.
18. From Xiaogan, in Raines and Maguire, *What Men Owe,* chap. 34.
19. Ibid., chap. 51.

When you know masculine yet hold on to femininity, you'll be the ravine of the country. When you're the ravine of the country, your constant virtue will not leave. And when your constant virtue doesn't leave, you'll return to the state of the infant.[20]

The imagination and language is that of the "mother/infant" relation. It recommends to all humans, both men and women, the practice of care, and of taking care, without trying to own or trying to be the boss. Dao rejoices not in issuing commands and ruling but in helping to mature.

In Genesis we find a different imagination and a different language. The picture it paints is of the Ruler and the ruled, a Sovereign demanding recognition and obedience and ready to punish infractions. It is the imagination of a male and it is written into the Western story of the beginning for the sake of males—not just any males, however, but those who enjoy hierarchy and benefit from its rule and intend to defend it.

From Daoism's originating texts we get a very different picture. It is one not of suspicion and jealousy concerning the exercise of power but of an encouraging nurturer delighted in an infant's advance in ability and independence. If that is how life is conceived in Daoism, then how does Daoism view death? Is death a punishment? Does death serve to remind us that we are not like the gods and face instead a grim and certain termination? When the writers of Daoism wrote about death this is what they said: "a leaf when it falls, falls close to its root." Death does not represent an end or a separation but a return—the flow of life inside returning to the larger flow of life outside.

In Daoism, we are never alone. We are always embraced and sustained. And when we die we return to the place we never really left and a place that never left us. This attitude is given strong voice in a passage where a Daoist sage, Master Chuang, whose wife has just died, is found by his friend, Hui Shih, squatting on the ground and pounding on a pot and singing. Hui Shih reprimands him for not showing proper grief. Master Chuang responds:

Not so. When she first died, how could I not grieve like anyone would? But on looking back into her beginnings, I saw that she originally had no life, and not only was she without life, she had no bodily form, and not only was she without bodily form, she had no qi [ch'i]. Scattered amidst the muddle and confusion, a change occurred and there emerged her qi, the qi changing, she emerged in bodily form, and her bodily form changing, she

20. Ibid., chap. 28.

emerged alive. Now, she has changed again, and has died. This is but to travel together with the passage of the four seasons from one to the next. When she was on the point of taking her repose in the great mansion of the world, I was in a state, trailing after her and howling. But it then occurred to me that this was a failing on my part to understand her circumstances. So I gave it up.[21]

Life and death and how we are to conceive of Ultimate Reality, and in response to those conceptions to shape our hearts and minds—this is presented in fundamentally different ways in the Western sacred texts and in Daoism. For one it is the Sovereign Lord and Master who rules all, for the other it is an enabler who does not want to rule. For one, the likeness of God in man is our human right to have dominion (over other animate and inanimate things here on earth). For the other, the way we should live our life is to live like water, staying in the flow.

In the whole world, nothing is softer and weaker than water. And yet for attacking the hard and the strong, nothing is better. There is nothing you can use to replace it. That the weak can overcome the strong—that the soft can overcome the hard—there is no one in the whole world who doesn't know it, and yet there is no one who puts it into practice.[22]

For Daoism, it is the nurturer/enabler that symbolizes Ultimate Reality. Life and death are not opposites at war with each other. Each embraces the other. And out of that embrace life renders itself alive, not fixed and finished but generative, always opening itself again to the new and unexpected. Here is a different kind of "resurrection of the body," one that can help tame our male fear and anger and our need to place blame and to control. This different resurrection reclaims our body as bodies that belong to a larger body, the Body of Livingness. It is the story of Ultimate Reality written as cosmic process and intimacy.[23]

Unfortunately, that more kindly view of life in the body has not for the most part taken root in our Western imagination. As a result we (men) continue to treat the bodies of women as dangerous and needing male supervision and control. And we are permitted to use violence, if necessary, to enforce that control.

---

21. Quoted from the chapter on Chinese views of death by Amy Weigand in *Death and Dying in World Religions*, an anthology edited by Lucy Bregman (Boston: Pearson Custom Publishing, 2004).
22. Quoted from Liu Xiaogan, in *What Men Owe*, chap. 78.
23. Process Philosophy/Theology, with its idea of panentheism, presents a Western alternative intellectual and religious imagination that has much in common with Daoism.

GUARDS, PRISONERS, AND FEMALE SACRIFICE

There are various ways of thinking about violence against women. We usually think about what seems to us *obviously* violent—the violence, for example, of dowry murder in India, or of honor rape and killing in Pakistan, or of clitoridectomy in Africa. Within the confines of their own cultural contexts, however, these acts are not seen as violent but as acts required by devotion. We in the West fall under the same judgment. For us there is a different kind of devotion and a different kind of violence against the female body. But as is the case of others, so for us inside our own culture, we do not see it as violence and instead practice that violence as an act of piety. I am talking about how the female body in our culture becomes the site of a sacrificial rite, where her body is treated as an open field of entrepreneurial exploitation.[24]

Living under the dominant and dominating male gaze, to modern women in the West their bodies become a commodity in a market of competing bodies, each needing an endless supply of other commodities (cosmetics, hair dye, hair spray, perfumes, depilation creams, hair relaxers, skin lighteners, teeth whiteners . . . you complete the list) to improve "how she looks." Walk into any supermarket and count the shelf space dedicated to products that promise to improve or correct the female body, and then compare that to the shelf space targeting the male body. What you are looking at in that comparison is the power of the gendered gaze made visible.[25]

But however "good you look," to get your value from how you look is always to experience yourself as out of control. The French existential-

---

24. My perspective in the following is clearly focused on the exploitation of women who are mostly middle class or above and disproportionately live in the Northern Hemisphere rather than the Southern. If instead I were to focus upon violence against women in the "two-thirds" world, I would need to talk about the crisis of undernourishment and poor or no health care, or the exploitation of female factory workers working along the global assembly line, or the sex industry that is spreading throughout the "two-thirds" world, and the exploitation of both legal and illegal immigrants who work as domestic workers in the households of the well-to-do. I have chosen the focus I have because it expands our notion of "violence" and reveals how patriarchy pursues domination of women who are thought of as privileged and liberated. It should be noted, however, that the global media is intent to expand through advertising the violence I document here to dependent female populations in the "developing" world. For an excellent summary of the globalization debate as it affects the lives of women, see Rebecca Todd Peters, *In Search of the Good Life* (New York: Continuum, 2004), especially chapters 1, 6, and 7.

25. I explored these ideas in a joint presentation with Anne Marie Hunter at the 1994 meeting of the American Academy of Religion under the title "Power and the Gendered Gaze." That presentation has not been published, but Hunter's exceptional insights can be found in her earlier article published in the Fall 1992 edition of *The Journal of Feminist Studies in Religion*. I will quote Hunter several times in what follows and those quotes are all drawn from our joint lecture.

ist Jean Paul Sartre put it this way: "I keep getting stolen from myself by the other person's eyes!"[26] To look at oneself through the eyes of others is to put oneself under the control of the other's eyes. But that is precisely what is expected of women living in Western societies and the eyes almost always belong to men. As Hunter complains: "Women learn to live their bodies from outside in." If your identity is constructed as a being who is a-being-to-be-looked-at, that fuels an endless anxiety to gain back control. Think of diets, workouts, cosmetic surgery—women persistently unhappy with their bodies and driven by a voracious appetite to discipline, to sacrifice, and to improve.[27]

Sandra Barkty comments on how women perform and experience their bodies under the dominant male gaze:

> The woman who checks her makeup half a dozen times a day to see if her foundation has caked or her mascara has run, who worries that the wind or the rain may spoil her hairdo, who looks frequently to see if her stockings have bagged at the ankle or who, feeling fat, monitors everything she eats, has become, just as surely as the inmate of the Panopticon, a self-policing subject, a self committed to a relentless self-surveillance.[28]

In talking about the Panopticon, Barkty is referring to the brilliant analysis of power and visibility in Michel Foucault's *Discipline and Punish: The Birth of the Prison* (New York: Pantheon Books, 1977).

Panopticon literally translates as "the all seeing" and describes a prison designed so that a single guard can effectively control hundreds of prisoners. The prison is circular in design with single cells on multiple floors around a guard tower in the center. Each cell is continuously backlighted, with bars facing the center and solid walls in between. The guard tower is always veiled in shade. Prisoners know that the guard can't be watching each of them all the time, but they also know that at any given moment he can be observing them. What happens under these conditions of persistent but uncertain visibility is that the prisoners internalize the

---

26 Sartre explores this idea in his play *No Exit*.

27. The evidence that many, perhaps most, women are unhappy with the way their body looks is overwhelming. It is reflected in the profit margins of the cosmetic and diet industries or the explosion of fitness centers. The fact that cosmetic surgeons are some of the highest paid in the medical profession, making more than twice the annual income of internists, is further evidence. Then there are eating disorders like anorexia and bulimia that each year strike some eight million Americans, overwhelmingly young women. Compulsive attitudes toward exercise and eating, or using surgery to address anxiety about appearance, leaves one, at the end of the day, still out of control, asking the appraising eyes of the other how much one can like oneself.

28. Quoted from the Hunter article mentioned previously.

gaze of the guard. They become their own disciplinarians, each prisoner becoming "the principle of his own subjection."

"I keep getting stolen from myself" is the everyday experience of women living under the dominant social gaze, and like prisoners in the Panopticon they internalize that gaze. Hunter complains: "media images of women have solidified and legitimated the gaze of the guards by surrounding us with what might be likened to photographs taken from the guard tower. Women have merely to look at those images to see themselves and their world through the eyes of the guards." And what they see is literally self-defeating; it defeats the self as the center of its own existence. In competing for a better looking body, or even just an acceptable body, women experience their lives as a self looking at itself through the eyes of the powerful stranger. The danger is, as Hunter puts it, "women do not live at the center of their own world. Indeed, some women seem in danger of being completely tangential and irrelevant to themselves."

I have called this "female sacrifice." It is a different kind of violence, one we usually don't see as violent but just the way things are and should be. Women live their bodies in our society as prisoners. The guard is patriarchy, and the discipline required is to live as a self perpetually unsure of itself, a commodity needing other commodities to shore up an uncertain market position, a body feeding the global profits machine.

This tragedy of the dominant gaze belongs in the end to both genders. For those who define themselves in terms of control are controlled by that need for control. It is a profound irony and truth that there are no guards without prisoners. Guards depend upon prisoners to recognize and respond to them as guards in order to be. Likewise, prisoners become prisoners by becoming those who know themselves and relate to themselves as those who are seen by the guards. What we are looking at then is a dance of mutual entrapment, where each gender performs a culturally scripted role. Both guards and prisoners are dancing together inside of a drama they usually don't see and therefore can't recognize. It is the dance of a world where all values, including the value of persons, have become values of competing commodities in a new and now global market. And the prayer of confession we are taught to pray is, "how much am I worth?"[29]

What we need are different eyes.

---

29. For a brilliant analysis of this new world culture see the chapter entitled "The Religion of the Market" by David Loy in *Visions of a New Earth: Religious Perspectives on Population, Consumption and Ecology*, ed. Harold Coward and Daniel C. Maguire (Albany: State University of New York Press, 2000). Loy shows how this new religion of the market has its own theologians (economists), its own missionaries (the global advertising industry), and a huge network of places of worship (the global shopping malls).

DIFFERENT EYES, DIFFERENT WITNESSES

Earlier I wrote with considerable enthusiasm about Daoism and its sense of Ultimate Reality as cosmic intimacy and process. But Daoism remains elitist and lacks a social ethic for transforming society and its institutions. For that, we must *turn again toward Jerusalem and its prophetic heritage*. However problematic that heritage is, it carries within it an indispensable truth. I have been critical of Christianity for its preoccupation with death, its suspicion of the body (projected onto women), and its consequent inner disengagement from our grounding in the material world.[30]

Here we Christians can learn something from our Hebrew forebearers. With their homeland occupied first by the troops of Alexander the Great and then by the Romans (333 BCE and after), those who would give birth to Jesus of Nazareth wrote a vision of a radical reversal—the eschatological drama of the Messiah, the resurrection of the dead and the kingdom of God. They did this *not* in response to the problem of mortality but in response to the threatened collapse of the moral meaning of history. Those ideas were written into the Hebrew Bible, and subsequently became part of the scriptures of Christianity and Islam, in order to *rescue the moral meaning of God*.

In its earliest period, members of the Jesus movement remained thoroughly Jewish in this respect. That is to say, the clear notion in the earliest writings in Christian Scripture is that the righteous dead are "asleep in God" and will stay that way until awakened for the final events—judgment day and the kingdom of God.[31] There was no idea of a purely spiritual, immediate-after-death eternal life—a reunion with lost loved ones in heaven. Loss of loved ones to death is painful, but in the first century for the Jews and for the members of the Jesus movement that was not the issue. The issue was the possible unwinding of the whole community done under by the assaults of moral despair, its giving up on itself by giving up on the always unfinished struggle for justice. Justice, not death, was the issue.

But as Christianity continued to develop and became less and less Jewish, and the return of the Messiah continued to be delayed, the origi-

---

30. Daniel Maguire in his book cowritten with Larry Rasmussen, *Ethics for a Small Planet: New Horizons on Population, Consumption, and Ecology* (Albany: State University of New York Press, 1998), puts this very nicely when he says: "If we have a claim on an afterlife, and the plants and the animals do not, we are not their kith and kin, nor do we share their perils. *Earth as prolegomenon* and *earth as destiny* are the ultimate in divergent worldviews and divergent ethics" (44–45).

31. The earliest writing of the New Testament is Paul's First Letter to the Thessalonians, dated around 45 CE. In the fourth chapter of that letter, beginning at line 13 and continuing to line 18, Paul refers to those who "sleep in death" and how at the return of the Messiah "the Christian dead will rise . . ."

nal ideas concerning death gradually became transformed, and the idea of immediate after-death immortality became inviting. The result today is that what the church seems mostly to sell is *death insurance*. Departing from the prophetic heritage, salvation has come to mean being saved from individual death, not being saved as a community from moral despair.

If Daoism leaves us without a social ethic and the church has become so preoccupied with personal death and immortality that it pays insufficient attention to issues of social justice, then where are we to go? Where can we find different eyes by which to see and guide our lives?

The idea of a "cloud of witnesses" is lodged deeply in the religious traditions of Abraham. It expresses a sense of identity with and responsibility for not just the self and its immediate loved ones but one that involves responsibility for the whole community. A "cloud of witnesses" is a remembered sense of all those who have struggled for justice, and mostly lost that struggle in their times, but passed that struggle on as their moral heritage to us. Why is that heritage important? Because it witnesses to an enduring truth, to something fundamental in human nature.

That truth is that we are, as humans, ineluctably social in our being, in our surviving and our flourishing. We depend upon each other to be dependable. We trust because we must. Thus, what terrorists try to destroy is not people but what as humans all people absolutely require. And that is a sense of taken-for-granted safety in our sharing of public space. Our everyday life together depends upon a mostly unquestioned and unquestioning sense of shared safety. And we almost always give that gift to each other.[32]

As humans we do not live primarily inside our individual skins, where some believe the punishment called death awaits us. Instead, *we live outside of ourselves in a double sense*: as material creatures dependent upon life processes that are outside of us before they are inside of us, and also as social beings dependent upon the dependability of others. That truth speaks to our male obsession with control and urges us to accept rather than deny being *the radically dependent animals* that we are. And that means we need to revise the stories we (men) write about our gods, because the religious roots of violence against women are often rooted in those stories, and in the end that becomes violence redirected against ourselves.

---

32. For a more detailed exposition of these claims see my chapter "Nature, Resistance, and the Kingdom of God" in *Resistance and Theological Ethics*, ed. Ronald H. Stone and Robert L. Stivers (Lanham, Md.: Rowan and Littlefield, 2004).

6

Rectification of the Four Teachings in Chinese Culture

HSIAO-LAN HU

esides the notorious practice of footbinding that has been abolished for well more than a century and yet continues to draw criticisms, violence against women in Chinese culture takes many other forms. The female is strongly associated with negative qualities and even evil forces, and is not considered a suitable carrier of the patriarchal lineage. In modern China since the 1970s, under the stringent population control policy that allows only one child in each nuclear family, the preoccupation for patriarchal lineage leads to female infanticide and abortion of female fetuses. In the year 2000, 117 boys were born in China for every one hundred girls.[1] The shortage of wives further results in women trafficking in poverty-stricken areas.[2] In the societies that are culturally Chinese but not governed by the Chinese government, girls and women are also subject to various forms of violence. They are either discouraged from seeking education or denied education altogether, especially those who are economically disadvantaged. Parents are worried that a high educational level would reduce their daughter's chance of fulfilling the tasks assigned to her by "nature," such as getting married, serv-

1. See the "China Population" website set up by National Population and Family Planning of China: http://www.chinapop.gov.cn/rkzh/zgrk/tjgb/t20040326_2836.htm.
2. Wang Man-na, "Chung-kuo nan-n, shih-heng-hsia-te jen-k'ou fan-mai ch'ang-ch,eh (The Rampant Human Trafficking under the Unbalanced Sex Ratio in China)," www.epoch times.com.tw/bt/5/3/12/n846389.htm (2005/3/12). The interrelation between the birth control policy and women trafficking in China is also noted by Christina Gilmartin in "Violence against Women in Contemporary China," in *Violence in China: Essays in Culture and Counterculture*, ed. Jonathan N. Lipman and Stevan Harrell (Albany: State University of New York Press, 1990), 214–17, as well as by Emily Honig and Gail Hershatter in "Violence against Women," in *Personal Voices: Chinese Women in the 1980's* (Stanford, Calif.: Stanford University Press, 1988), 291.

108

ing her husband (and his family), and bearing and rearing children, for a man is supposed to be the master of the household and he would not stand a wife better informed than he is. It is also popularly held that girls are not intelligent enough and therefore educational resources should not be wasted on them. Occupying the lower rungs in the economy and lacking education as their social leveler, many women are forced into menial labor or the sex industry, or thrown at the mercy of their husbands. They may be "disciplined" for not displaying their "natural" characteristics of being submissive and obedient, and on occasion are even told that it is due to their bad *karma* in past lives that they were reborn as women and/or are suffering from violence.

When dealing with the violence against women in Chinese culture, or cultures that have had close cultural connections with Chinese culture, a general tendency is to blame Confucianism and Confucius for the patriarchal ideology that treats women as nothing but the property of men. On the other hand, largely in reaction to the representation of Chinese culture that is static, backward, hierarchical, authoritarian, and patrilineal, some Confucian scholars, both ethnically Chinese and Western, have taken an apologetic approach, trying to restore the good name of Confucius and to reclaim the principle of reciprocity as the true spirit of Confucianism. Both parties, it seems, are falling into an either-or logic—Confucianism is either to blame or is not at all to blame—that does not exactly apply to Chinese culture in which the Three Teachings of Taoism, Confucianism, and (Chinese) Buddhism have been integrated into one and can hardly be distinguished, especially on the popular level, in the commoners' lives.[3] In other words, it is inadequate to analyze the roots of violence against women in the Three Teachings separately and then blame Chinese women's misery entirely on just one of the three or, conversely, to completely exonerate one or two of them. Rather, it is the combination of some elements from the Three Teachings that has condoned and perpetuated gender injustice in Chinese culture. Furthermore, rather than being Three-Teachings-in-One, Chinese culture is in fact Four-Teachings-in-One. That is, it is a combination of Taoism, Confucianism, (Chinese) Buddhism, and *Fa-chia/Fajia*[4] (commonly translated as Legalism or the

---

3. In my opinion, it is not even accurate to claim that one of the Three Teachings dominates one aspect of Chinese life and another dominates a different aspect, such as Confucianism dominating the political sphere and Taoism dominating the artistic sphere.
4. In this chapter, when a Chinese term or phrase appears for the first time, both the Wade-Giles transliteration and the *pinyin* transliteration will be given. For article titles, book titles, and the names of publishing companies, only the Wade-Giles transliteration will be given.

Legalist School[5]), a school that distrusts human nature, sees from the viewpoint of authorities, and dedicates itself to effective top-down control.

At a glance, Legalism has disappeared since the Emperor Wu (Han Wudi; r. 141–87 BCE) of the Han Dynasty (202 BCE–220 CE) elevated Confucianism to state ideology. However, it is common knowledge among students of Chinese history that, for two thousand years, "On the surface (yang) it is Confucianism; deep down (yin), Legalism (*yang-ju yin-fa/yangru yinfa*)," meaning that on the surface the state ideology is the Confucian morality of reciprocity, but in reality the state ideology has always reflected the Legalist concern about exerting top-down control. The root for violence against women in Chinese culture, I will argue, is this Legalist concern about control interwoven with conventions and practices in the other three teachings, namely, the Confucian concern of "rectification of names (*chengming/zhengming*)," the reified understanding of the analytical dichotomy of yin and yang, the emphasis of harmony shared by Confucianism and Taoism, and the misuse of the Buddhist concept of karma.

CONFUCIANISM: GUILTY OR INNOCENT?

In examining various forms of violence against women in Chinese culture and societies that have had strong cultural ties with Chinese culture, the majority of research has readily identified Confucianism as *the* cause. Female infanticide, footbinding, concubinage, wife-battering, the sex industry, and other forms of violence against women are all considered to be rooted in the misogynist Confucian values.[6] Confucianism is presented to be solely responsible for violence against women in Chinese, Japanese,

---

5. Traditionally, Chinese people did not have exact equivalents for "religious" or "sacred." They honored some teachings and schools of thought and saw them as grasping, to some extent, the operating principle of the universe that should also be guiding human behaviors (i.e., the *Tao/Dao*). For example, what is translated as Taoism/Daoism in the West was and is still understood as the Teaching about Tao (*Tao-chiao/Daojia*) or the School of Tao (*Tao-chiao/Daojiao*), and Buddhism was and is still called Buddha's teachings. None of these teachings, however, was taken as a self-contained "religion" with monopoly of truth. In this line of thinking and conceptualizing, Confucianism and Legalism, though lacking apparent "religious" elements, were put in the same category as Taoism and Buddhism, which bear elements that would be more readily recognized as "religious" by Westerners.

6. For examples, see Joan D. Chittister, "Divinely Ordained? Religious Creation Myths and the Relation of Militarism to Sexism," in *Winds of Change: Women Challenge the Church* (Kansas City: Sheed and Ward, 1986), 97; Jana S. Eaton, "Gender Issues in Transitional China," *Multicultural Education* (Winter 1998): 34; Vivien Ng, "Sexual Abuse of Daughters-in-Law in Qing China: Cases from the Xing'an Huilan," *Feminist Studies* 20/2 (Summer 1994): 373–91; and Catherine So-kum Tang, Shuk Han Pun, and Fanny Mui-ching Cheung, "Responsibility Attribution for Violence against Women: A Study of Chinese Public Service Professionals," *Psychology of Women Quarterly* 26 (2002): 176. For examples of the discussions about violence against women in societies adjacent to China, see Hilda Maria Gaspar-Pereira, "Patterns of Family Violence in Japan,"

Korean, and Vietnamese cultures, while possible influences from other major elements in Chinese culture such as Taoism and Buddhism are either disregarded or romanticized.[7] Counteractively, there have been attempts in revealing the "true" spirit of Confucianism and thereby arguing its innocence in the oppression of women. William Theodore de Bary, for example, contends that the key word in Confucian teachings is reciprocity and that, when Confucians differentiate and assign roles to men and women, more emphasis was intended to be put on the complementary natures of men and women and the need of union and combination, rather than on separate individual roles.[8] Terry Woo argues that sexist texts and practices in China predate Confucius[9] and that, if Confucius' teaching seemed androcentric, it was because men had held most of the political and military power and therefore it was men who needed to be stopped and transformed by *jen/ren* or benevolent relationships.[10] She also asserts that Confucius could not possibly have supported female infanticide or footbinding since he did not condone cruelty and inhumaneness on the part of the persons currently occupying authoritative positions.[11] Furthermore, she observes that Western feminists are prone to make gross generalizations based on their limited understanding of Confucianism for the purpose of establishing the inherent inferiority of Chinese culture and the progressiveness of the West.[12] Along a similar line of observation, in his monograph *Asian Values and Human Rights* de Bary detects a sense of Christian superiority behind the Western criticisms of Confucianism.[13]

In all fairness, given the central importance of *jen* in Confucius' teaching, it is unlikely that Confucius would have in any way tolerated

---

Wellesley Centers for Women Working Paper Series (Wellesley, Mass.: Wellesley Centers for Women, 2003), working paper no. 411, 8; Mee-Hae Kong, "Rethinking Women's Status and Liberation in Korea," paper presented at Conference on Asia-Europe Relations, Soest, October 31–November 2, 1997; Nguyen Thi Ngoc-Dung, "Violence against Women," summarized and trans. Le Minh Thinh, *Conference on Vietnamese Women in Canada*, Ottawa, 1996; and Ann D. Jordan, "Commercial Sex Workers in Asia: A Blind Spot in Human Rights Law," in *Women and International Human Rights Law*, vol. 2, ed. Askin and Koenig (Ardsley, N.Y.: Transnational, 2000), 534.

7. For instances, see Chittister, "Divinely Ordained?" 96, and Gaspar-Pereira, "Patterns of Family Violence in Japan," 20, 26.

8. William Theodore de Bary, "Women's Education and Women's Rights," in *Asian Values and Human Rights: A Confucian Communitarian Perspective* (Cambridge and London: Harvard University Press, 1998), 124–27.

9. Terry Woo, "Confucianism and Feminism," in *Feminism and World Religions*, ed. Arvind Sharma and Katherine K. Young (Albany: State University of New York Press, 1999), 114, 116.

10. Ibid., 113, 129.

11. Ibid., 115.

12. Ibid., 111, 116.

13. de Bary, "Women's Education and Women's Rights," 121–23.

any form of violence against women (it is unlikely that he would have tolerated any kind of violence), and it is true that there is no textual support for violence against women in Confucian classics, either. This, however, does not mean that Confucianism is not the least responsible for the violence against women in Chinese societies. The often male-centered and sometimes misogynist writings of Confucian scholars who served in the government undeniably have shaped Chinese culture by defining morality for the masses. Moreover, the usage of the word "Confucianism" as the translation of the Chinese term *Ju-chia/Rujia* is rather misleading. The word "Confucianism" equates Confucius' teaching with the whole tradition created and reinvented by the official-literati throughout Chinese history, and thereby holds Confucius accountable for all the renditions made during the twenty-five hundred years after his death. The Chinese language differentiates *Ju-chia* from *K'ung-chiao/Kongjiao*, with the former referring to the tradition of Chinese official-literati and the latter to the very own teaching of Confucius. It is therefore possible for Chinese speakers to denounce the corrupted elements in Confucianism qua *Ju-chia* without considering Confucius to be the initiator of all iniquities generated or condoned by the tradition, although Chinese speakers do not necessarily make that distinction.

CONFIGURATION OF THE MECHANISM SANCTIONING VIOLENCE AGAINST WOMEN

Legalist Propensity in State Confucianism

Confucianism qua *Ju-chia* (the school established by male official-literati) was different from Confucianism qua *K'ung-chiao* (Confucius' teaching) when it was adopted by the Emperor Wu of the Han Dynasty as the state ideology. Chinese historian Yü Ying-Shih comments that the Confucianism adopted as the state ideology since the Han Dynasty is more akin to Legalism than to early Confucianism.[14] Antonio L. Rappa and Sor-Hoon Tan's work also shows that prominent Han Confucians' prescription of hierarchical relationships in fact mirrors the Legalist discourse and deviates from the early Confucian thought of ethical mutuality.[15]

Legalism is one of the schools of thought that thrived in China in the fourth and third centuries BCE. It is also the school of thought that was ultimately responsible for ending the turmoil of the Warring States Period

---

14. Yü Ying-Shih, "Anti-Intellectualism and Chinese Political Traditions," in *History and Thought* (Taipei: Lianjing Publishers, 1976), 43.
15. Antonio L. Rappa and Sor-hoon Tan, "Political Implications of Confucian Familism," *Asian Philosophy* 13/2–3 (2003): 94.

(476–221 BCE) and building a huge empire for the first time in the history of China.[16] In *A Source Book in Chinese Philosophy*, Wing-Tsit Chan introduces Legalism in the following words:

> The Legalist School . . . rejected the moral standards of the Confucianists . . . in favor of power. . . . Its aim was political control of the state and the population, a control to be achieved through an intensive set of laws, backed up by generous rewards and severe punishments. According to their theory, aggression, war, and regimentation would be used without hesitation so long as they contributed to the power of the ruler. . . . [T]he Legalists were primarily interested in the accumulation of power, the subjugation of the individual to the state, uniformity of thought, and the use of force.[17]

Within early Legalism, there were three distinctive trends. One trend, represented by Shang Yang (d. 338 BCE), emphasized setting up laws and regulations and enforcing them through severe punishments. Shen Pu-hai (Shen Buhai; d. 337 BCE) represents a second trend that was interested in administrative methods and techniques. The third, represented by Shen Tao (Shen Dao; c. 350–275 BCE), was concerned with the demonstration of the ruler's power, the natural tendencies of the ruled, and the circumstances that would affect the exertion of power. The three trends of early Legalism were synthesized by Han Fei (d. 233 BCE), whose work was instrumental in setting up the dictatorship of the Ch'in (Qin) kingdom that would later conquer all other kingdoms and lay down the foundation of the subsequent empires in China. Han Fei provides the following reasoning for the Legalist control of human relationships: "The severe household has no fierce slaves, but it is the affectionate mother who has spoiled sons. . . . [V]irtue and kindness are insufficient to end disorder. . . . [T]he enlightened ruler does not value people who are naturally good and who do not depend on reward and punishment."[18] Han Fei's writing reflects the Legalist distrust of human nature.[19] For Legalists, an orderly society depends on

---

16. The very word "China" derives from the name of this first Chinese empire that Legalism helped build: Ch'in/Qin.

17. Wing-tsit Chan, tr. and comp, *A Source Book in Chinese Philosophy* (Princeton, N.J.: Princeton University Press, 1963), 251.

18. Ibid., 253–54.

19. Han Fei is a disciple of Hsün-tzu (Xunzi; 298–238 BCE), a Confucian who avers human beings are endowed with depraved nature and need education in order to be good. Hsün-tzu's view of human nature has never become *the* Confucian stance; mainstream Confucians have adopted the view of Mencius (Meng-tzu/Mengzi; 371–289 BCE), who believes human nature to be naturally good.

forcible and adamant top-down control. This line of thinking finds a striking resemblance in the work of Han Confucian scholar Tung Chung-Shu (Dong Zhongshu; c. 179–c. 104 BCE), because of whom the Emperor Wu dismissed non-Confucian scholars from the court and elevated Confucianism to the status of state ideology. In his work the *Luxuriant Gems of the Spring and Autumn Annals (Ch'un-ch'iu fan-lu/Chunqiu fanlu)*, Tung reasons:

> Man's nature being in sleep, as it were, and before awakening is the state created by Nature. . . . The people receive from Nature a nature which cannot be good [by itself], and they turn to the king to receive the training which completes their nature. . . . [G]oodness has to do with training and not with nature.[20]

Though Tung Chung-Shu does not assume human nature to be evil as Legalists commonly do, he does not believe people can be good by themselves, either. Therefore, contrary to the emphasis on self-cultivation in early Confucianism, Tung considers top-down regulations, such as the "Three Bonds" (*san-kang/sangang*), necessary in bringing forth the "good" (that is, orderly) side of the ruled.

Given the discernible affinity between Legalism and Confucianism à la Tung Chung-Shu, it is not surprising to know that the idea of the Three Bonds, the primal target of criticisms against Confucian authoritarianism, lacks firm basis in the early Confucian classics but is only mentioned for the first time in Tung's *Luxuriant Gems of the Spring and Autumn Annals*. The "Confucian" idea of the Three Bonds, which has been commonly understood as prescribing absolute obedience on the part of ministers, sons, and wives to their rulers, fathers, and husbands, finds its provenance in the "Three Accordances (*san-shun*)" or the "Three Services (*san-shih*)" in Han Fei, the aforementioned Legalist synthesizer: "Ministers serve rulers, sons serve fathers, wives serve husbands. When the three are in accord, the world is in order; when these three are reversed, the world is in chaos. This is the constant way of the world, even enlightened kings and worthy ministers will not change it. Even when a ruler is despicable, his minister will not dare go against him."[21] While the

---

20. Translation adapted from Chan, *Source Book*, 275–76. The Chinese word *t'ien/tian* can mean "sky," "heaven," "nature" in the sense of something inherent and thus natural, and "Nature" in the sense of the operating principle of the universe or the totality of "natures." Here I think the proper translation is "Nature."
21. Translation given by Rappa and Tan in "Political Implications of Confucian Familism," 94.

Chinese word for "bond" indeed allows ambiguity and can mean "main-stay," indicating the primacy of the three sets of relationships in all human relationships,[22] it is undeniable that the very idea of the Three Bonds carries a Legalist overtone. Therefore, if it is due to the idea of the Three Bonds that Chinese women have been rendered subservient down to this date, apparently Legalism has been very much alive and in fact should be held accountable for the authoritarianism that has existed in Chinese culture.

Confucius' and Confucians' Complicity

To recognize the Legalist origin of Tung's idea of the Three Bonds is not to exonerate either Confucianism qua *Ju-chia* or Confucianism qua *K'ung-chiao*, nor is it to place the blame solely on Legalism or on Tung. Both Confucius and later Confucians are complicit in countenancing, re-inforcing, or even adding to the patriarchal tradition that condones vio-lence against women. The very fact that the great Legalist synthesizer Han Fei was a disciple of, and derived at least part of his ideas from, a Confucian (namely, Hsün-tzu, albeit his position always having been a minority one within Confucianism), speaks volumes of the affinity of Confucianism and Legalism and is indicative of Confucianism's complic-ity in promulgating the Three Bonds in the Legalist sense.

To begin with, Confucius uncritically inherited the tradition and took for granted the patrilineal feudal norms that had been established as early as the beginning of the Chou (Zhou) Dynasty (c. 1050–256 BCE), possi-bly even earlier.[23] With regard to the relations between rulers and sub-jects, he instructed people to abide by the ancient feudal rites of the Chou Dynasty and condemned those noblemen who trespassed against the rites.[24] In terms of the parent-child relationship, he apparently maintained a distant and hierarchical relationship with his one and only son.[25] In the

---

22. De Bary argues that the word "bond" signifies "bonding" rather than "bondage," and that Han Confucians elaborate on complementarity and reciprocity rather than accepting the ab-solute inequality of power. See De Bary, "Women's Education and Women's Rights," 124–27.
23. Woo, "Confucianism and Feminism," 116–17.
24. For examples of the former, see *Analects* 2:3, 3:19, and 14:41; for examples of the lat-ter, see *Analects* 3:1 and 3:22.
25. In the *Analects*, Confucius' son, Li, was said to have never received any special in-structions from his father. Upon seeing his father, Li's reaction, which reflected the ex-pected behavior of a son at Confucius' time, was to quietly walk by without uttering any word unless he was talked to. Confucius stopped him to question if he had studied the *Book of Odes* and the *Book of Rites*, and then said that one could not establish himself as a human being without studying those two classics. Such were the only words Confucius ever spoke to his son as recorded in the *Analects*. *Analects* 16:13.

Analects he did not appear to be misogynist,[26] but that is only because he rarely discussed about or with women, which could imply that Confucius did not think that women were important or that they should learn or could understand what he taught. The only occasion that Confucius ever directly talked *about* (not *to*) women was the notorious remark "Women, and lesser men, are most difficult to deal with. If you get closer to them, they cease to be humble. If you keep a distance from them, they resent it."[27] In no records was he said to have ever associated with women, nor did he ever have a female disciple. He might or might not have been misogynist, but he was certainly androcentric and patriarchal.

Secondly, Confucius' concern for the "rectification of names" is consonant with the Legalist insistence on complete "correspondence between actuality and names (*hsing-ming/xingming*)"[28] and thus opens the door for a Legalist, prescriptive rendition. It is recorded in the *Analects* that, when Duke Ching of Ch'i (Qi Jinggong) inquired about government, Confucius taught, "Let the ruler *be* a ruler, the minister *be* a minister, the father *be* a father, and the son *be* a son."[29] Given the general spirit of his teaching, it seems this reply is urging people to take up the moral responsibilities in their own positions. However, it may as well mean to command people that they should play the roles assigned to them and fulfill the accompanying obligations without questioning. Wang Ping puts it this way in her study of footbinding: "The tight rein Confucius put on language indicates the dangerous wolf that lurks behind and inside words. Names are the incarnation of social law and authority, and the act of naming is theoretically constitutionalized, embedded with power, authority, and social status."[30] The doctrine of the "rectification of names" inevitably contains a Legalist element, for names carry with them certain

---

26. Richard W. Guisso comments, "There is little evidence of misogyny in the recorded sayings of Confucius, but in commentaries on the Odes, later exegetes have imposed their own more stringent patriarchy to the point of distortion." See Guisso, "Thunder over the Lake: The Five Classics and the Perception of Woman in Early China," in *Women in China: Current Directions in Historical Scholarship*, ed. Richard W. Guisso and Stanley Johannesen (Youngstown, N.Y.: Philo Press, 1981), 52. Although the second part of the sentence is tenable, the first half is a precarious argument based on silence.

27. Translation adapted from Chan, *Source Book*, 47. The word *hsiao/xiao* signifies "less" in the physical, socioeconomical, or moral aspects. Thus the term *hsiao-jen/xiaoren* can be used to refer to people who have not fully grown (that is, children), people who have lesser socioeconomical resources (such as servants or lower-class people), or people who have little virtue.

28. Chan, *Source Book*, 256–57. Chan also offers a detailed discussion on the translation and mistranslation of the term in footnote 17 on pages 256–57 as well as in the Appendix, pages 787–88.

29. Chan, *Source Book*, 39 (*Analects* 12:11).

30. Wang Ping, *Aching for Beauty: Footbinding in China* (Minneapolis and London: University of Minnesota Press, 2000), 110.

rights and obligations that are allowed or prescribed by the whole society. Thus regarded, Confucius has planted the seed for the misuse and abuse of his teaching. However, the preoccupation with rectification of names and right understanding of the concepts embedded in names, in as much as it has been widespread in Chinese culture, can also play a crucial role in rectifying the tradition and righting the wrongs done to women, which will be shown subsequently.

Thirdly, even though some later Confucians did stress reciprocity in the three sets of relationships, as de Bary shows, none of them seemed to question Tung on his hierarchical understanding of the relation between yin and yang, nor did they reject Tung's reifications of the analytical dyad. Tung's Confucianism is often termed "Yin-Yang Confucianism" by later Confucian scholars because Tung's writing is replete with ideas borrowed from religious Taoism,[31] in which the yin-yang dyad is reified and has manifestations in the natural world, in the human body, and in human social relationships. For instance, in the *Scripture of Ultimate Equilibrium (T'ai-p'ing ching/Taipingjing)*, the earliest religious Taoist scripture available, it is stated:

> There are three primordial energies: the Ultimate Yang, the Ultimate Yin, and the Harmonic Neuter. There are three kinds of embodied entities: Heaven, Earth, and Human. There are three types of celestial bodies: the Sun, the Moon, and the stars, with the Polar Star as the center. There are three types of terrestrial bodies: mountains, rivers, and plains. There are three types of human beings: fathers, mothers, and children. There are three categories in politics: rulers, ministers, and subjects.[32]

Although the appearance of the written form of this scripture postdated Tung, the belief in natural-human correspondence had been existent since

---

31. William Theodore de Bary, Wing-tsit Chan, and Burton Waston, comp., *Sources of Chinese Tradition* (New York and London: Columbia University Press, 1960), 1:191. At Tung's time, religious Taoism and philosophical Taoism were still different enough to be distinguished from each other. Within the few hundred years after Tung, religious Taoism would have absorbed philosophical Taoism into itself and it became increasingly meaningless to distinguish the two.
32. "Ho san-ch'i hsing ti-wang fa (Method of Harmonizing the Three Energies for the Rising of the Ruler)" in *T'ai-p'ing ching ho-chiao (The Scripture of Ultimate Equilibrium* [collated]), comp. Wang Ming (Pei-ching: Chung-hua shu-chü, 1960), 18–20. My translation. *T'ai-p'ing ching* is otherwise known as *T'ai-p'ing ch'ing-ling shu (Taiping qingling shu)*. It was said to be revealed by the deified Lao-tzu to a man living in the Eastern Han Dynasty called Kan Chi/Gan Ji (in some versions, the man's name is Yü Chi/Yu Ji, as the Chinese characters for "kan" and "yü" look very similar). According to the Standard History of the Later Han, originally the whole scripture contains one hundred and seventy scrolls, but now there are only fifty-seven extant.

the pre–Ch'in era (that is, before 221 BCE).[33] Tung's understanding in chapter 56 of his *Luxuriant Gems of the Spring and Autumn Annals* certainly betrays his absorption of the belief of religious Taoism as illustrated in the preceding text:

> The material force of Heaven is above, that of Earth below, and that of man in between. . . . The body's 366 lesser joints correspond to the number of days in a year, and the twelve larger joints correspond to the number of months. Internally the body has the five viscera, which correspond to the number of the Five Agents. Externally there are the four limbs, which correspond to the four seasons. . . . Man's conduct follows the principles of human relations, which in fact corresponds to the relationship of heaven and earth.[34]

For Tung, yin and yang are no longer simply abstract conceptual pairs but are materialized as real phenomena in the world, and the harmony (or order) of the world relies on yin functioning as yin and yang functioning as yang. Moreover, in his system, yang is clearly reified as positive qualities, yin as negative qualities: yang is good nature, yin is evil feelings;[35] yang is health, yin is sickness; yang is happiness, yin is sadness; yang is light and wisdom, yin is dark and stupor.[36] Following this logic, yang is obviously superior since it is positive, while yin is inferior given its negative nature. Combined with the belief in the correspondence between the natural and the human world, it follows that Heaven is superior and Earth inferior; the ruler is superior and the ruled inferior; fathers are superior and sons inferior; and men are superior and women inferior.[37] By extension, all that is positive (such as purity, cleanness, honesty, wisdom, and construction) is male and all that is masculine is superior, while all that is negative (such as impurity, filth, deceit, stupor, and destruction) is female and all that is feminine is inferior. And, just as "Earth serves Heaven with the utmost loyalty,"[38] so should the inferior in all other sets of relationships, such as a wife, serve the superior, such as a husband. Through such homology, a hierarchy is built, and gender inequality is firmly grounded in the "natural" law of the proper relation between Heaven and Earth.

---

33. Chan, *Source Book*, 244–45.
34. Ibid., 282.
35. Ibid., 276.
36. Ibid., 283.
37. Ibid., 277–78.
38. Ibid., 279.

Later Confucians or official-literati (since the state ideology is supposed to be Confucianism, all official-literati are *de jure* "Confucians") may disagree with each other and have indeed contended with each other over many points, but the reified and hierarchical (mis)understanding of yin and yang is simply taken for granted and taught to the people. That is, if Confucius is androcentric for not addressing women and is patriarchal for uncritically adhering to the patrilineal feudal norms, and if Tung Chung-Shu is sexist for assigning essences to male and female, and misogynist for assigning negative qualities to the female, later Confucians are no less culpable for continuing the tradition and even making the tradition more misogynist. By the same token, later Taoists are equally blameworthy for embracing, or at least not correcting, the misuse of the yin-yang concept. The rectification of the yin-yang concept is also much needed in dismantling the mechanism that condones violence against women, as will be discussed subsequently.

Misuse of Yin-Yang and Karma

On the popular level, religious Taoism even added to the misassociation of yin with base, negative, demonic qualities. To make things worse, on the popular level, the Buddhist idea of karma has been understood in a rather passive sense, under which mistreatments are explained away as the fruits of one's bad karma in past lives and injustice is left unchecked. Tang and associates observe that "finding 'fault' with victims for negative events is in line with Chinese cultural thinking. Chinese are taught since youth that they need to think carefully about their behaviors and conduct themselves properly all the time, otherwise they have only themselves to blame if bad things or misfortune happen to them."[39] Women, in particular, are taught to be accepting of the misfortunes they suffer, since it was the bad karma they accumulated in past lives that caused their rebirth as women.

When the Confucian concern for the rectification of names interlocked with the Legalist concern of exerting control by inflicting punishments to bind people to their assigned positions, when the yin-yang concept is not only reified but hierarchically arranged, and when the concept of karma is mainly used to blame the victim, the idea of the Three Bonds in effect allows not only domination but tyranny on the part of whoever is supposed to be in the position of yang, and victimizes and then blames those who are in the position of yin. The implications for those who are labeled yin are dreadful. Wife abuse, for instance, becomes "a legitimate

---

39. Tang et al., "Responsibility Attribution for Violence against Women," 182.

means to discipline Chinese women when they are perceived as failing to meet the prescribed cultural and social standard of obedient wives."[40] Also, anything embodying "femaleness" is forbidden to appear in the public sector or even in a shared space in the private sector (such as the living room and the dining room), lest the yin force contained in those female-related objects contaminate the fortune of the master of the house, or the town, or the kingdom. This taboo takes a drastic form in a battlefield practice named *Yin-men-chen* (*Yinmenzhen*) in late imperial China. Based on the association of women with yin, and therefore with impure and demonic forces, women's bodies, particularly their reproductive organs that are the most yin of all, are considered capable of effectively counteracting the yang force of the all-male military. From the late sixteenth century until the late nineteenth century, in many (men's) rebellions against the government (run by men), women were stripped naked and forced to stand in front of the government's army during wars. In some cases women were raped, slaughtered, stripped naked, and planted into the ground upside down so that the government's army would be surrounded by the sight of female reproductive organs.[41] By exposing the most yin to the enemy, it was believed that the impure, filthy, demonic forces of the yin could cause the enemy's weapons to malfunction.[42] Even more shocking, in the eighteenth century, this barbarous practice was adopted by the government's army, and its effect was believed not only by uneducated ordinary people but by the official-literati who served in the court (the *de jure* Confucians), as well.[43]

Not all violence against women sanctioned by the twisted combination of the Four Teachings took this drastic a form as *Yin-men-chen*. More frequently, it takes the forms of locking women up in their assigned gender roles under the excuse of maintaining the harmony of yin and yang. Not unlike the combination of Legalism and Confucianism, religious Taoism can produce the effect of confining women to their "natural" place of being soft and weak, bearing and nurturing children, enabling men without asking anything in return, and assuming low positions. Even though there *are* female immortals in Taoist hagiography, which certainly makes religious Taoism appear to be less androcentric, the exemplariness

---

40. Ibid., 176.
41. Chiang Chu-shan, "Nü-t'i yü chan-cheng: Ming-Ch'ing yen-pao chih shu, 'Yin-men-chen' tzai-t'an (Women's Body and Warfare: The Re-exploration of *Yin-men-chen* in Late Imperial China)," *Hsin Shih-Hsüeh* (*New Historical Studies*) 10/3 (September 1999): 165–67.
42. Ibid., 175–83.
43. Ibid., 168–71.

of the female immortals-to-be still lies in their being docile, living in the shadows and under the commands of their husbands and fathers.[44]

The misuse of the yin-yang concept can also make women feel dirty and unworthy, deprive women of opportunities, silence women's protests, and, if all of the above still do not keep women in their subservient positions, sanction tyrannies from men and blame the victims for whatever goes wrong, be it the disharmony of the household or the disorder of the nation.[45] For example, in the second century, Cheng Hsüan (Zheng Xuan; 127–200 CE), a prominent Confucian annotator, used a poem from the *Book of Odes* (*Shih ching/Shijing*), one of the Confucian classics, to prove women's destructive nature and to justify the exclusion of women from education and intellectual activities. While the original context of the poem quoted, "Looking Up (*Chan-yang/Zhanyang*)," was in fact a complaint against a particular woman living in the eighth century BCE, Pao Ssu (Baosi), Cheng passed a universal judgment: "Man is *yang*. *Yang* is active in nature, and therefore when he abounds in reasoning and consideration, he can establish the kingdom. Woman is *yin*. *Yin* is passive in nature, and therefore when she abounds in reasoning and consideration, she can put the kingdom into disorder."[46] And in the eleventh century, Chu Hsi (Zhu Xi; 1130–1200 CE), the renown synthesizer of neo-Confucianism thanks to whom the standardized Confucian curriculum was established in China for nationwide examinations, further added to Cheng's commentary: "Women are good when they are without dissent or opinion; smartness is not good for them. Their smartness only leads to the collapse of the kingdom."[47] Bettine Birge rightfully points out that "Chu did not believe that women had the same intellectual capabilities as men" and was convinced that the bedrock of Confucian ethics depended on keeping women in the interior of the house.[48] By this line of reasoning, Chinese women were largely denied education, or dis-

---

44. Eva Wong, "Taoism," in *Her Voice, Her Faith: Women Speak on World Religions,* ed. Arvind Sharma and Katherine K. Young (Boulder, Colo.: Westview Press, 2002), 122.

45. Wives have also been verbally and physically abused for "failing" to produce male progeny to carry on the patriarchal lineage of their husbands' families, especially in modern China since the implementation of the one-child-only policy. Gilmartin, "Violence against Women in Contemporary China," 209, 215, and Honig and Hershatter, "Violence against Women," 275, 294.

46. Cheng Hsüan, *Mao-shih Cheng-chien* (*The Mao's Commentary on the* Book of Odes, *with Cheng's Subcommentary*), chüan 18, 24a. My translation.

47. Chu Hsi, *Shih chi chuan* (*Collected Commentaries on the* Book of Odes), 897. My translation.

48. Bettine Birge, "Chu Hsi and Women's Education," in *Neo-Confucian Education,* ed. William Theodore de Bary and John W. Chaffee (Berkeley: University of California Press, 1989), 331.

couraged and not taken seriously in terms of intellectual development. Given fewer resources and discouraged, women could not but stay ignorant. The association of women with yin, and yin with stupor, thus becomes a self-fulfilling prophecy. Even to this date, there are still parents who, with limited resources, would willingly invest on their sons' education and readily recognize their sons' intellectual prowess, and yet say to their daughters, "What do girls have to do with studying?"[49]

RESOURCES FOR DISMANTLING THE MECHANISM RESULTING IN VIOLENCE

Put together, elements from Legalism, Confucianism, Taoism, and Buddhism, misconstrued or not, can constitute a cruel mechanism that sanctions violence against women. However, each of these Four Teachings also contains resources that may help reduce the iniquities. With the widespread Confucian-Legalist obsession with correctness in place, it may be helpful to propagate the correct understandings of *jen*, yin-yang, and karma.

Among the four, Legalism may be the one that has the least to contribute in stopping the violence against women. However, Wing-tsit Chan points out, "It was the only ancient school that was consistently and vigorously anti-ancient. . . . It looked to the present rather than the past, and to changing circumstances rather than any prescribed condition."[50] Legalism demands renovation and refuses to preserve corrupt customs in the name of tradition; how things have been by no means justifies how things should be done. In addition, Legalism "insisted that laws must be applicable to all" regardless of one's social station or one's closeness to the ruler.[51] "A prince who commits a crime," a Legalist slogan goes, "is to be given the same punishment that is given to a commoner who commits the same crime." It demands that a ruler (or anyone in an authoritative position, for that matter) should not set up any law he himself cannot abide by. Thus Legalism promotes fairness and equality, though rather inadvertently. Furthermore, to add to Chan's observations, Legalism forbids

---

49. This bias is manifested when the numbers of male illiterates and female illiterates are juxtaposed, and in the percentage of females among the receivers of advanced education. For instance, according to the statistics provided by the Ministry of Education in Taiwan in 2003, among Taiwanese above the age of fifteen, 78,460 men were illiterate, and the number of illiterate women was 470,107. In the same year, female students constituted 50.99 percent of the body of all college students in Taiwan, and yet of all those pursuing master's degrees, only 37.82 percent were female, and only 24.85 percent of all Taiwanese doctoral students were female. http://www.edu.tw/EDU_WEB/EDU_MGT/STATISTICS/EDU7220001/overview/brief/index.htm?TYPE=1&UNITID=197&CATEGORYID=0&FILEID=126373&open.
50. Chan, *Source Book*, 251.
51. Ibid., 252.

"private disciplinary measures (*ssu-hsing/sixing*)," so wife-battering under the pretense of "disciplining" the wife is not to be tolerated.

Confucians at later times may differ from each other and Confucianism qua *Ju-chia* may have deviated from Confucianism qua *K'ung-chiao*, but all Confucians still look up to Confucius himself and consider him the primal saint. That is, what Confucius said still carries considerable weight. It is generally agreed that the key word in Confucius' teaching is *jen* (benevolence or humaneness), which is none other than *chung* (*zhong*; conscientiousness) and *shu* (consideration or reciprocity).[52] The concept of *chung* can be ambiguous and is often misconstrued as "loyalty," thereby becoming the reason that people are taught to follow closely their assigned social roles. However, the concept of *shu* is far from ambiguous: "not do to others as you would not wish done to yourself"[53] and "a man of humanity, wishing to establish himself, seeks also to establish others; wishing to be prominent himself, he seeks also to help others be prominent."[54] Therefore, even though Confucius might be androcentric in that he only addressed men, he did not preach any double standards and did not condone inhumanity on the part of anyone in any position. Violence does not have a place in Confucius' own teaching. In addition, judging from the fact that Confucius values humaneness over rites[55] and on occasions even encourages his disciples to trespass the preconceived boundaries,[56] it is unlikely that by *chung* he means one should be loyal to whatever role assigned to him/her or conform to social expectations. Besides, he may have valued harmony (*ho/he*), but he has also made it clear that harmony should be distinguished from conformity (*t'ung/tong*).[57] In other words, absolute conformity to rigid social regulations is not at all what Confucius would require of his followers or would think his (male) followers could require of others.

Claiming to be a follower of Confucius, Tung Chung-Shu may be convinced that femininity is base and inferior, and later Confucians or re-

---

52. *Analects* 4:15.
53. James Legge, trans., *The Four Books: Confucian Analects, the Great Learning, the Doctrine of the Mean, and the Works of Mencius* (New York: Paragon Book Reprint Corporation, 1966), 157 (*Analects* 12:2).
54. *Analects* 6:28. Translation adapted from Legge, *The Four Books*, 77.
55. "If a man is not humane, what has he to do with rites?" *Analects* 3:3. Translation adapted from Chan, *Source Book*, 24.
56. "When it comes to the practice of humanity, one should not defer even to his teacher." Ibid., 44 (*Analects* 15:35).
57. "A gentleman seeks harmony but not conformity; a lesser man seeks conformity but not harmony." *Analects* 13:23. My translation.

ligious Taoists[58] may have accepted Tung's reification without questioning, but not all Chinese have understood femininity in this way. Drastically different from Tung's typology, early philosophical Taoism extols the qualities stereotypically identified as feminine and even upholds femininity to be the normative virtue that all people should cultivate.[59] It is much celebrated that the *Tao Te Ching/Daodejing* (the *Classic of the Way and Its Power*) likens Tao to a mother and presents as positive the qualities conventionally considered feminine, such as softness, weakness, nurturing, enabling, assuming low positions, and not asserting the self. The "behavior" of Tao is described in the following words: "It gives them life and rears them. It gives them life yet claims no possession; it benefits them yet exacts no gratitude; it is the steward yet exercises no authority. Such is called the mysterious virtue."[60] Being the "mother of the myriad creatures,"[61] Tao nurtures her children and lets them be themselves when they are grown and able to stand on their own, without demanding obedience or imposing her authority. She "retire[s] when the task is accomplished."[62] Such "femininity" (or, in fact, maternity) of Tao is highly praised and recommended as the model for all, especially for those (men) who are in power—in the *Tao Te Ching*, the term "Sage" (*Shen-jen/Shenren*) is used to refer to a ruler who emulates Tao in nurturing all and yet not exercising authority.

Taoism as a religious system reveres *Tao Te Ching* as one of the most sacred texts and follows its teaching *in principle*. In practice, however, its attitude toward women is at best ambivalent. On the one hand, based on the supposed affinity between females and Tao, many Taoist masters reckon it easier for women than for men to control the flow of energy, achieve tranquility, succeed in "internal alchemy," and be united with Tao.[63] Quite a few of the prominent male Taoists are even said to have

---

58. The two terms, in reality, may very well denote the same group of people, for, generally speaking, different teachings are not considered mutually exclusive by Chinese. Confucianism and religious Taoism, in particular, are very compatible in that they both inherited much from ancient Chinese culture, such as the concept of *yin-yang*, the respect for Nature, and the veneration of ancestors.

59. Liu Xiaogan made the same observation in "A Taoist Perspective: Appreciating and Applying the Principle of Femininity," in *What Men Owe to Women: Men's Voices from World Religions*, ed. John C. Raines and Daniel C. Maguire (Albany: State University of New York Press, 2001), 243.

60. D. C. Lau, trans., *Lao Tzu: Tao Te Ching* (New York: Penguin Books, 1963), 65 (chap. 10).

61. Ibid., 57 (chap. 1).

62. Ibid., 64 (chap. 9).

63. Karen Laughlin and Eva Wong, "Feminism and/in Taoism," in *Feminism and World Religions*, ed. Arvind Sharma and Katherine K. Young (Albany: State University of New

learned from female teachers or deities.[64] On the other hand, women are expected to display their "nature" of yin and complement the yang nature of their husbands, so that in the grand scheme the yin and yang are balanced and harmony is reached. "Although Taoism does value such qualities as softness and fluidity, which are traditionally understood as feminine," Karen Laughlin and Eva Wong rightly remark, "this does not mean that Taoism favors a feminine model or can be seen as a stronghold of feminism."[65] If the element in Taoism that has contributed to the mechanism sanctioning violence against women is the reified understanding of the analytical dyad of yin and yang, simply reasserting philosophical Taoism's elevation of the feminine will not help much—as long as women are considered the embodiment of the yin force, they are still expected to, and in effect *forced* to, display the yin qualities, and are still subject to violent "disciplinary" measures when they "deviate" from their yin nature and thereby disturb the harmony in the grand scheme.

The Taoist resource in dismantling the oppressive mechanism, in my opinion, does not lie mainly in its appreciation of the feminine, but more in its dynamic understanding of what may appear to be opposites. Feminine and feminist imagery may be appropriated and applied in helpful ways (cf. John Raines, chapter 5 of this book), but I turn to the Taoist depiction of yin and yang in the "Tai Chi Fish," which shows the interdependent relation of any two things that differentiate from one another. Just as the black and white halves are divided by a meandering line that leads white into black domain and allows black to lap back into the white, Huston Smith explicates, "the opposites are bonded; banded together by the encompassing circle that locks both black and white in inseparable embrace." Moreover, just as "a white dot stakes its claim in the deepest recesses of black, while a black dot does likewise in the central citadel of the white, . . . [a]ll things do indeed carry within themselves the seeds of their own antitheses."[66] The relation between any two particulars that differentiate themselves from each other is like the dynamic relation between yin and yang: mutually generating, mutually defining, mutually sustaining, mutually complementing, mutually penetrating, mutually yielding,

---

York Press, 1999), 165–70. Also noted in Liu, "A Taoist Perspective," 250; Kristofer Schipper, *The Taoist Body*, trans. Karen C. Duval (Berkeley: University of California Press, 1993), 239; Hong Jianlin, ed., *Daojia yangsheng miku* (*Treasury of the Taoist Secrets for Nurturing Life*) (Beijing: Dalian Chubanshe), 245.

64. Wong, "Taoism," 123.

65. Laughlin and Wong, "Feminism and/in Taoism," 149.

66. Huston Smith, "Tao Now," in *The Ways of Religion: An Introduction to the Major Traditions*, 3rd ed., ed. Roger Eastman (Oxford and New York: Oxford University Press, 1999), 248–49.

and mutually containing. Thus yin and yang are simply makeshift names that signify the process of differentiation as well as of the relationship between particulars that are (being) differentiated. Once the dynamics of the reality is grasped, the names are to be disregarded, just as, to use Chuang-tzu's metaphor, a fishing basket is to be put aside once the fish is caught.[67] Yin and yang should not be understood as a primordial pair that have ontological existence, nor are they necessarily opposites. To dichotomize the reality, or to equate yin and yang with static qualities or particular people, is to misunderstand the reality and to fall apart from the Way. Therefore, the opening sentence of *Tao Te Ching* reads, "The way that can be spoken of is not the constant way; the name that can be named is not the constant name."[68] All systematic categorizations fall short of grasping the dynamic reality, and therefore rigid categories such as gender stereotypes need to be deconstructed. In fact, as Liu Xiaogan notes, in *Tao Te Ching* the words for "man" and "woman" are never used, and "[a]ll terms concerning gender . . . are repeatedly mentioned only in a metaphorical sense."[69] Thus women are not the embodiment of yin and are not prescribed to display only the stereotypical feminine qualities, nor are men the embodiment of yang. In this regard religious Taoism fully agrees with philosophical Taoism, and part of the training in religious Taoism "involves letting go of attachments even to the forms of masculinity and femininity as well as to notions of what a man or woman can or should do."[70]

Buddhism cautions against the reifying, and hence trapping, effects of names or conceptual categories, too. The historical Buddha and many later Buddhist masters constantly remind people that the raft is not the shore but the means that takes one to the shore, and *Ch'an (Chan)* Buddhism keeps saying that the finger pointing at the moon is not the

---

67. "The fish basket exists because of the fish; once you've gotten the fish, you can forget the basket. The rabbit snare exists because of the rabbit; once you've gotten the rabbit, you can forget the snare. Words exist because of meaning; once you've gotten the meaning, you can forget the words." *Chuang-tzu*, chap. 26. Translation adapted from Burton Watson, *Zhuangzi: Basic Writings* (New York: Columbia University Press, 2003), 141. Although named after the philosopher Chuang-tzu, scholars suspect that *Chuang-tzu*, instead of representing one person's voice, may actually be a collection of the writings of a group of thinkers. Many scholars believe that only the seven Inner Chapters were written by Chuang-tzu himself, and the fifteen Outer Chapters and eleven Mixed Chapters were written by his disciples and followers. Some speculate that the distinction of the Inner, the Outer, and the Mixed was merely imposed by an anonymous editor. However, the reality is, the content of Chuang-tzu is mostly treated as an integral whole, and when citing from the book Chinese people still use "Chuang-tzu said," rather than "*Chuang-tzu* the book said . . ."

68. Lau, *Lao Tzu*, 57.

69. Liu, "A Taoist Perspective," 252, 245.

70. Laughlin and Wong, "Feminism and/in Taoism," 159, 175.

moon. The Buddhist resource that more directly pertains to the current discussion of violence against women, however, is the meaning of karma. Since two chapters in this book are devoted to Buddhism, I do not intend to be redundant. It is sufficient here simply to point out that the popular understanding of karma neglects the active dimension of the concept. The Buddha uses the word to refer to ethically accountable acts in the present moment, not to teach people to blame the victims.

Separately viewed, none of the Three Teachings of Confucianism, Taoism, and Buddhism condones violence, and one cannot find textual support for violence against women in any of the classics or scriptures of the Three Teachings. Violence against women is generally condemned, even on the popular level. For example, a Taiwanese saying goes, "He who cherishes his wife is truly a great man; he who beats his wife is no better than a swine, a dog, or a cow." That saying, however, does not effectively curb wife battering in Taiwan. Continuing to feel that by "natural" law they should be indefinitely superior and absolutely in control, many Taiwanese men prefer to buy an uneducated, docile bride from some other poorer countries in Southeast Asia such as Vietnam, Indonesia, Philippines, Cambodia, Malaysia, and Thailand, rather than dealing with Taiwanese women who are in general much better educated and have minds of their own. And yet those foreign brides, who are noticeably more obedient and dependent (partly because they are thrown into an alien society whose official language they do not speak), are still much abused. In the year 2000, twelve out of one hundred brides in Taiwan were from poorer Southeast Asian countries,[71] and one out of five of these foreign brides suffered from domestic violence.[72] Questionably, social workers in Chinese culture tend to convince the battered wives to display their yin quality of endurance for the sake of the "harmony" in the household, shifting the responsibility of violence against women to the victims.[73]

The general condemnation of violence in early Confucianism, philosophical Taoism, and Buddhism, obviously, is ineffective in the face of the monstrous combination of Legalist control, Confucian rectification of names, reification of the yin-yang concept in Taoism, misunderstanding of the Confucian and Taoist definitions of harmony, and a distorted interpre-

71. Hsüeh Ch'eng-t'ai, "T'ai-wan ti-ch'u hun-yin de pien-ch'ien yü she-hui ch'ung-chi (Transition of Marriages in Taiwan and Its Impacts on Society)," *National Policy Forum Periodicals, Fall 2003* (Taipei, Taiwan: National Policy Foundation): 254.
72. Hung Hsiao-hsing, "Wai-chi hsin-niang Pao-tao meng (The Formosa Dreams of Foreign Brides)," *The Epoch Times Taiwan* 91 (2002/12/26–2003/1/1).
73. Ibid. Also see Tang et al., "Responsibility Attribution for Violence against Women," 181.

tation of karma. To blame Confucianism alone (as many Western and Chinese feminists have done) or to denounce Confucianism in its entirety (as has been done in mainland China since the Cultural Revolution) has not helped. To restore the good name of Confucianism or to idealize Taoist teachings may in effect justify the Three Bonds and reinforce rigid gender roles. Under the unseen influence of Legalism, Confucianism has created certain obsession with "correct" understanding. It may therefore be useful to assert the "correct" understandings of those teachings and concepts that ended up being the components of the mechanism of violence. The misuses of rectification of names, of yin and yang, of harmony, and of karma, moreover, need to be grappled with and corrected simultaneously since they have been supporting and reinforcing one another. More importantly, it needs to be acknowledged that Chinese culture is in fact Four-Teachings-in-One, that Legalism has had persistent presence and has deflected the understandings of the Three Teachings of Taoism, Confucianism, and Buddhism. Otherwise, it will continue to have tremendous control over Chinese culture, for power is the most powerful when it is unseen.

PRIMARY SOURCES[74]

Chan, Wing-tsit, trans. and comp. *A Source Book in Chinese Philosophy*. Princeton, N.J.: Princeton University Press, 1963.

Cheng Hsüan. *Mao-shih Cheng-chien* (*The Mao's Commentary on the* Book of Odes, *with Cheng's Subcommentary*). In *Ssu-pu pei-yao* (*Essentials of the Four Branches of Literature*), *ching-pu* (*The Branch of Classics*). Taipei: Taiwan Chung-hua shu-chü, 1983.

Chu Hsi. *Shih chi chuan* (*Collected Commentaries on the* Book of Odes). Taipei, Taiwan: Yi-wen yin-shu-kuan, 1967.

de Bary, William Theodore, Wing-tsit Chan, and Burton Waston, compilers. *Sources of Chinese Tradition*, vol. 1. New York and London: Columbia University Press, 1960.

Lau, D. C., trans. *Lao Tzu: Tao Te Ching*. New York: Penguin Books, 1963.

Legge, James, trans. *The Four Books: Confucian Analects, the Great Learning, the Doctrine of the Mean, and the Works of Mencius*. New York: Paragon Book Reprint Corporation, 1966.

T'ai-p'ing ching ho-chiao (*The Scripture of Ultimate Equilibrium* [collated]), compiled by Wang Ming. Pei-ching: Chung-hua shu-chü, 1960.

Watson, Burton. *Zhuangzi: Basic Writings*. New York: Columbia University Press, 2003.

SECONDARY SOURCES

Birge, Bettine. "Chu Hsi and Women's Education." In *Neo-Confucian Education*, ed. William Theodore de Bary and John W. Chaffee. Berkeley: University of California Press, 1989, 325–67.

---

74. These are the main sources used in this chapter.

Chiang, Chu-shan. "Nü-t'i yü chan-cheng: Ming-Ch'ing yen-pao chih shu, 'Yin-men-chen' tzai-t'an (Women's Body and Warfare: The Re-exploration of *Yin-men-chen* in Late Imperial China)." *Hsin Shih-Hsüeh (New Historical Studies)* 10/3 (September 1999): 159–86.

Chittister, Joan. "Divinely Ordained? Religious Creation Myths and the Relation of Militarism to Sexism." In *Winds of Change: Women Challenge the Church.* Kansas City: Sheed and Ward, 1986, 89–107.

de Bary, William Theodore. "Women's Education and Women's Rights." In *Asian Values and Human Rights: A Confucian Communitarian Perspective.* Cambridge and London: Harvard University Press, 1998, 118–33.

Eaton, Jana S. "Gender Issues in Transitional China." *Multicultural Education.* (winter 1998): 32–36.

Gaspar-Pereira, Hilda Maria. "Patterns of Family Violence in Japan." *Wellesley Centers for Women Working Paper Series*, Working Paper No. 411. Wellesley, Mass.: Wellesley Centers for Women, 2003.

Gilmartin, Christina. "Violence Against Women in Contemporary China." In *Violence in China: Essays in Culture and Counterculture*, ed. Jonathan N. Lipman and Stevan Harrell. Albany: State University of New York Press, 1990, 203–25.

Guisso, Richard W. "Thunder over the Lake: The Five Classics and the Perception of Woman in Early China." In *Women in China: Current Directions in Historical Scholarship*, ed. Richard W. Guisso and Stanley Johannesen. Youngstown, N.Y.: Philo Press, 1981, 47–61.

Hong Jianlin, ed. *Daojia yangsheng miku* (Treasury of the Taoist Secrets for Nurturing Life). Beijing: Dalian Chubanshe, 245.

Honig, Emily, and Gail Hershatter. "Violence Against Women." In *Personal Voices: Chinese Women in the 1980's.* Stanford, Calif.: Stanford University Press, 1988, 273–307.

Hsüeh Ch'eng-t'ai. "T'ai-wan ti-ch'u hun-yin de pien-ch'ien yü she-hui ch'ung-chi (Transition of Marriages in Taiwan and Its Impacts on Society)." *National Policy Forum Periodicals, Fall 2003*: 245–59.

Hung Hsiao-hsing. "Wai-chi hsin-niang Pao-tao meng (The Formosa Dreams of Foreign Brides)." *The Epoch Times Taiwan* 91 (2002/12/26–2003/1/1).

Jordan, Ann D. "Commercial Sex Workers in Asia: A Blind Spot in Human Rights Law." In *Women and International Human Rights Law*, vol. 2. Ed. Askin and Koenig. Ardsley, N.Y.: Transnational, 2000, 525–85.

Kong, Mee-Hae. "Rethinking Women's Status and Liberation in Korea." Paper presented at Conference on Asia-Europe Relations, Soest, October 31–November 2, 1997.

Laughlin, Karen, and Eva Wong. "Feminism and/in Taoism." In *Feminism and World Religions*, ed. Arvind Sharma and Katherine K. Young. Albany: State University of New York Press, 1999, 148–78.

Liu Xiaogan. "A Taoist Perspective: Appreciating and Applying the Principle of Femininity." In *What Men Owe to Women: Men's Voices from World Religions*, ed. John C. Raines and Daniel C. Maguire. Albany: State University of New York Press, 2001, 239–57.

Ng, Vivien. "Sexual Abuse of Daughters-in-Law in Qing China: Cases from the Xing'an Huilan." *Feminist Studies* 20/2 (summer 1994): 373–91.

Nguyen Thi Ngoc-Dung. "Violence against Women," summarized and trans. Le Minh Thinh. Workshop in the Conference on Vietnamese Women in Canada, Ottawa, 1996.

Rappa, Antonio L., and Sor-hoon Tan. "Political Implications of Confucian Familism." *Asian Philosophy* 13/2–3 (2003): 87–102.

Schipper, Kristofer. *The Taoist Body*, trans. Karen C. Duval. Berkeley: University of California Press, 1993.

Smith, Huston. "Tao Now." In *The Ways of Religion: An Introduction to the Major Traditions*, 3rd ed., ed. Roger Eastman. Oxford and New York: Oxford University Press, 1999, 246–54.

Tang, Catherine So Kum, Shuk Han Pun, and Fanny Mui-ching Cheung. "Responsibility Attribution for Violence against Women: A Study of Chinese Public Service Professionals." *Psychology of Women Quarterly* 26 (2002): 175–85.

Wang Man-na. "Chung-kuo nan-nü shih-heng-hsia-te jen-k'ou fan-mai ch'ang-chüeh (The Rampant Human Trafficking Under the Unbalanced Sex Ratio in China)." www.epochtimes.com.tw/bt/5/3/12/n846389.htm (March 12, 2005).

Wang Ping. *Aching for Beauty: Footbinding in China*. Minneapolis and London: University of Minnesota Press, 2000.

Wong, Eva. "Taoism." In *Her Voice, Her Faith: Women Speak on World Religions*, ed. Arvind Sharma and Katherine K. Young. Boulder, Colo.: Westview Press, 2002, 119–43.

Woo, Terry. "Confucianism and Feminism." In *Feminism and World Religions*, ed. Arvind Sharma and Katherine K. Young. Albany: State University of New York Press, 1999, 110–47.

Yü Ying-Shih. "Anti-Intellectualism and Chinese Political Traditions." In *History and Thought*. Taipei: Lianjing Publishers, 1976, 1–46.

7

Muntu, Kintu, and the Pursuit of *Bumuntu*: Reflection on the Roots of Violence against Women in African Traditional Religions[1]

MUTOMBO NKULU-N'SENGHA

Despite the spread of "modernity" in postcolonial Africa and the multiplications of local human rights organizations, violence against women remains a major social problem in Africa as elsewhere in the world. From the case of women raped and buried alive in the recent Congolese war in Kivu, to Catholic nuns frustrated by a patriarchal church that rejects the ordination of women, to women who live in fear in their marriage, to girls terrorized by the fear of rape, excision, and other forms of abuses, violence condemns millions of women, and their families, to die silent psychological, spiritual, intellectual, and violent physical deaths. It is worth noting, however, that violence against

---

1. The terms *muntu* (a human being), *kintu* (a thing), *bumuntu* (the essence of authentic personhood), and many other African words in this study are taken from Kiluba, the language of the Baluba people of Congo (Democratic Republic of Congo, or DRC). The Baluba are one of the Bantu people who inhabit much of central and southern Africa. The Baluba developed an important empire from 500 C.E. to the twentieth century. Their thought was the basis of *Bantu Philosophy,* the work published by Placide Tempels in 1945, which is considered by many as the starting point of modern debate over the existence of an African philosophy. This book was also instrumental in the development of enculturation theology and the Africanization of Christianity. Luba religion and Luba philosophy are centered on the key concept of *bumuntu,* an encompassing concept that is not easy to translate in Western language. Its semantic field is closer to the ancient Egyptian moral principle of *maat,* to the Chinese notion of *chun-tzu* and *jen,* or to the golden rule as articulated by Jesus and Confucius. It includes love, compassion, justice, harmony, peace, dignity, self-respect, reciprocity, and solidarity with our fellow human beings, and even with the whole created world.

women should not be regarded as a mere sociological or cultural mistake. In cases where violence is perpetrated in the name of tradition or the will of the ancestors, the solution to the problem requires a serious exploration of the religious roots of structural sexism that condones or banalizes violence against women.

The aim of this chapter is to reflect on the religious foundations of violence against women in sub-Saharan Africa and to suggest a "way out." Indeed, in Africa, one of the fundamental characteristics of religion is healing. And it is from this perspective that we will address the issue of violence against women. Will the religion that heals be regarded as genuine and as evil the one that "hurts" and "kills"? We shall thus examine the role of African traditional religions in the oppression of women as well as the potential flexibility for the invention of new traditions capable of enhancing a kind of "liberation feminist theology" based on African religious resources. In this context, Max Weber's insight is worth recalling:

> When a man who is happy compares his position with that of one who is unhappy, he is not content with the fact of his happiness, but desires something more, namely the right to this happiness, the consciousness that he has earned his good fortune, in contrast to the unfortunate one who must equally have earned his misfortune. Our everyday experience proves that there exists just such a psychological need for reassurance as to the legitimacy or deservedness of one's happiness, whether this involves political success, superior economic status . . . or anything else. What the privileged classes require of religion, if anything at all, is this psychological reassurance of legitimacy.[2]

In our context, this means that religion is often used to legitimize "gender privileges" and rationalize violence used to maintain such patriarchal privileges.

But what is meant by violence in this context? It is worth noting from the outset that violence against women takes myriad forms. In this regard, we can identify, among others, "ten plagues" of sexism in Africa: (1) polygamy, (2) excision, (3) dowry burden and "forced marriages" of young girls to men chosen by their parents, (4) menstruation stigma, (5) disregard for barren women, (6) wife battering, (7) various religious taboos, especially dietary laws, (8) marginalization of women in the political arena, (9) marginalization of women in the sphere of religious

---

2. Manu's *Dharmashastra* may be another source that spells out an inferior position for women but it is a social and legal rather than a sacred text.

power, and (10) rigid gender roles ("girls don't do that") and the burden of domestic work and domestic stagnation.

A detailed analysis of these "ten patriarchal plagues" goes beyond the scope of this brief format. I have already elsewhere analyzed in detail the issue of sexism in African traditional religions.[3] I shall limit myself here to a special case study of the issue euphemistically called "female circumcision" or what is often called genital mutilation, excision, or cutting.

This phenomenon, which has become for foreign audiences the paradigmatic symbol of "African oppression of women," is one of the most controversial and also the most misunderstood elements of "African tradition." The very fact that after more than a hundred years of steady war on female excision terror the practice has survived and even gained momentum calls for a deeper rethinking of the roots of this custom. This is a matter of great concern when we know that female cutting is no longer limited to a few isolated villages in some lost jungles. In a kind of ferocious backlash against modernity, female genital cutting has gone global, thriving not only in the modern metropolises of Asia, Africa, and South America, but also in Europe and the United States. Indeed, female circumcision is not a thing of the past. That female excision occupies a central role in the world's perception of African mistreatment of women is confirmed by the overwhelming presence of such an issue in cyberspace, where many sites state plainly that female genital mutilation "originated in Africa." A Google search provides 1,160,000 hits for excision alone, 551,000 for genital mutilation, and 31,200 hits for clitoridectomy. This cyberlibrary also makes it clear that female genital mutilation (FGM) is not merely an African problem, but a tradition widespread in many parts of the world.[4]

HOW RELIGION IN AFRICA SHAPES ATTITUDES TOWARDS WOMEN

Over the past one hundred years, African intellectuals, including Christian theologians, have pointed out that African traditional religions constitute the soul of "black civilization" (negritude or African Personality). Moreover, many scholars agree that the importance of traditional African religions goes well beyond what the statistical affiliation figure of 20 percent of the total African population may suggest

---

3. See Daniel Maguire and John Raines, eds., *What Men Owe to Women* (Albany: State University of New York Press, 2001), 69–105.
4. It is not the aim of this author to engage in the controversial question of where the practice originated. Our only concern is that excision exists in Africa and that some Africans claim it is a fundamental element of African cultural identity that should be preserved, while many others argue it is a harmful tradition that is not essential to African authenticity.

since, for many Christians and Muslims, the basis of moral values still derives more from the old cosmology than from the new beliefs. In this context, the study of the religious foundation of violence against women requires a careful examination of "the will of the ancestors" (*kishila-kya-bankambo*).

Moreover, in Africa, as elsewhere, religion plays a crucial social role. It is "an eminently collective thing" (Emile Durkheim) that defines the role and relation between various individuals in a society. Religion helps people understand their identity as people or as a community. Moreover, religion has been defined as the heart or the soul of African civilization. It shapes the identity and self-esteem of the people. As Laurenti Magesa rightly pointed out, African traditional religions are "the moral power that shapes and directs the lives of millions of people in their relationship with other human beings, the created order, and the Divine."[5]

In other words, religion is the way by which a society defines what it means to be male or female, and what responsibility and right behavior is expected from each one. More specifically, religion shapes the way men have to behave toward women and viceversa. It is in this context that the role of religion in shaping violence against women becomes critical. As Mercy Amba Oduyoye, Anne Nasimiyu-Wasike, and many other African feminists have pointed out, African religions have been marred by rampant sexism, and patriarchy has shaped even the articulation of creation myths and religious proverbs.[6] But what is meant by violence in reference to patriarchy and sexism?

EXCISION AND THE CONCEPT OF VIOLENCE

Religion, in the mind of many devotees, is fundamentally about love and universal brotherhood. It is thus perceived as radically antithetical to violence. In this context claims about religious foundations of violence against women require a clarification of the critical concept of violence.

Violence is defined in many dictionaries and encyclopedias as an act or instance of aggression or hostility that inflicts harm or injury on another. More often it is an abusive or unjust exercise of power. To do violence implies to violate, to offend, to do harm, to go against, to break with, to disregard, to disturb peace and harmony. Violence also refers to

---

5. Laurenti Magesa, *African Religion: The Moral Traditions of Abundant Life* (Maryknoll, N.Y.: Orbis Books, 1997), 18–19.
6. See Mercy A. Oduyoye and M. R. Kanyoro, eds., *The Will to Arise: Women, Tradition, and the Church in Africa* (Maryknoll, N.Y.: Orbis Books, 1992); Mercy Amba Oduyoye, *Daughters of Anowa: African Women and Patriarchy* (Maryknoll, N.Y.: Orbis Books, 1995).

coercion and injury to freedom. Violence violates another person's dignity. It frustrates or destroys another person's life and sense of well-being. Violence is the enemy of freedom, peace, harmony, and happiness. Violence implies hate and injustice. As such, violence is antithetical to love; it is not in the realm of virtues. It is rather found in the frame of crimes, disorder, evil, the insane, the pathological, and the hateful.

In light of this semantic field, we call religious violence a harmful religious behavior, or a religious thought or principle that support attitudes or practices that harm other human beings. In order to better grasp the harmful nature of excision, we shall turn to a brief analysis of the procedure of excision and the testimony of physicians who have worked with excised women.

The lexicon of female genital cutting is vast and complex. It loosely refers to a number of procedures performed on the female genitalia, for a variety of reasons. Professionals who make a distinction between various forms of female circumcision often use three technical terms: "excision," "clitoridectomy," or "infibulation."

Clitoridectomy refers to surgical removal of the clitoris or excision of the clitoris. The expression "female genital mutilation" refers to the removal of some parts of the female genitalia. Scholars have identified three major forms of this procedure, some more dramatic than others:

1. "sunna circumcision" (from the Arabic word for tradition) consists of the removal of the tip of the clitoris.

2. "clitoridectomy." This brutal surgery consists of the removal of the entire clitoris and the removal of the adjacent labia.

3. "Infibulation," also referred to as "pharonic circumcision," is a more dramatic type of clitoridectomy. It consists of removal of all or part of the labia minora, and the labia majora. This is then stitched up, allowing a small hole to remain open to allow for urine and menstrual blood to flow through.

Some researchers estimate that in Africa 85 percent of female genital mutilation cases consist of clitoridectomy and 15 percent of cases consist of infibulation. In Sierra Leone, for instance, no ethnic group practices infibulation. Most, however, practice clitoridectomy and excision.[7]

There is no doubt that the nature of mutilation involved in female excision points to a violent and harmful practice. We have to turn to

---

7. Olayinka Koso-Thomas, *The Circumcision of Women: A Strategy for Eradication* (London: Zed Books, 1987), 19.

medical doctors to better grasp the crippling consequences of this surgery. Faithful to our non-Eurocentric principle of finding African solutions to African problems, I shall follow here not the novelist Alice Walker, but the rigorous guidance of Olayinka Koso-Thomas, a Nigerian female medical doctor who treated for many years women of Sierra Leone suffering from the physical and psychological problems directly attributable to excision. From her own experience, Dr. Olayinka became an active proponent of the total eradication of female cutting and published in 1987 a detailed program with practical proposals for the eradication of the practice over a period of twenty years. Dr. Olayinka identified immediate, intermediate, and late health complications. Immediate problems involved, among others, acute hemorrhage, tetanus, urinary infection, septicemia, and possible death. Intermediate problems include among others, pelvic infection, dysmenorrhea, cysts and abscesses, and dyspareunia. Late gynecological complications include infertility, lack of orgasm, hematocolpos, recurrent urinary tract infection, calculus, and depression.[8]

Because such cutting is excruciatingly painful and handicaps women for the rest of their life, often seriously jeopardizing their health, many African women and men have for decades waged a campaign to abolish this practice, while other African men and women claim that the abolition of this custom is a terrible attack on "African ancestral values" and is ultimately tantamount to religious heresy.

It should be noted however that African reaction to "war on FGM terror" is often complicated by the Western claims of the superiority of Western civilization and the Christian religion. It is thus indispensable to engage in a careful investigation of African tradition beyond Eurocentric "civilizing" mission ideology and beyond romantic African nationalism.

Since the publication of the novel *Possessing the Secret of Joy*[9] by the African American womanist Pulitzer Prize laureate Alice Walker, the postcolonial war on excision has gained momentum in the United States. However, while excision became over the last three decades a focus of Western scholarship and political discourse as the paradigmatic symbol of African oppression of women, the struggle against this practice is not new. The whole practice of FGM was the primary target of the civilizing mission of colonial empires between 1850 and 1950. Christian missionaries supported by colonial officials waged a determined war to eradicate excision. In an effort to better understand the

8. Ibid., 25–28.
9. Alice Walker, *Possessing the Secret of Joy* (New York: Harcourt Brace Jovanovich, 1992).

reasons behind this practice, there were numerous studies led by Western anthropologists and Christian missionaries, most of whom were simply amateur anthropologists.[10]

The "attack" on the clitoridectomy custom by outsiders provoked in two major phases a powerful reaction by African thinkers, politicians, and religious leaders that contributed largely to clarifying African vision of the relationship between excision and religion, and between religion and violence against women. During the colonial era, the attack mounted by Christian missionaries and European colonial agents provoked an African reaction that found its best expression in Jomo Kenyatta. Very recently the postcolonial attack spearheaded by Alice Walker provoked another African reaction that Emmanuel Babatunde articulated well in his work *Women's Rights versus Women's Rites.*[11]

By examining the response articulated by two African men, Jomo Kenyatta and Babatunde, one can better grasp how African "patriarchal tradition" approaches the issue of excision. We thus find two antithetical schools of thought. The conservative or traditionalist school embodied by Kenyatta claims that excision is a fundamental component of ancestral values and should be preserved. The "progressive" school embodied by Babatunde and most feminists and human rights activists argue for the eradication of the practice. This school, however, is divided in its understanding of the African nature of the custom. For some, the practice is part of African ancestral tradition, but should be rejected since fidelity to the tradition should imply endorsing only those "positive" values, and rejecting "the sins of our fathers." Others, however, claim that female circumcision is not an intrinsic component of ancestral wisdom, since it is not attested in many African traditions.

It should be noted however that the fact that excision has survived and even gained momentum despite more than one hundred years of war to outlaw it means that it carries a deep meaning that needs to be better understood. As Babatunde rightly pointed out in 1998, it is crucial to understand the "religious justification" of excision if the practice is to be efficiently eradicated. Failure to understand this aspect has led some feminist and human rights activists to problematic strategies that have contributed to a backlash, which strengthens the practice:

---

10. The result of such studies is synthesized in various "dictionaries of African civilizations" like the one edited by Georges Balandier and Jacques Maquet, *Dictionnaire des civilisations Africaines* (Paris: Fernand Hazan, 1968).

11. Emmanuel Babatunde, *Women's Rights versus Women's Rites: A Study of Circumcision among the Ketu Yoruba of South Western Nigeria* (Trenton: Africa World Press, 1998).

As a Nigerian anthropologist trained in England and working now in America, I have watched with fascination and concern the efforts to curb the sad practice of clitoridectomy in my home continent. In this country genital mutilation has become a hot issue in newspapers, magazines, the talk show circuit and was even featured recently on Nightline. Some have advocated granting asylum to women trying to escape this practice in their own countries. To me this outpouring of Western concern over genital mutilation offers a case study in how the well-intentioned efforts of Americans to improve the lot of oppressed people elsewhere in the world can have precisely the opposite effect intended. In at least some of the societies targeted by this movement, the practice has increased.[12]

Babatunde went on to stress the need to overcome superficial views of clitoridectomy and to investigate the deep foundation of its meaning:

Concerned Americans have a tendency to place issues in a context which they understand, but which may have little relevance to Africa. . . . Feminists have interpreted genital mutilation as a simple expression of male domination. They have created a perception in America that the only reason why this practice continues is to reduce a woman's pleasure in the hope of ensuring against promiscuity. Instead of making an effort to understand why this evil practice continues, Americans express surprise and dismay and then unleash strategies which have proven effective in forcing change here, but which can have [the] opposite effect there. Anyone interested in helping individuals of both genders reach their full potential should be horrified that clitoridectomy endures. But reducing the practice to a bizarre expression of male chauvinism just limits the wider cultural understanding needed to stop it. Cultural practices endure because they make sense to individuals in a society. Sacrifices are made willingly only when individuals believe their loss is offset by some greater gain.[13]

What is then the African religious foundation of female circumcision?

SACRED VIOLENCE: The Religious Foundation of Female Circumcision

We shall here turn to the "traditional school of thought" as well articulated by Jomo Kenyatta. One of the earliest studies of circumcision by

---

12. Ibid., 179.
13. Ibid., 179–80.

African scholars was published in 1953 by Kenyatta, the former president of Kenya, under the title *Facing Mount Kenya*.[14] Kenyatta belongs to the first generation of Africans trained in Western anthropology, and his book, which was tellingly prefaced by the famous anthropologist Bronislaw Malinowski, carries at once the traces of Eurocentric perspective and African patriarchal epistemology. In his book, which was based on his doctoral dissertation written in London, Kenyatta denounced the war waged by colonial officials against excision as an attack on African values.

> It should be pointed out here that there is a strong community of educated Gikuyu opinion in defence of this custom. . . . The real argument lies not in the defense of the surgical operation or its details, but in the understanding of a very important fact in the tribal psychology of the Gikuyu—namely, that this operation is still regarded as the very essence of an institution which has enormous educational, social, moral, and religious implications, quite apart from the operation itself. For the present it is impossible for a member of the tribe to imagine an initiation without clitoridectomy. Therefore the abolition of the surgical element in this custom means to the Gikuyu the abolition of the whole institution. The real anthropological study, therefore, is to show that clitoridectomy, like Jewish circumcision, is a mere bodily mutilation which, however, is regarded as the conditio sine qua non of the whole teaching of tribal law, religion, and morality.[15]

According to Kenyatta, for the Gikuyu who use the same word *irua* to signify the "circumcision" of both men and women, *irua* is fundamentally a rite of passage from childhood to adulthood. This *irua* plays a fundamental role in Gikuyu's sense of personhood and selfhood.

> In the matrimonial relation, the rite of passage is the deciding factor. No proper Gikuyu would dream of marrying a girl who has not been circumcised, and vice versa. It is taboo for a Gikuyu man or woman to have sexual relations with someone who has not undergone this operation. If it happens, a man or woman must go through a ceremonial purification, '*korutwo thahu*' or '*gotahikio megiro*'—namely, ritual vomiting of the evil deeds.[16]

---

14. Jomo Kenyatta, *Facing Mt. Kenya*, with an introduction by B. Malinowski (New York: Vintage Books, 1965).
15. Ibid., 128.
16. Ibid., 127.

Thus to the question why enforce excision on women, we find a multitude of reasons, some theological, while others are more sociological, psychological, or esthetic. In her study of the defense of the practice of excision, Dr. Olayinka Koso-Thomas summarized the various reasons in ten points: 1) maintenance of cleanliness, 2) pursuance of aesthetics, 3) prevention of still-births in primigravida, 4) promotion of social and political cohesion, 5) prevention of promiscuity, 6) improvement of male sexual performance and pleasure, 7) increase of matrimonial opportunities, 8) maintenance of good health, 9) preservation of virginity, 10) enhancement of fertility.[17] It is, however, the religious reason that is crucial in the continuing survival of female circumcision:

> The problem of female circumcision does not fall easily into that category of health problems for which solutions may be found through actions outside the domain of the culture of the country affected. It has a strong religious and cultural base without which it would not exist today. . . . The eradication of female circumcision must, therefore, involve the social, religious, and cultural transformation of certain communities, rather than overturning or uprooting this base by rapid legal decrees.[18]

This religious foundation of female excision is well clarified in the Dogon cosmology, which suggests that the practice should not be regarded merely as a foreign custom introduced by Arab Muslims. Kenyatta's tradition in East Africa, the Dogon cosmology in West Africa, and evidence (according to some scholars) of the practice in ancient Egypt indicate that excision is an indigenous phenomenon, at least in some areas of the continent. Among the ethnic groups that practice excision since immemorial times, scholars have identified specifically the Masaai of Kenya, some ethnic groups of Nigeria, and most importantly the Dogon and the Bambara of West Africa. Among these two ethnic groups, excision is deeply rooted in the traditional religion practiced in that area.

The cosmology of the Dogon of Mali and that of the Bambara starts with the notion of the ambiguity of human identity. According to their beliefs, at birth men and women are alike. But since reproduction requires male and female, a "surgery" had to be performed at puberty, during the rites of passage, in order to prepare boys to assume without ambiguity their "masculinity" and prepare girls for their "femininity." Bambara mythology explains this phenomenon with a "theory of the

---

17. Koso-Thomas, *The Circumcision of Women,* 5.
18. Ibid., 1.

soul." According to Bambara anthropology, before the initiation of male circumcision and female excision, every human being has four "spiritual principles," which include two souls (*ni*) and their two "doubles" (*dya*).[19] In each person there is a "feminine" soul and a "masculine" soul.[20] Likewise the "doubles" are divided into a feminine double and a masculine double. The souls (*ni*) are the principles of the unconscious, while the "doubles" are the conscious principles of will and intelligence. The "location" of these four principles in a human body explains why the Bambara think that both male circumcision and female excision are indispensable. According to their understanding of human nature, before the initiation the "feminine soul" (*ni*) and the "masculine double" (*dya*) reside in the foreskin of the penis of the boy, while in each girl a "masculine soul" (*ni*) and a "feminine double" (*dya*) reside in the clitoris. Circumcision and excision intervene to correct this situation and in such a way that the boy is left only with "male principles" (*ni* and *dya*) and the girl is left only with the "female principles."[21] An excised woman loses the clitoris, which is regarded as a "male organ." She becomes authentically female by keeping only a feminine *ni* and a feminine *dya*. Likewise the circumcized boy loses the foreskin of the penis, which represents "feminine secretions" and keeps only a masculine soul (*ni*) and a masculine double (*dya*). Thus, among the Dogon and the Bambara, after the initiation during which circumcision and excision are performed, boys and girls are no longer treated as children. Those who used to go naked have now the obligation to cover their genitals in a special way and avoid "playing with them."[22] The relationships between the mother and her sons and between the father and his daughters are completely transformed. A certain "distance" is established among them.

The second alleged raison d'être of circumcision and excision is to facilitate the sexual act and the fecundation. Dogon mythology refers excision to the first act of creation. When the Supreme God Amma attempted to unite with his wife (the earth), the clitoris stood up and blocked the entrance. As a result the pregnancy went wrong and the firstborn children were abnormal. It is only when Amma cut off the clitoris that the "second creation" succeeded, giving birth to the Nommo twins, the ancestors of humankind. Seen in this cosmological context, clitoridectomy is understood as an essential element of African identity, and any campaign to abolish it

---

19. Louis-Vincent Thomas and René Luneau, *La terre africaine et ses religions: traditions et changements* (Paris: L'Harmattan, 1986), 223.
20. Ibid.
21. Ibid.
22. Ibid.

may be perceived by some as a violation of the cultural and religious rights of the African people. It plays a role as an indispensable rite of passage that guarantees the growth of individuals into manhood or womanhood in Africa, and most importantly, it is considered as an indispensable ritual of fertility, as the explanation of the Ketu Yoruba makes it clear:

> The logic of the practice is couched in the anthropological term of prestation, a gift that you give under pain of sanction, for which you receive a greater gift in return. The logic of clitoridectomy is that by taking a tiny bit of the sacred instrument of fertility as an offering, the god of fertility will bless you with more children and easier childbirth.[23]

Thus, among the ethnic groups where female excision is a component of ancestral tradition, the practice has a deeply religious foundation. It is presented as institutionalized by the creator for the benefit of procreation. Therefore, circumcision is viewed as the embodiment of the will of God and the will of the ancestors. An integral part of the very gift of life from God, the circumcision of both men and women becomes people's religious response to God, a worship through the ultimate sacrifice of one's own life, the offering of one's own blood to God. It is thus evident that "circumcision violence" is enshrined by African traditional religions as a sacred activity, intimately linked to fertility and the act of reproduction. In other words, the eradication of "circumcision" is viewed as tantamount to "blocking life from flourishing." Since in African traditional religion life is the most sacred of all divine gifts, the challenge to the religious character of female excision requires a careful examination of claims about the fertility virtues of this custom. Since many non-"circumcised" African women are fertile, it clearly appears that the connections between circumcision and respect for the sacredness of life are baseless.

The only meaningful way of addressing the validity of the practice is to examine whether it contributes to the protection and promotion of the life of women. For all intents and purposes, it clearly appears that this is a bad religious practice that requires change for the sake of African religion itself. The second helpful consideration is whether all forms of African traditional religions endorsed this practice.

Kenyatta, who used the words "circumcision" and "clitoridectomy" interchangeably, claimed that "this custom is adhered to by the vast majority of African peoples and is found in almost every part of the continent."[24]

---

23. Babatunde, *Women's Rights versus Women's Rites*, 181.
24. Kenyatta, *Facing Mt. Kenya*, 128.

Careful scholarship has disproved Kenyatta's claims. In their diction-ary on African civilizations, Georges Balandier and Jacques Maquet have analyzed the issue of excision in various traditions.[25] Their conclusion, confirmed by my research on the Baluba and some other ethnic groups, is that there are three traditions: a) there are ethnic groups who practice both male circumcision and female excision, b) there are people who only practice male circumcision, and c) there are those who practice none.

From this analysis comes two important considerations: a) what is widespread in Africa is the circumcision of men rather than the excision of women, and b) those who practice neither circumcision nor excision are very few. It can then be safely argued that excision is part of "some" African traditions, but is not coterminous with African religious tradition as a whole. In her careful and meticulous study on "the female circumci-sion controversy," Ellen Guenbaum (professor of anthropology and dean of social sciences at California State University at Fresno) made a clear distinction between African societies that practice female cutting and those to whom such a custom is alien. Out of fifty-three African coun-tries, she identified twenty-eight countries as the cultural areas that prac-tices female circumcision.[26] These countries are concentrated in northern, eastern, and western regions of Africa. Central and southern parts of Africa are rather the kingdom of the "Hottentot Venus"[27]—in other words, they are among the regions that ignore excision. With the excep-tion of a small territory in the north, Congo is largely among regions that do not practice female excision.

The prevalence of female cutting in Africa is found in seven countries of northeast Africa; these countries contain half of all the circumcised women and girls in Africa: Somalia, Egypt, Djibouti, Ethiopia, Eritrea, Sudan, and Kenya.[28] The rest are largely found in Nigeria, which, because of its large population, accounts for nearly a third of the cases—that is 30.6 million of the 114.3 million cases identified in the whole African continent.[29]

Most cases of clitoridectomy pointed out by scholars are found in some regions of west Africa and east Africa. Central Africa and many re-gions of the southern part of the continent are rather dominated by an

---

25. Georges Balandier and Jacques Maquet, eds., *Dictionnaire des civilisations Africaines* (Paris: Fernand Hazan, 1968).
26. Ellen Gruenbaum, *The Female Circumcision Controversy: An Anthropological Perspective* (Philadelphia: University of Pennsylvania Press, 2001), 8.
27. On the popularity of the exhibition of the "Hottentot Venus" in Europe, see Nicolas Bancel, dir., *Zoos humains: de la vénus hottentote aux reality shows* (Paris: La Découverte, 2002).
28. Gruenbaum, *The Female Circumcision Controversy*, 8.
29. Ibid.

opposite custom, known in the West as the "Hottentot Venus." Kenyatta himself acknowledged in his work that there are Gikuyu men who marry unexcised girls from different "tribes."[30]

The fact that traditional religions practiced in most parts of Africa share many features in common—from ancestor veneration to healing to communication with nature—and yet diverge on female circumcision points to the dynamic and complex nature of African traditional religion, which is not coterminous with "female genital mutilation." In other words, the abolition of female genital excision is not blasphemous to many Africans, since the custom was not condoned by the whole of African religious tradition.

IS THERE ANY HOPE?

Since the question of female genital mutilation raises the ethical problem of the definition of good and evil conduct, and subsequently the discernment between good and bad ways of being a religious person, we have to turn to the fundamental question of African theological anthropology: what does it mean to be a genuine human being in Africa, to be that holy person loved by the gods and the ancestors?

Bumuntu and the Religious Response to Violence against Women

Once we have established that violence against women is sanctioned in some parts of Africa by religion, the end of violence requires the deconstruction of religion itself. In the same way that African wisdom established a distinction between *muntu* (genuine human being) and *kintu* (a bad person, a worthless being), there is also a deep-seated tradition of critical thinking that makes a clear distinction between "bad" and "good" religion. Because religion—despite divine revelation—is to some extent always human-made, wisdom requires a constant discernment by which a genuine religious person struggles to grasp the will of God amid this confusing institution where moral values, principles, and pious practices are often shaped by human selfishness and mistakes.

The transformation of religious views is made possible by 1) the non-dogmatic nature of traditional religions, 2) the pervasive tradition of critical thinking, 3) the vision that creation is not yet over, 4) the notion that divine revelation continues through all ages, 5) the centrality of *bumuntu* (genuine personhood) and *mucima muyampe* (good heart, good character) as the African vision of the essence of religion, 6) the centrality of *bumi* (life, respect for life) as essential criterion of good character, and, fi-

---

30. Kenyatta, *Facing Mt. Kenya,* 127.

nally, 7) the fundamental African belief that wisdom and virtues are accessible to all human beings, men and women, young and old. These concepts constitute a kind of check and balance on the religious ideologies produced by one single class of people. This is well expressed in what I term the African allegory of the cave, so wonderfully formulated in the folktales of Ghana.

In Ghana, the Akan expressed this critical approach to wisdom in a tale about Ananse Kokrofu, the Great Spider, who wanted to keep wisdom for himself and hide it from everybody, but wisdom escaped from his hand and fell on the ground, thus becoming available to everybody. The legend goes as follows:

> Ananse collected all the wisdom in the world and shut it up in a gourd. Then he began climbing the trunk of a tree so as to keep this precious gourd safe at the top. But he got into difficulties only half-away up, because he had tied the gourd to his front, and it hampered him in his climbing. His son Ntikuma, who was watching at the bottom, called up: "Father, if you really had all the wisdom in the world up there with you, you would have had the sense to tie that gourd on your back." His father saw the truth of this and threw down the gourd in a temper. It broke on the ground, and the wisdom in it was scattered about. Men and women came and picked up what each of them could get and carry away. Which explains why there is much wisdom in the world, but few persons have more than a little of it, and some persons have none at all.[31]

As this tale clearly indicates, in the African way of thinking, wisdom is not the private property of a small male elite. Wisdom is available to many; this idea includes the acknowledgement of the wisdom of women. As the Akan proverb put it, "Wisdom is not in the head of one person" (*Nyansa nni onipa baako ti mu*), "Wisdom is like a baobab tree, a single person's hand cannot embrace it." Two important lessons derive from these proverbs and the Ananse tale: first there is a relativization of the wisdom of men. In other words, it is not contrary to the will of the ancestors for a woman to challenge the wisdom of men or men's interpretation of religious laws or the will of the ancestors.

Second, there is the acknowledgement of other segments of society as "wisdom agents." In other words, the recognition of the wisdom of

31. Basil Davidson, *West Africa before the Colonial Era. A History to 1850* (London, New York: Longman, 1998), 148.

women means that it is legitimate for women to challenge men's inter-pretation of African tradition. This conception of wisdom is critical for understanding an African view of the relationship between religion and excision. It means that those who depart from the practice of excision do not necessarily commit a blasphemy. They may well be acting in con-formity to the will of the ancestors, whose fundamental article of faith is that the descendent have abundant life. As our brief historiography of cir-cumcision has shown, female genital mutilation has never been part of the entire African religious tradition. This opens a door to healthy dis-agreement within the ethical framework of African traditional religions. Moreover, even where excision has always been practiced, a change is al-ways possible without committing a blasphemy.

Indeed, one of the peculiar aspects of world religions is the "self-cor-rective" nature of religion. Religious traditions are highly ambiguous and contain at once antithetical value systems. Thus people can appeal to the tradition to justify oppressive rules and customs or to foster rebellion and advance the cause of liberation and justice.

We thus turn to African traditional religion to find sources for a cri-tique of violence against women. At stake here is the question of what it means to be a genuine human being, for it is clearly understood that a man who abuses women cannot be praised as a model of genuine per-sonhood. In other words, the fundamental question is, what is meant by good character? Central to African theological reading of violence is the notion of sainthood translated into the category of *mucima muyampe* (good or pure heart). A genuine religious person is a person of good heart (*muntu wa mucima muyampe*). Such a person is essentially a prince of peace, a peaceful person and a peacemaker. This notion of personhood is intertwined with that of the essence of religion. In other words, what are the values that constitute the essence of an African way of being reli-gious? The answer lies in what the Baluba people refer to as *bumuntu* (genuine human being) and *mucima muyampe* (pure heart).

As John Mbiti rightly pointed out, the notion of *bumuntu* refers to the African principle of interconnectedness with others: "I am because we are, and since we are, therefore I am." This is also well expressed in var-ious proverbs, such as the Zulu dictum "*Umuntu ngumuntu ngabantu*" (It is through others that one attains his full humanity) or the Luba proverb "*Bumuntu I buntu*" (Genuine humanity is fulfilled through the expression of generosity toward other people). This humanity is never given once for all, it has to be built up, increased, preserved and pro-moted. We are not human, we have to become human through a relent-less moral struggle.

In African theological anthropology being human oscillates between *muntu* (an authentic human being, a person replete with *bumuntu*) and *kintu* (a thing, a person empty of *bumuntu*). The *kintu* is a mode of existence as false consciousness, baseness, estrangement. It is a state of moral and spiritual chaos. The *kintu* is a human being replete with immorality or harmful behavior. It is a mode of being as a tool, dull, and ignoble. It is a mode of existence as a matter without manner, as platitude without positive attitude. The *kintu* is a human being who has fallen into moral lawlessness, into the category of things without conscience, through lack of respect for the life of others and that person's own life. This is a human being who has lost the *bumuntu*. The concept of *bumuntu* refers to the "quintessence of personhood, the essence of genuine selfhood, that fundamental authentic mode of being human and humane. Its chief characteristics are respect and dignity or self-respect, which are rendered in Kiluba with one single word: *buleme* (weight, content). *Bumuntu* is that ontological authenticity that governs the African quest for well-being and the African celebration of the humanity of other fellow humans. It is the ability to feel the pain of others. A person of *bumuntu* is the one guided by love and compassion for others. The motto is clear: "your pain is my pain, and your joy is my joy." Becoming *muntu* is overcoming the *kintu* status, which is a mode of reified existence, that is, a state of hostility. The *kintu* is a thing, not a person. Becoming *muntu* transcends the *kintu* by reconciling being with other beings, that is, through hospitality and solidarity with others.

This implies solidarity with women who suffer terribly from genital mutilations. The *bumuntu* is grounded in the article of faith in *bumi* (life). Life, abundant life, is the primary reality. Hence, the *bumuntu* theology is fundamentally a vision of permanent celebration of life in its multifarious forms, life in men and women, old and the young, family members and strangers, humans and nature. The man of *bumuntu*, the man who honors his own life, is therefore a man who honors life in women by denouncing practices that humiliate, frustrate, and even destroy women. And in this category we place female genital mutilations. In this religious worldview, men fulfill their *bumuntu* by treating women with respect and dignity, by rejecting all forms of violence against women.

For the Baluba, as for many other Africans, to be is to be ethical. This implies not only the capacity to distinguish good from evil, but the ability to choose to do good. An unethical person is *muntu wa bumvu* (a man of shame), *muntu bituhu* (a zero-person). In Kiluba language, ethics is expressed by the expressions *mwikadilo muyampe* (a good way of being in the world) or *mwendelo muyampe* (a good way of walking on the road of life).

In African philosophical anthropology, a human being can increase or lose humanness. The quality of a human being does not stem from gender or ancestry, but rather from personal behavior. It is not even enough to be created in the image of God! This means that in Africa to be a human being is a project to be fulfilled by each individual. An individual is not truly a human being simply by the fact of being born from human parents. One has to "become" a real *muntu*. This happens according to one's "way of life" (*mwikadilo*) or ethics. This ethic is based on a clear distinction between the notion of *bubi* (evil, ugliness) and the notion of *buya* (goodness, righteousness, purity, beauty). The criterion of distinction is the attitude toward human life. Everything (word, thought, and action) that threatens, destroys, and belittles human life (*bumi*) and human dignity (*buleme*) is considered evil. Being a human being is an ongoing process; and we become more fully human by behaving more ethically. Luba religion identified four main modes of behavior (through thought, speech, eyes, and action), as the following figure shows:

BUYA (GOODNESS) *mwikadilo muyampe*	BUBI (EVIL) *mwikadilo mubi*
The *mu-ntu* category (good human)	The *ki-ntu* category (thing)
mucima muyampe (good heart)	*mucima mubi* (evil thought)
ludimi luyampe (good speech)	*ludimi lubi* (evil speech)
diso diyampe (good eye)	*diso dibi* (evil eye)
bilongwa biyampe (good deeds)	*bilongwa bibi* (evil actions)

According to this ethical logic, violence against women can be performed in four different ways: a) through violent ways of thinking about women (*mucima mubi*), b) through violent language (*ludimi lubi*), c) through violent actions (*bilongwa bibi*), and through violent body language or evil eye (*diso dibi*). Although female genital mutilation falls explicitly in the category of *bilongwa bibi*, it also carries with it other forms of violence, namely the violent ways of thinking that justify the practice. It is worth noting here that for the Baluba a man who abuses women forfeits his own humanness. Thus he loses his being "*muntu*" and falls into the category of "*kintu*" (a thing). He becomes an empty man, a person without weight, a being without content, that is, a "nonperson," for as a Yoruba proverb put it explicitly, "a handsome man without good character is nothing more than a wooden doll."[32]

---

32. Cited by George Anastaplo, "An Introduction to 'Ancient' African Thought," in *The Great Ideas Today, 1995; Britannica Great Books of the Western World*, Encyclopedia Britannica, 1995, 176.

Thus we may conclude that female circumcision, like many other forms of violence against women, violates the will of the ancestors. It should be eradicated in the very name of African religious tradition whose focus at its best has always been human flourishing and the respect and protection of life and human dignity. As the Nigerian anthropologist Emmanuel Babatunde rightly pointed out: "Cultural differences are not excuses for violations of human rights, and the damage that clitoridectomy does to women suffices to make it alone the object of attack."[33]

All this points to the centrality of ethics in African tradition. Although African traditional religions include a plethora of taboos and rituals, from libation and sacrifices to trance and incantations of various types, good character or pure heart (*mucima muyampe*) remains the essence of the authentic spirituality. Indeed, rituals and prayers are deemed inefficient and even offensive when performed by a "*muntu wa mucima mubi*" (a man with evil intent or evil heart). Good character is regarded as the essence of humanity. A man without good character is regarded as dead, as an empty envelope. As one proverb put it, "Good character, good existence, is the adornment of a human being" (*Iwa rere l'èso eniyan*).

It is also good character that makes the distinction between a genuine religious person and a phony. The centrality of good character and, most importantly, goodness toward our fellow human beings and other creatures is clarified in Yoruba religion. Yoruba spirituality teaches that since God is the father of the whole universe—the creator of black and white people, albinos and hunchbacks, the Yoruba people, and all other nations as well[34]—prayers and invocations offered in *ile-ife* are deemed incomplete until prayers are offered for the people of the entire universe (*agbala aye gbogbo*), who are regarded as having had their origin in *ile-ife*.[35] Likewise, in Kenya, a "Meru Prayer" reminds us that concern for the welfare of all the people of the world is the heart of good religion. Thus holy persons do not only pray for themselves or their countrymen but even for people and nations whose existence they do not know:

> *Kirinyaga* (God), owner of all things,
> I pray to thee, give me what I need,
> Because I am suffering, and also my children,
> And all the things that are in this country of mine.

---

33. Babatunde, *Women's Rights versus Women's Rites*, 180–81.
34. Wande Abimbola, "The Attitude of Yoruba Religion Toward Non-Yoruba Religion," in Leonard Swidler and Paul Mojzes, eds., *Attitudes of Religions and Ideologies toward the Outsider* (Lewiston: Edwin Mellen Press, 1990), 137.
35. Ibid., 138.

I beg thee, the good one, for life,
Healthy people with no disease.
May they bear healthy children.
And also to women who suffer
Because they are barren, open the way
By which they may see children.
Give goats, cattle, food, honey,
And also the trouble of the other lands
That I do not know, remove.[36]

That good heart or good character is the essence of religion is also well stressed by the notion of *iwà*.

Where did you see *iwà*? Tell me!
Iwà, iwà is the one I am looking for.
"A man may be very, very handsome
Handsome as a fish within the water
But if he has no character
He is no more than a wooden doll."
Iwà, iwà is the one I am looking for.
If you have money,
But if you do not have good character,
The money belongs to someone else.

Iwà, iwà is the one we are searching for.
If one has children,
But if one lacks good character,
The children belong to someone else.

Iwà, iwà is the one we are searching for.
If one has a house
But if one lacks good character,
The house belongs to someone else.

Iwà, iwà is what we are searching for.
If one has clothes,
But if one lacks good character,
The clothes belong to someone else.

Iwà, iwà is what we are looking for.
All the good things of life that a man has,
If you have money,

---

36. A. Shorter, ed., *The Word That Lives: An Anthology of African Prayers*, mimeo, n.d., 32. Cited in Magesa, *African Religion*, 197–98.

If he lacks good character,
They belong to someone else.
Iwà, iwà is what we are searching for.
Each individual must use his own hands
To improve on his own character
Anger does not produce a good result for any man
Patience is the father of good character
If there is an old man who is endowed with patience
He will be endowed with all good things
It is honesty which I have in me,
I do not have any wickedness
Iwà ièsin, Good character is the essence of religion
(Yoruba religion)

It is worth noting that traditional spirituality insists on the need for each human being to improve one's character. It calls for personal responsibility in the process of religious maturation. The *Ifa* corpus states explicitly that "Each individual must use his own hands to improve on his own character" (*Owo ara eni, Là afi I tunwa ara enii se*). This concept of free will and personal responsibility finds an interesting echo in the Luba proverb, "*Vidye wa kuha buya nobe wa mukwashako.*" As Chinua Achebe pointed out, in Africa, "age was respected, but achievement was revered,"[37] and young people had to strive for their own excellence and greatness since the ancestral wisdom teaches that "a man who pays respect to the great paves the way for his own greatness"[38] in a society that ridicules lazy people and where "a man is judged according to his worth and not according to the worth of his father."[39] This means that traditional spirituality does not call for a blind obedience to a religious gerontocracy. As many proverbs put it, to have grey hair does not imply that one is wise or more spiritual, for there are indeed wise and spiritual people among the youth. The notion of free will calls for a mature discernment in the interpretation of the will of the ancestors. Because it admits free will and critical thinking, traditional religions make it legitimate to challenge the religious authenticity of excision.

CONCLUSION: The Golden Laughter of African Gods

Our detailed analysis of the nature of excision and its impact on the mental and physical health of women has clearly shown that we are dealing

---

37. Chinua Achebe, *Things Fall Apart* (New York: Anchor Books, 1959), 8.
38. Ibid., 19.
39. Ibid., 8.

here with a tradition of extreme violence. The question then is whether "the will of our ancestors" is faithfully upheld by "abolitionists" or their opponents.

The tragedy of patriarchy in Africa is such a paradoxical phenomenon in the midst of African traditional wisdom of *bumuntu* that the only better way to approach it is to learn from the wisdom of laughter. Unlike Thomas Hobbes and many British gentlemen who tried to bring laughter into bad repute in all thinking minds by claiming, "Laughing is a bad infirmity of human nature, which every thinking mind will strive to overcome" (Hobbes), Africans are fond of laughter. They do not see laughter as a spiritual and intellectual infirmity. They laugh all the time, anywhere and for any reason. Laughter is a great teacher of the path of becoming fully humane, and a great therapy for human soul. It is, indeed, a gift from the gods; it is a good spiritual exercise. Indeed, among the multitude of theophoric names and divine attributes found in African traditional religion, one stands in an astonishing uniqueness. God is referred to as "the Father of Laughter."[40] The African God is a "Laughing God!" He mocks all those who equate violence with holiness, sexism with the will of the ancestors, those who take themselves too seriously to the point of absolutizing their particular understanding of the will of God. Violence against women can never be equated with the divine modus vivendi, nor should female genital mutilation be identified with the divine modus operandi. Ideologies, like the Negritude of Jomo Kenyatta, that glorify female genital mutilation as fidelity to the will of the ancestors should be regarded as a delusional and dangerous fundamentalist humbug and a farcical parody of a shameful and misguided patriarchal tradition that betrays the authentic will of the ancestors. The ancestor tradition calls for the promotion of the welfare of both men and women. Indeed, African gods look upon the solemnity of excision and other brutal (and certainly sexist) traditions as a spiritual disease. That too is my argument in this chapter.

---

40. Joseph Healey and Donald Sybertz, *Toward an African Narrative Theology* (Maryknoll, N.Y.: Orbis Books, 1996), 81. This divine attribute of laughter is recorded among the Yoruba people of Nigeria. But it is also found among the Baluba people of Central Africa and in many other African cultures.

8

Sita's Epic Journey: Reflections on the Violence in the Lives of Hindu Women in North India

VEENA TALWAR OLDENBURG

IN the continuing dig for the roots of that ubiquitous phenomenon—violence against women—in the realm of religious texts, I suspect that we will strongly endorse what feminist scholars and theologians unearthed some three decades ago: the consistent privileging of the masculine in the construction of gender that informs, in varying degrees, *all* religions. Male anxiety about the power of female sexuality and reproduction is reflected in all cultural traditions and it is only logical that texts produced in these environments will indubitably be similarly tainted. These texts wrestle, with uneven success, in establishing laws, prescriptions, and doctrines to establish men's control over the minds and bodies of women and political and social control over society. Male moral authority enjoins codes of honor that enforce female chastity and exclude and seclude women from access to sacral functions or the very texts themselves. In an ironic and convoluted twist, the threat of female sexuality is transmuted into men's will (or sacred duty) to protect women (sisters, wives, and daughters) from the uncontrolled and dangerous intentions of men at large! Can we explore a multicultural world that India represents and find a powerful enough Hindu text that shapes attitudes towards women or prescribes violence against women?

The bewilderingly vast set of ideas, beliefs, philosophies, epics, and legal and social treatises that constitutes the Hindu canon does not offer its believers the same core features as other religions do: *a* founding figure, *a* single god with a capital G, an assortment of texts that are packaged as *the* Book, or *an* indisputable set of fundamentals, commandments, or pillars of the faith. The astonishing spread of textual options confounds the search for textual material that actually enables or sanctions male aggression against women; it is safer to assume that nothing happens between two human beings that has not been noticed and commented upon somewhere in that immense literature. It is possible but futile to make a case for violence against women rooted in one text and strenuously refute it by quoting from another.

Equally intriguing, like the chicken-or-the-egg question, is whether sacred texts shape society or whether historical and social contexts inspire these texts in the first place. The notions of "sacred" and "text" are also complicated in Hinduism. Only the Vedas have been rigorously maintained letter perfect by astounding mnemonic methods for three millennia; all other texts are often rewritten, revised, changed, with interpolations added and sections deleted. So Hindus have no other equivalent "Ur" texts, such as the Torah or the Qur'an, nor the fixity and certainty that other religions have in what they regard as the core of their scriptures. The Epics, whose stories are familiar to a great many Hindus since there are many, many *Ramayanas*[1] in oral, print, and now film and televison versions, were composed over the last 2,000 years; they also traveled and spread across space from the subcontinent to the farthest islands of the present day Indonesian archipelago—north Indian Hindus may have upwards of three hundred versions and more being minted. It is therefore presumptuous to suggest that I speak for "Hinduism" as a "Hindu."

For the sake of simplicity most scholars of Hinduism point to at least three disparate strands woven into the tapestry that is known as the Hindu tradition today—the *Shakta*, the beliefs and praxis associated with the Mahadevi or Great Goddess; *Shaiva*, with texts, cults, rituals, and austerities associated with Shiva, including *Tantra* (both consider power a female attribute); and the *Vaishnava*, with Vishnu and his nine realized *avataras* or incarnations. The two most popular of Vishnu's incarnations are the gods Krishna and Ram who are the focus in the great epics, the *Mahabharata* and the *Ramayana*. It is chiefly in the epic literature, where gods take human form and come down to live human lives, that we will find the misogyny that flavors social norms and behavior.[2] These texts have generated a vast literature comprising translations, exegeses, inter-

---

1. Paula Richman has edited two volumes, *Many Ramayanas* and *Questioning Ramayanas* (Berkeley: University of California Press, 1991 and 2001) that bring together excellent essays on the variants, the resistance, and the questioning this bottomless story inspires.
2. Manu's *Dharmashastra* may be another source that spells out an inferior position for women but it is a social and legal rather than a sacred text.

pretations, film and drama scripts, and debates, from both within the tradition by believers and by scholars.[3]

Given this variety, I propose to do something very arbitrary and finite by concentrating on my own reading of the *Ramayana* or the Sita-Ram *katha*, a text that lends itself easily to feminist analysis.[4] Quite unobtrusively one was exposed to recitations of it with explanatory and didactic extrapolations by local pundits, or from watching dramatic performances of it in village or city settings. A comic book–style version made it a popular account in the hands of school children, and I have used sections of R. K. Narayan's translations of the Valmiki text for my course on gender and violence. In the 1980s the serialized television version had created a gigantic following and (although I saw only the odd segment or two on visits to Lucknow) it brought the story forcibly into the living rooms of urban India and set off passionate arguments about episodes that set gender and caste hierarchy in stark relief.[5] Furthermore, Hindu nationalists, who are so unequal to the task of understanding Hinduism in all its richness, are stubbornly pushing the *Ramayana* as *the* Hindu bible (in their version of it) to make Hindus a people of a single book.

"My" version is a composite that memory has welded together. I heard it, read bits of it, and remember it (chiefly) from the various recitations in its

---

3. I am extremely grateful for the generous help I have received from several quarters: U.S. scholars of Hinduism who know many of these *Ramayana* texts best and have overawed me with papers, e-mail, and telephone conversations—Robert Goldman and Sally Sutherland Goldman, Linda Hess, and Philip Lutgendorf, who sent me their own relevant and inspiring articles on the subject; Mary McGee, who lent me books and cheered me along; and John S. Hawley and Rachel McDermott, who answered questions. Michael Fisher and Philip Oldenburg read a draft and made excellent suggestions. Ruth Vanita shared with me her soon-to-be-published paper on the *Adbhut Ramayana*, a truly strange Shakta version of the story that resonates with my own irreverent telling of the story to a friend's son; and, of course, my mother, who religiously intones Tulsidas's exquisite *Avadhi* verses in his *Ramcharitmanas* in a haze of blue-grey incense smoke every single morning in our home in Lucknow to this day. She made Ram and Sita as familiar to me as members of our extended family and tolerated my frank questioning of gender relations in the *Manas*. Thus, it is with great trepidation that I attempt to refract their lights through my prism.

4. My choice of the Sita-Ram story is deliberate for the purposes of this chapter. I would much rather have chosen the most celebrated and beguiling adulterous affair in sacred literature, the immortal *katha* of Krishna, the blue god and his beloved, Radha. There is no talk of chastity and high-minded patriarchal duty in the Radha-Krishna *katha*.

5. Linda Hess, in an important essay, "The Poet, the People and the Western Scholar: Influence of a Sacred Drama and Text on Social Values in North India," *Theatre Journal* 40 (1988): 236–53, has gone through the text with a fine-tooth comb and found an astounding catalogue of "disturbing" passages against women in the *Ramcharitmanas*. After reading them I, as a Hindu woman, found them not only very disturbing but also truly offensive, even pathological. While these despicable and chiefly Brahmanical attitudes do not go unquestioned in the culture and society, they insidiously inform the socializing that young boys and girls receive to prepare them for their marital roles as adults.

vernacular and most widely know forms, Valmiki's *Ramayana* and the *Ramcharitmanas* of Tulsidas; from recalled fragments of the theatrical and dance performances of it called the *Ram Lila* I saw on chilly November nights that ended in the blazing and crackling immolation of the towering effigy of the demon Ravan; from Wadia's film *Sampurn Ramayan* with its operatic power; from pundit Sheetala Prashadji, who sang and explicated several *chaupais*, or verses, accompanied by his harmonium in our living room twice a week; and from the repeated episodes, frequently out of sequence my *ayah* (nanny), grandmother, and mother told from it as bedtime stories. Now I want to see how it speaks to the contemporary existential violence against women that I encountered in my own research into the subject.

The position of Hindu women in India is equally intricate. Indira Gandhi's tenure as the world's most powerful woman, serving as she did for sixteen years as the prime minister of the world's largest democracy, ended in her own brutal murder. Reported around the same time in Delhi were the gruesome killings of young brides, drenched with kerosene and burned to death in their kitchens. Can both these severely opposed trajectories—one of an indomitable world actor and the other of wives burned alive—be *sanctioned* by Hindu texts? While the tradition is comfortable with the idea of female power and conceptualizes the notion of power in the abstract as *shakti*, the female principle glorified in several sacred texts, it also sees female sexuality as dangerous, fickle, polluting, and potent, even emasculating and in strong need of male control. There are other representations of female power that one encounters in everyday life in India—of Kali with her garland of skulls dancing on the corpse of Shiva; of Saraswati, whose power is knowledge in all its forms; of Lakshmi, whose worship ensures prosperity, success, and domestic harmony and has the Indian corporate world in her thrall. How then do we explain the spate of deaths of married women—mostly murders, with a few credible kitchen accidents and suicides—that have surpassed an average of five thousand annually (in a population of over a billion) for the past decade and a half? Is there something specifically Hindu going on here? How do we account for the murders of Sikh, Muslim, and Christian women included in that statistic?

I will explore and analyze selected events, moments, or junctures from the plot in the story of Ram and Sita that resonate with the modern patriarchal and legal constructions of gender I encountered in the archives and in the field while interviewing victims of violence at Saheli, a women's resource center in Delhi. The Sita-Ram *katha* was often alluded to as an unembarassing way of explaining sexual misgivings.[6] Robert P. Goldman has

---

6. My own work on the subject was published as *Dowry Murder: The Imperial Origins of a Cultural Crime* (New York: Oxford University Press, 2002).

pointed out the importance of analyzing the *Ramayana* for comprehending the construction of gender and caste because he finds Valmiki's text "a paean to conformity, obedience and an handbook of social integration" and yet, he goes on to say, "it is the very quality of social normativity, and its resulting status as the family text par excellence and the ideal medium for the acculturation of children . . ." that makes any departures from the norm rather significant.[7] It is in the statement of the norms and their ruptures that one will look for answers.

A brief, spare adumbration of the action might be in order here to make my arguments intelligible. It is a grand plot in the genre of Indo-European epics; it is a tale of love and war, abduction and pursuit and heroic battles. A beautiful woman (or two, or three as in this case) becomes the catalyst for the action-packed poetic narrative while heroes and demons settle scores, predictably ending in the rout of the latter. The story begins and ends in an earthly setting, Ayodhya. The present-day town of that name still exists on the banks of the Saryu River in eastern Uttar Pradesh and gives the epic a historical plausibility.

As the tale goes, Ravan, the ten-headed demon-king of Lanka, through his devotion to Shiva, won himself a boon of invincibility against the gods, vulnerable only to the bravest of men. He sets about destroying the world's peace and dares to shake even Mount Kailash, the abode of the gods, knowing that none can subdue him. Vishnu is persuaded by the divine parliament to incarnate himself as a man to annihilate this demon-king.

In Ayodhya, Dasharath, the aging king, has with great difficulty produced four sons from his three queens. Kaushalya, the eldest queen, gives birth to Ram, the elected incarnation of Vishnu, with the earthly duty to slay Ravan. Sumitra gives birth to twin boys, Lakshman and Shatrughan, and the youngest, beautiful wife Keikeyi bears the goodly son, Bharat. Ram goes off into the forest, as royal *kshatriyas* (of the warrior caste) must, to help the hapless Brahmins by slaying Ravan's obstreperous and cannibalistic emissaries.

Beyond the forest to the east in Mithila, King Janak finds an infant girl in the furrow of a ploughed field and lovingly rears her as his daughter, Sita. As a child she astonishes her father by lifting an enormous bow with ease and playing with it. She grows into a beautiful and virtuous young woman, and her father holds what was customary at that time, a *swayamvar* (literally, the bride's selection of a groom), a gathering of all eligible princes. He announces that the prince who breaks the enormous

---

7. Robert P. Goldman, "Resisting Rama: Dharmic Debates on Gender and Hierarchy and the Work of the Valmiki Ramayana," unpublished paper, forthcoming.

bow will wed Sita. Ram, who is on his demon-ridding exploits, wanders into this contest and wins the lovely Sita as his bride and takes her home to Ayodhya, leaving Ravan, who is also a suitor, sorely defeated.

The action then cuts to Ayodhya where Dasharath is ready to retire and appoints his beloved Ram as his successor. The youngest wife, Kaikeyi, who has ambitions for her own son, wishes instantly to redeem the two boons Dasharath granted her, when, once, she saved his life in the field of battle. She demands Bharat's ascension and Ram's banishment to the forest for fourteen years. Dasharath dithers, but Ram salvages his distraught father's honor by promptly agreeing to leave for the forest. Kaushalya wants to leave with her son but he refutes her wish. Sita wins the argument to accompany Ram and his younger half-brother Lakshman into exile.

On their journey through the forest they encounter Ravan's long-taloned and ugly sister, Surpanakha. She assumes the form of a beautiful woman who tries to seduce Ram while threatening to devour Sita. He rebuffs her advances with rude jests and the headstrong Lakshman slashes her nose. An enraged Surpanakha proceeds to Lanka to her brother, the demon-king Ravan, and reports the indignities and the assault she suffered at the hands of the princes. She also describes the ravishing Sita, whom she wanted so much to devour. Ravan vows to avenge his sister's humiliation by abducting Sita and making her his queen.

Reconfiguring himself as a single-headed holy man, accompanied by a fellow demon in the guise of a golden deer, he heads for the forest hermitage of the exiled royals. Sita spots the deer, craves it strongly for its meat and golden pelt, and cajoles Ram and Lakshman to pursue it. Soon after the brothers leave for the hunt, Ravan appears as a hungry ascetic at Sita's door, and she dutifully prepares to feed him. He grabs her and transports her back on his flying chariot to his island kingdom.

Anguished to find Sita gone, her jewelry strewn as clues of her struggle against her abductor, Ram begins the long and difficult search for her. The brothers traverse a kingdom ruled by monkeys, whose general, Hanuman, instantly becomes a devotee of Ram and marshals his army of monkeys to battle against Ravan. He then flies to Ravan's garden with Ram's signet ring to reassure Sita of Ram's determination to rescue her. He finds her harangued by terrifying demons attempting to induce her to yield to their lustful king. Hanuman manages to exchange Ram's ring for the precious jewel she is wearing. The eventual engagement is bloody, with many casualties on both sides; Ram finally kills Ravan in ferocious combat and appoints Vibhishan, Ravan's brother who has defected to Ram's side, as king of Lanka.

After his triumph and with Sita at his side, Ram is filled with jealous misgivings. He obliges her to submit to an *agni pariksha*, a public trial by fire, to prove her chastity. Sita walks into the flames and passes the test unscathed. Yet, trouble persists.

They return to Ayodhya where Ram assumes the throne. I have heard two endings that compete to finish this tale. My ayah always insisted on the first one found in Valmiki's original Sanskrit version. The suspicion about Sita's relationship with Ravan festers among the people of Ayodhya and a low caste washer man's taunt about her chastity riles King Ram. In response he instructs Lakshman to take Sita away and leave her in the forest without a word of explanation or farewell. She is pregnant and is cruelly abandoned in the forest. Brave and dignified, she finds shelter with a learned ascetic, the self-same Valmiki who listens to *her* story and writes it down as his great Sanskrit epic. She brings up her twin boys (who strongly resemble Ram, which ends the suspense about their paternity). Ram chances upon this trio and entreats Sita to come back with him, but she, in defiance of cultural expectations, refuses to forgive his behavior. Instead she wills the Earth, her mother, to crack open a fissure and disappears into it. Ram, now rejected and miserable, sheds his mortal coil and returns to the world of the gods.

Tulsidas alters the ending and makes it a happy one. An uncharacteristically docile Sita agrees to a second trial in Ayodhya, which she passes again, quelling all doubts and rumors, and the divine pair initiates an ideal reign. Tulsidas omits the Valmiki ending of an unreconciled wife when writing it in 1574, roughly twelve hundred years later in the reign of Mughal Emperor Akbar, but emphasizes, instead, the glories of an ideal and wishfully eternal Hindu kingship.

THE *KATHA*, WOMEN, AND VIOLENCE

Before I present my analysis of the *Katha* I might briefly recapitulate the position I have taken in my book and the central findings that I would like to "test" against the grain of the moral and patriarchal universe found in the *Ramayana*. I have rigorously argued against the common perception that the custom of dowry is a "social evil" that accompanies hypergamous marriages among high caste Hindus and is responsible for female infanticide in the natal home and for "dowry murder" in the marital home. Instead I have shown that the custom of giving jewelry, clothes, household furnishings, livestock, and occasionally property as dowry to a daughter at the time of marriage was created by women for women as a safety net and a marker of the status and affection they enjoyed in their natal homes, and is found in many other cultures, including the European. This custom changed radically in meaning and function in colonial India after the British redefined communally held agricultural land as private property, instituted an inelastic revenue demand that was fixed for fifteen to thirty years, and insisted that the newly minted peasant proprietors deposit their dues in cash on fixed dates at the district headquarters. It wrought a revolution that remade the moral economy of the Punjab countryside. I also discovered that the almost obsessive "preference for sons" in the Punjab was not because of ritual or caste rules of Hindus, but a general preference shared also by Muslims and Sikhs in the agrarian political economy of a larger northwestern historical war zone. The control of land was perennially contested; men fulfilled the existential imperatives of defending and tilling the land as warriors and agriculturalists. The corollary to this reality was female infanticide, widely committed in the Punjab across castes and creeds. The preference for sons was discernibly deepened with the creation of male property rights and opportunities for employment in an economy shaken by the inelastic revenue demand. Indebtedness, land auctions, and market forces reengineered social relations, substantially changing the equation of power to gender. This gave the entire region—covering Afghanistan, Pakistan, and northwest India—the lowest female sex ratios, on average 875:1000.

Given the enormous shortage of employed (and educated) men who were most sought after as grooms, the custom of dowry (for some families with eligible grooms) would degenerate into a plain and simple opportunity for extortion, leading, in some of those cases, predictably to violence and even murder. I have argued at length that these gender crimes increased because of an unevenly modernizing political economy that *exacerbated* gender inequalities rather than because of cultural practices (identified as hypergamy and the high caste custom of dowry) sanctioned in religious texts.

One of my key arguments is that the less articulated problems of sexuality—infidelity, sexual abuse, and sexual jealousy—often underlie the violence we see at the quotidian level. The sexual factor is easy to ignore since dowries were legally banned in 1961. Amended and strengthened two decades later, this law, while giving women a chance to seek justice, has also silenced the real stories of many women. Almost every case of violence against women is framed as a case of dowry-related violence, as a matter of individual greed rather than of structural defects in the social and legal construction of gender. How, then, does the Ramayana story I know speak to this summary of my major conclusions?

THE PREFERENCE FOR SONS

Let me begin with the gendered destinies of boys and girls. The disparate stories of the births of Ram and Sita are emblematic even in our modern times. If we set aside the divine reincarnation, Ram and his three half-brothers are products of more than biological processes—they are conceived after many fasts and prayers undertaken by the childless wives of an aging king (with a low sperm count?) and the critical ministrations of rice pudding by an obliging sage. The "preference for sons" is apparent in a plot where there are four sons and no daughters. The three wives are transformed, quietly and painlessly, without any of the travails of pregnancy, labor, and childbirth, into the receptacles that bring forth these boy-children, to save the royal lineage from extinction and Avadh from enemy attack. Today fasting and praying are supplemented by modern science—in vitro fertilization for conception and the expensive method of amniocentesis, which detects the sex of a fetus with precision. This has been more recently replaced by safer, cheaper, although less accurate, sonograms. Both methods are now banned, just as much as dowries are banned, but flourish illegally in this same war zone from where the Indian army continues to draw it greatest number of recruits.

In contrast to the much-heralded male births, it is interesting how Sita is introduced to this world as a foundling. She lies in a furrow of a field—it was mysterious to me as a child and is ominous to me now as to why this particular unorthodox "birth" forms such a part of the story.

There is, however, a more troubling connection to be made with Sita's foundling status. In the precolonial and colonial period we know that the killing of unwanted female infants was widespread and in flagrant transgression of religious law that considers it the most heinous of crimes. A common method was to simply expose the newborn to the elements, in a distant field where she would die of cold and starvation. Was Sita abandoned as an infant by a family who did not want her and hoped that she would be found by Janak, the king of Vadeha, as he tilled his field during the seasonal ritual?[8]

The women in three villages in Gurgaon district, whom I had occasion to question on my several trips there in the 1980s and 1990s, confirmed what the archives had already revealed: the decision to kill the female child if one or two sisters already existed. This dispatch prevented the onset of lactation and cleared the way for another pregnancy. Nursing a

---

8. In another version, Sita is Ravan's daughter through his wife Mandodari, who abandons the child because she fears that the lustful Ravan is not beyond incest. This only underscores female sexual vulnerability as a building block of gender relations.

child is practiced as a device to space the birth of children. In order to make it emotionally less brutal for the mother, she never sees or holds the female infant marked for death. A more pitiless logic was never at work.

Infanticide then was the primitive "sex determination test." When a newborn emerged from the womb and its genitals became visible, its fate was sealed; a penis saved the infant. Now the absence of a penis in a fetus made visible by a sonogram is tantamount to a "birth defect" and the fetus will be aborted. Birth order was the destiny of the girl child. Daughters early in the birth order had the lower chances of survival, since the priority was to produce an optimum number of five or six boys as early as possible. I marveled at the zeal with which the women played the role of the secret agents of patriarchy. The size and composition of families, overtly referred to as *kismat* or "God's will," are actually the products of patriarchal power systematically deployed through women against women for the alleged welfare of the family. Educated women, other research has shown, are even more efficient at achieving a gender-targeted family than their uneducated sisters.

WAS DOWRY THE PROBLEM?

It is interesting to note that when Sita is to wed, the groom's parents have little to do with "choosing the bride"—the act is almost entirely managed by the bride's family. Her father tests the physical prowess of the princely suitors and Ram, god incarnate, who is the only one capable of breaking the enormous bow, is found worthy of the beloved daughter's hand. The wedding is celebrated grandly, as befitting the status of the royal family. There is absolutely no whisper of dowry negotiations or the level of hospitality expected by the bride-takers. Instead we are told King Dasharath, Ram's father, arrives for the occasion with a small customary male entourage (no ostentation then, even among kings). He distributes the gifts he has brought from Avadh for the people of Janakpuri or Maithili, almost obliterating the line between dowry and bride price. The dignity and mutual agreement that marked the proceedings match the precolonial baseline I constructed for the custom from archival and literary sources. They are in striking contrast to the petty greed and bargaining that attends the arrangements in families where violence occurs in the consumer societies that replaced a simpler world. Hypergamy too is not in evidence then as now, as mistakenly alleged by the scholar-bureaucrats of the colonial period when they were investigating the motives for female infanticide. The marriage alliance is between two royal Kshatriya families of *comparable* status, which is still the norm with most marriages arranged some two millennia later.

Sita receives a dowry made up of splendid clothes and jewels from her father and these are described at great length in several tellings of this story; I remember my own tellers lingering over this wedding and the catalogue of precious jewels she is given. The dowry will play a vital role in Sita's life when misfortune befalls her. Fully bedecked even in exile (her mothers-in-law do not take control of her dowry), she strategically sheds some of her jewelry as she is abducted by Ravan. To find her precious jewels scattered on the forest floor signifies to Ram that she has been forcibly taken and points him in the direction in which her abductor has taken her. She keeps one jewel hidden close to her breast, and it plays a vital role as a signifier of her love and fidelity when she exchanges it for Ram's ring, brought to her by Hanuman. This jewel also has the power to remind her of her loving father who gave it to her.

Sita's story unequivocally reaffirms my basic argument that the traditional dowry was and still is a supportive institution for a majority of Hindu women in virilocal marriages (where the bride leaves her natal village and goes to live with her husband) among upper castes and classes. Wedding expenses were, and still are, for the majority, in proportion to the means of the bride's family, and the modern escalation of costs of both these items can be traced to the changes wrought in the traditional economy and society in the colonial period. It was surprising to see how much of the precolonial tradition of dowry that I had reconstructed in my book (chapter 3) was a closer match to what existed two thousand years ago than to what existed after swift and sweeping changes only a few decades into colonial rule.

Compulsory virilocality and its effects, alas, continue to be part of the patriarchal package of *kanyadan*, or gifting the virgin bride to the groom. It increases the vulnerability of women and reifies them as property. It is hard for anyone to argue that an arranged marriage to a virtual stranger followed immediately by the abrupt relocation of the bride in her distant marital home and the erasure of her identity and the assumption of her husband's family name are customs that have a daughter's interests at heart. The sending off of the bride is a tearful ritual at Hindu weddings, as emotional as it is inevitable, and perhaps a part of the greater Indo-European tradition that reifies women as property, since they are gifted or "given away." This Sita, too, endures and never in her distress does she consider a return to her father's home. The uncompromising nature of virilocality enforces the patriarchal idea that a woman must unconditionally stay with her husband. This is bleakly spelled out by Ram and Sita as the core of *stridharma* (a wife's code); Hindu women are still socialized to believe and accept this custom and it is psychologically very difficult, even when conditions absolutely warrant it, for women to leave their marital homes or countenance divorce (which is legal since 1956) as a way of escaping an abusive marriage. It also creates that rootless, even homeless state that women describe when they talk about the marriages they were forced to leave, and thoughts of suicide are common. It is still a strong part of the acculturation of young women to accept that, ideally, a married woman leaves her marital home only on an *arthi* or bier after her death, and this condition informs the *Ramayana* as much as it does the minds of millions of women in India today.

A woman's place and her wifely duty in the patriarchal context emerge in stark relief as Dasharath's royal household is thrown into turmoil after he grants Kaikeyi's covetous boons. She is the opportunist, albeit aided by her wicked low-caste maid, who unleashes her physical beauty against her weak and sensual husband to subvert the legitimate succession of Ram in favor of her own unsuspecting son. She chooses the moment when he is away visiting her family and brings the preparations being made for Ram's ascension to a jolting halt. With this twist several articles of *kshatriyaharma*, or the warrior code, are tested and have to be explicitly reordered to cope with this unusual crisis.

Ram, the model and obedient son who must obey his father's command, finds his mother, Kaushalya, and brother, Lakshman, in powerful alignment against him. A feeble patriarch, given to lust and reckless promises, Dasharath must be saved from ignoble collapse. The iron rule of the Kshatriyas, of preferring death to a breach of promise, has to be upheld; Ram has no option but to accept his own exile so that his father's honor will not be compromised; thus he must disobey his mother. As an obedient and loving son, he opts to uphold the patriarchal order and refuses his mother's orders to stay or to take her with him.[9] At this juncture Kaushalya, senior wife and now bereft mother, wishes to abandon her dotard husband. She tells Ram that if he insists on his exile she either accompanies him or kills herself. Ignoring the politics of co-wives, Ram tactlessly argues that in the scale of things a father's word carries more weight than a mother's, and that *she* must obey the supreme *dharma* of a

9. My tellers always praised Ram as a loving son whose intransigence against his mother's wish to go with him was out of concern for the dangers in the forest and a consideration of his father's fragile health. Goldman's superbly sensitive and nuanced discussion on this business of *dharmic* imperatives in his essay "Resisting Rama: Dharmic Debates on Gender and Hierarchy and the Work of the Valmiki Ramayana" (esp. 8–18) has helped me enormously to understand the contradictions one sees played out within the dynamics of an extended Hindu family; the extension of this argument with Sita, which follows, can be extrapolated to explain the unresolved daily struggle a man endures in the opposing duties he owes a mother and wife.

wife and stay by her husband's side; her place as a wife, he iterates, is unconditionally beside her husband. He cites bloodcurdling examples of the fate of errant wives and insistent mothers. Whether this dictum has its provenance in this religious text or merely reflects a hoary rule of society long before the *Ramayana* was ever dreamed up, most women do believe it to be their duty to stay and obey, even when their husbands are wrong, unfaithful, and, possibly, violent. I would, however, add that this foundational rule of social conditioning is greatly assisted by the material fact that more often than not, *women often have nowhere to go* and frequently have no independent means to actually vote with their feet. Socioeconomic constraints working in tandem with social conditioning render a woman captive to the patriarchal ideal of a "good wife."

Lakshman, fuming at his father's irresponsible indulgence of their stepmother, urges his brother to fight (by the authority of the same Kshatriya code) for his birthright as the eldest son and destroy those (his stepmother and half-brother) who stand in his way. Ram juggles these imperatives and tells Lakshman that the true dharma is to obey, with all the husbandly authority he can summon, his father's edict. Ram is actually helping his father to uphold *kshatriyadharma* by keeping his word given to his wife. Underneath all this *dharmic* high dudgeon between brothers I read a very sly subtext. Dasharath, the patriarch, is implicitly impugned for having indulged his passion in having taken on a young wife and given her unlimited power over him and the future of his dynasty. His regret and grief over his own actions will soon kill him. Later we see, in the Surpanakha episode, that both brothers are capable of disregarding *kshatriyadharma* entirely, while in the final episode, both *pitrdharma* and *stridharma*, patriarchal and wifely duty, are stood on their heads.

Next, in dealing with Sita's reaction to the same news, we see Ram contorting dharmic logic once again. He authoritatively *forbids* Sita to accompany him, saying that her proper dharma is to stay at home, not by his side in exile! Sita counters Ram's equivocation vociferously. She scoffs at his high-minded peroration to his mother about a wife's place being by her husband's side, so there is no question that she will accompany him. One appreciates her spirited rejoinder, her impeccable entrapping common sense, but shudders at how forcibly she articulates and underscores the patriarchal ideal of wifehood. This is the precisely the place at which we need to point the accusing finger—the mechanism whereby women internalize the defeating and pitiless logic of patriarchy that makes women act against their own best interests. Sita does come to a profound realization of this at the end, but she pays an enormous cost meanwhile, as we shall see.

Sita is brought up to be the exemplary ideal wife. Her girlhood is sketchy, although her pluck and unselfconscious physical strength is noticed by her father, but life really begins for her after her marriage to Ram. This is a pattern I traced in the stories I heard from women who came to Saheli, a women's resource center in Delhi, with severe marital problems. I was a researcher and volunteer there for ten months in 1985–1986, and at the end of that period I had listened to or read about three hundred stories of violence, hate, and broken lives. I noticed that on almost every form in the case files at Saheli, the space that was to be filled with information describing the problem the woman was having invariably began with the day the woman was betrothed or married, as if her past in her natal homes had been abruptly erased, her identity derived entirely from her husband. These narratives, not unlike the popular tellings of the *Ramayana*, also have very sketchy information on the women characters before they were married and expose how marriage becomes the defining moment in a woman's life; only men seem to have a serious apprenticeship to manhood. Dasharath's four queens really become people after their sons are born; even Kaikeyi's presence on the battlefield, where she saves his life and wins two unconditional promises from him, doesn't get told or acted out on the stage like the rest of the *Katha*. Lakshman never speaks of his wife who is left behind, and Ram, even in spurning Sita, never suggests her father might want her back. Are male epic story tellers unable to conjure the lives of women with any completeness or depth? The "discontinuous life" of the average Hindu woman, I have argued elsewhere, is largely a product of compulsory virilocal marriage.[10]

SURPANAKHA'S MUTILATION

This key episode is fraught with sexual tension and moves the plot into high gear. It is limned into my memory from a Ramlila performance in 1957 as the gas lights created shadows and sparkling contrasts and the stage bristled with sexual tension. This encounter indubitably encourages violence against women who are sexual transgressors. It also illustrates, par excellence, the lengths to which men may go to assuage their primal fear of unrestrained female sexuality. I remember that Surpanakha, the taloned demon, removes her mask to be transformed into a strikingly beautiful and stunningly bejeweled woman before she does a sexually provocative dance as she approaches the handsome pair of brothers standing amid a clump of potted trees on the stage at the Ramlila grounds in Delhi. The brothers look on, dazzled; Sita appears nervous and fidgety. For

10. Oldenburg, *Dowry Murder*, 216–17.

several minutes the audience is in thrall of an unrestrained and aggressively sexual woman; the men in the audience give cat calls and wolf whistles.

She accosts these *dharmic* Kshatriya brothers who have talked too long of honor, kingly behavior, duty, and piety. Surpanakha now makes a lascivious thrust of her pelvis at Ram, suggests that he become her husband and that she can devour both Sita and Lakshman to clear their way to a blissful union. He rejects her advances with an ambiguous jest and points to Sita as a restraining factor, but urges her to approach Lakshman instead, whose wife is not with him. Lakshman at first enjoys the teasing but also rebuffs her. Surpanakha, unable to fathom their intentions, lunges towards the cowering Sita in order to eat her. Lakshman draws his sword and threatens to kill her. Drums roll and fall silent. Here the brothers take pause because the code of the Kshatriyas *expressly forbids the killing of or violence against women* under any circumstances. Lakshman then reminds his brother that they had killed a female demon when appealed to by their Brahmin guru. Ram, with inexcusable cruelty, signals to Lakshman to cut off her nose.[11] A wounded and irate Surpanakha flies first to one brother, who is briskly dispatched in battle by Ram, and then to brother Ravan, who decides to abduct Sita in revenge for his sister's humiliation. This encounter endorses a social rule with enormous clarity: a sexually reprobate woman must be punished. Violently marking the face, like the stamping of the A for adultery on a woman's forehead or stoning to death, is a similarly primitive patriarchal formula to keep women's sexuality in check—on which male honor seems to depend.[12] A great deal of prescriptive violence against women who are deemed sexual offenders is the result, and a whole subgenre of so-called "honor crimes," including murder, flourishes in Afghanistan, Pakistan, India, and elsewhere. What is even more galling is that in all sexual encounters it is the woman who bears the moral burden (and physical disfigurement) because

---

11. For a far more textually learned and detailed treatment of this episode in several versions of the story see Kathleen M. Erndl, "The Mutilation of Surpanakha," in *Many Ramayanas*, ed. Paula Richman (Berkeley: University of California Press, 1991), 67–88. The precise words in the Valmiki text that Ram speaks to Lakshman are: "Mutilate this ugly, unvirtuous, extremely ruttish, great bellied" demon (71). Commentaries have been written to exonerate or explain away this unchivalrous behavior on Ram's part. Surpanakha had to be mutilated, they claim, so that Ravan would be provoked to abduct Sita, which would lead to his final destruction at the hands of Ram.

12. That the science of rhinoplasty developed in India and moved on to Egypt in this early period testifies to the fact that this kind of retribution was common for both men and women. Indian laws do not permit punitive mutilation today but *naak katvana* (literally, get your nose mutilated) is still a popular metaphor in contemporary Hindu and Urdu usage for something that brings visible and enduring shame to the person who has been mutilated thus.

it is her virginity or chastity that has to be protected; even rape is often believed to be the consequence of a woman's dangerous desire.

TRIAL BY FIRE

This leads us to the climactic episode that conflates Ram's decisive victory against Ravan with his doubt about Sita's chastity. The events that lead up to a verdict on the character of Sita subtly gesture towards the true nature of Ram, and thus, in an abstract sense, on the nature of gender relations. After the blood, smoke, and dust of the battle settle and the listeners expect an unmitigated and joyous reunion, a vividly painful denouement unfolds: Ram accosts Sita coldly and tells her that he has sought her so desperately only to vindicate his own family honor. He angrily rejects her because she lived in the house of strange man! He seems to have instant amnesia about her abduction and his own torment to find her gone. This development, in the erstwhile gripping story of love and heroism, suddenly debases their love and tarnishes the hero. The *Katha*— of the mutual love at first sight, the idyll of their romance, Sita's passionate argument to accompany her cruelly exiled husband into the forest, her uncompromised devotion and struggle against the threats and abuse in the demon-filled garden in Lanka—abruptly shifts registers. Sita, in the wishful twist of the male imagination, must have given in to her lustful and fickle nature.

The scenario of Ram accusing his wife of infidelity after her abduction and captivity is a familiar climax in the world of failed marriages. In this flash of temper I see Ram revealed, not as the god-king or *ideal man* he has been playing, but as an *ordinary* man, whose sexual suspicions muddle his judgment and expose ordinary male anxieties. Sita also seems an *ordinary* woman, suffering first the ignominies of abduction and sexual harassment and then the accusation of sexual betrayal. She now has to endure the humiliation of a public trial by fire to prove her sexual purity. The great macrocosmic battle of good versus evil is transformed into the microcosmic human scenario of the common doubt of a husband of his wife's faithfulness. At this juncture the *Katha* unravels the miraculous from the mundane, separating the god-hero from man-husband, Ram. After following him in his desolation at Sita's disappearance, and his unsparing effort to destroy her abductor, he now sends a chill through the world of gods and humans alike (and, perhaps, a knowing and weary shrug through the bodies of women in the audience) with his doubt.

Sita, humiliated and rejected, offers no defense, makes no counter-argument as she has done on previous occasions. This silence is often interpreted to imply Sita's submissiveness or powerlessness, but for me her speechlessness is perfectly apt; it proclaims her refusal to dignify such ridiculous misgivings with comment. She is disconsolate, does not wish to live, and requests a funeral pyre to be made for her and it is into these flames she walks but remains unscathed. Ram claims that Sita's *agni parisksha*, or trial by fire, was a ruse on his part to wipe out any doubts the onlookers in Lanka may harbor about her relationship to Ravan. Tulsidas chooses to see the royal couple home and living happily ever after. Valmiki's ending is perhaps more plausible because such a public demonstration of mistrust is hard to obliterate.

SITA'S STORY

Valmiki pulls no punches because Sita, pregnant and abandoned, finds him in his hermitage and tells him what happened after they retuned to Ayodhya. I imagine this is what inspired the sage to sit up, take notice, and distil his poetic inspiration into the *Ramayana*. This *is* her story in all its painful detail, which Tulsidas simply truncates, substituting devotional fervor and fairy tale evasions to bring matters to a happy close in the *Manas*. Yet he could not suppress Sita's truth, for it lives on in theatrical performances, in the blockbuster television serial, and in several local tellings of the *Ramayana*, but most strongly it is a story in itself told, heard, and believed in the company of women.

It is that final wrenching plot twist that highlights even more intensely not only the long-suffering quality of women's lives but the fragile nature of male honor, predicated as it is on female sexual behavior. After their journey back to Ayodhya, Sita is pregnant and a spy reports to Ram that rumors about her chastity and pregnancy persist; a washer man is overheard casting aspersions on Sita's character. This single bit of information induces Ram, who is fully aware of Sita's purity, to ask her if she would undergo yet another trial by fire to appease the citizens of Ayodhya. Sita categorically refuses and Ram exhibits moral cowardice of a calibre that makes total mockery of the kingly warrior's protocol. He has displayed these baser instincts before, but he now surpasses himself by using the prerogative of an elder brother and king to do his dirtiest and inexcusable deed. He orders Lakshman to trick Sita to go with him into the forest and abandon her there. As Goldman points out, there is no room for *dharmic* debates now because Ram's *dharma* as king must override his personal devastation, more so because he knows that Sita is utterly pure and blameless. "Suddenly Rama, who has permitted and even praised debate, even angry debate, of his most critical ethical decisions," writes Goldman, "declares his ethically most questionable choice to be beyond discussion, silencing any criticism with a thinly veiled threat of violence. There is no doubt because the issue at hand is none other than the very deeply imbedded one of female sexuality and male honor that lies at the heart of the patriarchal culture of the epic and its audiences."[13] He goes on to say that Valmiki gives several examples of kings who subordinated their dharma to "the emotional and sensual power of women and so come to grief"; Ram knows this well from the examples of his own father and Kaikeyi or the libidinous Ravan, who came to grief. So Ram will forsake his wife and the twins she is carrying in order to protect his kingly honor and his duty to his subjects.

And just when we think that we have understood the *dharmic* priorities in the *Ramayana* we are treated to the ultimate set of *dharmic* reversals in quintessential Hindu style. Many years later when Ram finds Sita and their grown twin sons in the sage Valmiki's hermitage, he requests they all come back to Ayodhya with him. The boys feel insulted on their mother's account and do him battle, reasserting, as it were, matriarchal over patriarchal authority that Ram had once so memorably flouted. Sita, resolute, never again wants to be by Ram's side, as she had once memorably argued, and sets the imperatives of *stridharma* aside. She begs her mother Earth to accept her back; she disappears into a fissure that opens up to receive her. Ram, defeated and repentant, ascends back into the realm of the gods with his assorted retinue.

SO WHAT CAN WE MAKE OF THIS?

Is this a *dharmic* conclusion or a subversion of the moral and social order?

As the story unfolds it is less the story of dharma and all its pious upholding and more a tale of sexual transgression, exploitation, suspicion, and tension. In pondering the subject I was astonished to find how strongly a two-thousand-year-old story still reflects the construction of gender in contemporary Indian society, with many of the sexual mores and behavioral expectations traceable in the present. The power of the *Ramayana* story is deployed today by women, not so much to celebrate the ideal marriage or polity, but as an apt metaphor for their own suffering at the hands of their husbands and a celebration of Sita's endurance and resistance, first of Ravan and then of Ram. It becomes for them, not the heroic epic of a distant age, but an immediate domestic drama in which sexually fraught episodes have catalytic impact on the plot as they do in their own lives. Sita remains very relevant to Hindu women: of course she is the good wife, but she is not just the silent, submissive wife—women see her as strong willed, outspoken in her views against violence, ready to speak out against perceived sexual ha-

---

13. Goldman unpacks this episode in a masterly fashion in "Resisting Rama," 24–29.

rassment (even from Lakshman), unflinching in her resistance against a demon-king even as he threatens to ravish or to kill her, and a hurt but dignified survivor even after her beloved husband abandons her. The many stories I heard from the women's shelter in Delhi as part of my research invoked her as a survivor of the inequality and violence built into a woman's condition rather than the meek and contented wife of the ideal man.

These key episodes diagram gender relations in the overarching context of a patriarchal society. While *kshatryadharma* is no longer germane in a multicultural parliamentary democracy that has officially abolished caste, the *Ramayana* still finds its deepest relevance in domestic relationships. The culture and purport of the extended family emerges in the relationship of wives to husbands in different circumstances: the Ram-Sita relationship stresses faithful monogamy, even though Dasharath, Janak, and Ravan are all polygamous kings. The obedience of a wife is expected, although both Kaikeyi (clearly a selfish wife) and Sita (clearly a model wife) express themselves strongly and boldly when needed and win difficult points against their husbands. While there is no marital violence in the *Katha*, there is mental cruelty and abandonment of a pregnant wife—both unequivocal causes for divorce in the India of today.

In an utterly stupefying soliloquy in *Manas*, Ram addresses the sage, Narad, on the "nature" of woman and why he prevented Narad from marrying. Only a few lines will reveal the profound misogyny that informs the protagonist:

> Lust, anger, greed, pride, and the like are powerful forces in the army of ignorance,
>> but the cruelest of all, the greatest cause of grief,
>> is the personification of *maya*: woman.
> Listen, sage, the Puranans, Veda, and saints say
>> that in the forest of ignorance, woman is the Spring season.
> For the pools of prayer, penance, and piety,
>> Woman is the hot season: she dries them all up.
> Lust, anger, jealousy are frogs, and she
>> is the rainy season that alone delights them. . . . So say the wise.
> A woman is the root of all evil, a source
>> of torment, a mine of sorrows.
> Therefore, sage, understand this, I held you back.[14]

---

14. Cited in full and discussed in Hess, "For the Sake of Brahmans," 9. This is not an obscure verse in the *Manas* but elocuted in the Ram Lila with great verve. Yet, this poem had little effect on my mother and she certainly suppressed it when telling me the story. I telephoned her to ask her what she thought and she admitted that she simply skips the bits she does not like.

I realize that these offensive verses may well reflect a Brahmanic position regarding women rather than a view of Hindu society as a whole, but the popularity of the *Manas* and its accessibility to an enormous base of devotees certainly helps to sustain the bias against women.

The fear of female sexuality is beautifully illustrated in the Surpanakha episode, and even the Kshatriya brothers cannot resist violently punishing a woman who has been sexually provocative. Ram clearly sanctions or tolerates Lakshman's action and seems to contravene his own *kshatriyadharma*—something that he will spend a great deal of his time upholding, discussing, and redeeming. It came up for discussion at Saheli several times and Surpanakha was seen as the agent who destroys Ram and his happy marriage. Sita's refusals, first of Ravan and then of Ram, are a source of inspiration for women who have suffered enormously in their marriages; Sita's refusal to go back to Ram after he abandons her in the forest can also be interpreted as the endorsement for modern divorce. Sita emerges with enormous dignity, self-respect, and power in rejecting subservient wifehood at last, transforming for many women who pay attention to these details the very essence of *stridharma*, imbuing them with courage and finding the *shakti* to endure or fight marital oppression. Suspicion of adultery, sexual jealousy, and related problems of infidelity or incompatibility are as often the cause for violence as drunkenness or money problems or dowry demands.

Women are increasingly aware of their rights; they speak out and seek justice with courage. I will end with a recent case, reported by Pamela Philipose, to show the long and hard journey that lies ahead for women to reject the entrenched patriarchal values that pervade Indian society:

> On September 7, '03, a nurse at the Shanti Mukund Hospital in Delhi was brutally raped by Bhurra, a ward boy in the same hospital. He also gouged out her right eye for good measure. When the case came up in court last week [almost two years later], Bhurra gave an undertaking to marry the nurse to make good his act of assault. The additional sessions judge did not dismiss this out of hand. He asked the assaulted woman for her response to it. She rejected the offer in unequivocal terms. How can she accept a beast who has "handicapped my very sense of being, more than my physical self, as my husband?" she asked. She went on to say that Bhurra's application "is to further humiliate, insult and denigrate my dignity. He committed a crime which should not be repeated." The judge, perhaps chastened by the protests that greeted his decision, then awarded a life term to the accused

after observing that Bhurra's was a "false, frivolous, mischievous and defamatory application with mala fide intention to evade punishment and mislead the court."[15]

What is different here is that the woman did not have to go like Surpanakha to her brother to seek revenge for rape and mutilation. She spoke for herself and the errant judge had to withdraw his obscene suggestion and sentence the violent rapist to a life term in prison. It might be too optimistic to think that patriarchal values and norms can be totally eradicated in India; but there is hope if we can remind the establishment of Valmiki's ending to demonstrate that even Sita, that long-suffering paragon of wifehood, finally passed up the chance to be with Ram. While there are local women's *Ramayanas*, Sita's story needs to be retold from a woman's point of view in print, film, and a blockbuster television series. Violence against women will only cease when women reject the patriarchal conditioning and become the writers of our laws and the retellers of our epics.

---

15. *Indian Express*, Monday, May 9, 2005.

9

Buddhism and Violence against Women

OUYPORN KHUANKAEW

This chapter is written based upon my experience as a Buddhist practitioner who works professionally on issues involving violence against women.[1] My work has involved facilitating educational workshops on violence against women with various Buddhist groups in South and Southeast Asia since 1997. These women and men, both ordained and lay, are from Thailand, Cambodia, Burma, India, Nepal, Bhutan, and Tibet. An autobiographical note will shed light on my provenance. I grew up in a very violent family. As a result I was living in fear and anger throughout my childhood and early adulthood. For so long, I did not trust any man, because if I could not trust my father, the man I loved the most, it was very difficult to trust any men that came along later in my life. I lived with the anger and rejection toward my father even some years after his death.

Although I was born into a traditional Buddhist culture, I was a feminist before I became a Buddhist practitioner. There was nowhere and no one from whom I could learn to understand the domestic violence that I experienced until I discovered feminism during my studies for a master's degree while in my late twenties. Although at some level of my consciousness I knew (even as I knew at a very young age) that my father was

---

1. Sources for this chapter include Walpola Sri Rahula, *What the Buddha Taught* (Bangkok: Haw Trai, 2004); my Buddhist training and understanding is much influenced by Thich Nhat Hanh, a renowned Buddhist teacher, through participating in his retreats and reading his books. To learn more about him and his community see www.plumvillage.org. This chapter is written with lots of support and contribution from my Buddhist activist circle: Kathryn Norsworthy, Ginger Norwood, Kristen Beifus, Ven. Bhikkuni Dhamanandha, and Venerable Bhikku Paisal Visalo. I am grateful for their patience and wisdom.

wrong, that my mother was a good wife and a good mother, and that we were all good children, no one ever told me that I was right. It was a very powerless experience to know that, while I was right, I could not do anything to protect myself and the people I love. Feminism helps me understand why my father was violent and why no one and no institution helped my family when we were in such suffering. Feminism helps me understand violence against women, to know why my family and millions of families around the world live with domestic violence. It helps me to know that it is not my fault when I experience gender-based violence any time anywhere. This wisdom and strength motivate me to study and to work to end violence against women.

Traditional Buddhist culture did not help me understand the suffering that my family and I went through. It did not help me to reconcile with my father. It is only after I became a feminist and learned of the suffering of other women in the Buddhist context that I began to understand how traditional Buddhist culture is one main cause of violence against women. However, when I learned the essence of Buddhism and my practice deepened, I found that Buddhism helped to liberate me from my childhood suffering.

I started to practice meditation because I wanted to have peace and harmony in my personal life. This led me to become a practicing Buddhist in my early thirties. It is the Buddhist practice that helps me work on my anger toward my father. I began to understand that my fear, anger, and alienation from men originated from the relationship with my father. While feminism helps me understand violence against women through my head, it is the Buddhist practices that help me understand it from my heart. Through Buddhist practices I cultivate understanding, compassion, and loving kindness toward my father and myself. I was able to let go of the anger and fear that lay deep inside of me. I learned to know my father not only through my anger and fear but also in his compassion and loving kindness. This is how I continue to be reconciled with him and become healed.

Through my life experiences I learn that the unique principle that feminism and Buddhism share in common is that truth and wisdom are drawn from personal experiences. I use the principles, methods, and practices from Buddhism and feminism as the guiding path to work for peace and justice.

BUDDHISM CONTRIBUTES TO VIOLENCE AGAINST WOMEN

In truth, Buddhism teaches only one thing: suffering and the way to end the suffering. When we do workshops on violence against women with

Buddhist groups we use the Four Noble Truths, the core teachings of Buddhism, as a tool to help participants understand this problem and work together to find ways to end the suffering. The Four Noble Truths consist of suffering, the root causes of suffering, the cessation of the suffering, and the path that leads to the cessation of the suffering. Although there are eighty-four thousand discourses that the Buddha used to teach his disciples for forty years, all of them are expansions and details of this core teaching, particularly the Fourth Truth, the Eightfold Noble Path.

THE FIRST NOBLE TRUTH: The Suffering of Women

In the workshop with Buddhist men and women we draw a picture of an island in the water and discuss with them the nature of the island. For example, it originates deep in the earth. Though we only see the top, the part we call an island, there is the foundation underneath that holds it up. If we want to destroy an island we have to remove the earth underneath it. Then we ask the women participants to identify the forms of suffering that they themselves or other women experience in their family, community, or society. With each form of suffering we ask the participants to decide if the suffering is natural or unnatural. Most of the women with whom we work internalize that the suffering they are experiencing is natural, and thus they cannot do anything about it. They often see the suffering as a result of their past life karma, so they do not believe they can change it. Our questions help them see clearly that being women is an identity that makes a big difference in their life experience. We write those forms of women's suffering on the part of the island that is above the water.

The following are forms of suffering identified by the participants to be caused by Buddhism itself:

- Young girls do not have the opportunity for education in temple.
- Women are told, often by a monk, that the reason they were born as women is because they did not accumulate enough merit in their previous lives; thus, they could not be born in a male form.
- Women are often told by monks to be patient with abusive husbands.
- Women who experience suffering, especially sexual violence, are not able to seek spiritual help from monks because they are not sure of their safety and are not sure the monks have the experience to help them.
- Women are not allowed to enter certain buildings or areas inside temples.
- Women are told that they are an obstacle to the monks' celibate life.

- In some temples paintings about Buddhism depict women as inferior.
- Some temples note in their chanting books that certain sutras are exclusively for monks and male novices to chant.
- The institution of Buddhism defines women who have abortions as religiously immoral.
- Generally women are not selected to be part of the temple committee. The roles they are assigned are merely bringing offerings to the monks, and cooking and cleaning when there is a temple festival.
- Monks and religious institutions are silent about gender-based violence.
- In Thailand it is common to hear news about a monk who exploits women sexually or financially by misleading them into believing that he has a spiritual power to make them attractive to men or to bring back a husband who left his wife for another woman.

Workshop participants described the following special forms of suffering for Buddhist nuns:

- Their identity is not legally and socially accepted; they have no educational or financial support from the government, religious institutions, temples, the public, or their families.
- They have little or no access to living in a temple with food, decent shelter, or guidance from spiritual teachers. Or, if they have these facilities, the conditions are very poor.
- When they go for alms in the morning (within the Theravadha tradition), they are often treated badly. Often parents force their daughters to put aside the robe and return home to take care of them.
- Generally, nuns do not receive respect even if they have been living ascetical lives for a very long time and have undergone long meditation practice or academic Buddhist training.
- Nuns who live in the temples are totally controlled by the monks.
- In Thailand nuns are required to cook for the monks and do the cleaning, often in exchange for living in the temple.
- Some Thai temples put signs outside their temple saying "This temple does not accept nuns."
- In some communities in the Shan state inside Burma, the nuns are not allowed to pass through or stay in the community because it is thought that they bring bad luck to the community and to the people who meet them.

- The Thai interior ministry does not allow the nuns to vote, saying they are not lay women, yet the transportation ministry charges them full fare on public transportation, saying they are not ordained (monks pay only half fare).

- In Thailand some nuns and lay women have been raped or sexually harassed by the monks who were their meditation teachers. Some women were verbally, sexually, and spiritually abused by the monks living in the same temple.

- In Ladakh, northern India, many nuns still live with their families and work on the farm or as the maid of the household. They often have little or no Buddhist training.

THE SECOND NOBLE TRUTH: Ignorance, the Root Cause of the Suffering

After the participants name the various forms of suffering we ask them to think further about the root causes of the existence of this island, what holds it up, and what causes this island of suffering to expand. They identify the factors and institutions that cause, sustain, and reinforce the different forms of violence against women. We locate these root causes in the part of the island submerged beneath the water. The participants reveal that the root causes of violence against women are found in patriarchy, religion, politics, war, consumerism, globalization, media, military dictatorship, poverty, education, law, and the legal systems. In this chapter I will stress patriarchal culture and religion as a source of gender-based violence against women.

It is very important for women to clearly understand the root causes of the violence they face because it helps them to see the big picture. It helps them understand structural violence of the problem, to understand that this is neither their fault nor their karma, nor is it natural. This understanding liberates them from self-blame, passivity, and fault acceptance. We share with workshop participants that the Buddha taught his disciples to remove the root causes of suffering in order to end the suffering. Understanding the root causes and how they reinforce each other also helps women see the necessity of working together collaboratively to end the problem.

Cultural and religious factors that cause women's suffering include:

- Misinterpretation of the texts by monks.
- Misinterpretation of karma.
- Male dominant culture within the Buddhist institutions, state, and society.
- Poor education of monks.

The Misinterpretation of the Texts by Monks

The Buddha's teachings were passed down orally and then recorded by monks from the meeting that was held about four hundred years after the death of the Buddha. Additionally, the texts were translated and written into the languages that are spoken today (Thai, Burmese, Khmer, and Tibetan) by monks. With the internalization of the male dominant culture it was inevitable that the meaning of the Buddha's teachings would be altered, selected, and emphasized according to the worldview and the belief system of the writers and translators. Thus, the texts do not purely express the true spirit of the Buddha's teachings.

As an example, it is common for women in Thailand to be told orally and in writing that they are the enemies of the monk's celibate life. Venerable Dhammananda, the first female monk of Thailand, knows the language of the original text and tells the story behind this verbal abuse. She reports, "Ananda, the close disciple and personal attendant of the Buddha, was a very charming monk. He also had much compassion toward women. Many women knew of this kind monk so they came to see him to seek support. Because Ananda had not attained enlightenment yet, he was impacted by the encounters with beautiful women. The Buddha knew the challenges in Ananda's mind. Then one day the Buddha summoned him and said, 'Ananda, if your mind is not yet strong, you should not stay close to women because the contact could make your mind go astray.' The Buddha meant to teach Ananda to watch and train his mind when he contacted women. The Buddha did not teach Ananda to tell women to keep their distance from him as if women were the enemy of Ananda's practice. The Buddha taught Ananda to take responsibility for his own behavior."

Karma: A Cultural Misinterpretation Perpetuated by Monks' Teachings That Reinforces and Sustains Violence against Women

I first heard the word "karma" from my family when I was quite young. When my father was violent, my desperate mother, unable to protect her children, would cry out loud and keep saying, "What kind of karma have I done? When will this karma end?" My father had many wives and that added more suffering to our family. Eventually I believed that our family had very bad karma because other families did not experience as much suffering as we did.

A close friend of mine had a ten-year marriage with a husband who was an alcoholic. With immense suffering she went to see the monk to ask for spiritual guidance. The monk said to her, "Be patient and keep doing more merit so that one day the accumulated merits will help improve your life." That same monk gave similar advice to her friend whose husband was having an affair with another woman. The monk told her friend, "There is nothing you can do about it, keep being nice to him, do not ever challenge his behavior because you have done bad karma to him in your previous life." Thus the religion is used to blame the victim. Just as Christian women are often taught to bear their cross, Buddhist women are taught to accept their karma.

This is what Buddhist women, not only in Thailand but elsewhere, too, hear over and over again. Here we can see the problem of monks who generally have no knowledge or experience of domestic relationships and have never been trained in counseling, especially with respect to women's or gender issues. With no social knowledge of domestic violence, the monks further reinforce and sustain it by advising the women to be patient and to accept it in order to keep false peace and harmony in the family. Women not only hear these messages from monks but also from their family, friends, neighbors, and the mass media.

What are the consequences for women after hearing these messages? First, women start to internalize self-blame, that the violence is totally their fault, and that they are solely responsible for this problem. Second, women are even more disempowered and even less able to challenge and change the situation. Third, women will continue to suffer in the abusive relationship. The husband will continue his behavior because no individual or institution takes any action to stop him. The children will internalize the problem as normal, seeing their fathers abuse their mothers or abandon them. Boys will eventually do the same thing to their wives when they grow up. Girls will accept this violence as normal if it happens to them the same way it did to their mothers.

This notion of karma as understood and internalized by most Buddhists, women and men, ordained or lay, is the result of the internalization of the male dominant culture. Karma is viewed as permanent and fixed, something from the past life that people who are abused cannot do anything in the present life to change. Instead, one must be patient, accepting, and forgiving. This misinterpretation of karma leads to total ignorance. Furthermore, abusers do not have to take responsibility for their own actions.

At the social level, this wrong and narrow view of karma causes government agencies, religious institutions, and society as a whole not to look seriously at violence against women. Ignorance of the problem leads to the continuation and expansion of violence at every level of society.

The Male Dominant Culture

An essential component of our workshop includes the understanding of the gender roles in cultural contexts. We want women and also men to be able to discover the Buddha's true teachings, to acquire the true spirit of Buddhism toward women. Our goal also is to help people understand the male dominant culture's teachings and its negative influence on Buddhism. Focusing on gender roles in their cultural contexts is also a way to help participants understand the male dominant culture and feminism. This is important because one way people resist the feminist movement in Asia is by saying that this theory and knowledge comes from the West; thus, it is not only irrelevant to our culture but it will destroy our traditions.

We ask participants to name the images, roles, and expectations of men and women in their society. The following are some of their answers, which are very similar across all the countries and ethnicities with which we work.

Man: protector, leader, willing to sacrifice, person with honor, brave, trustworthy, strong, smart and decisive, the breadwinner of the family, the one who takes risks, likes challenges and is very determined, the one whose roles are in the public realm and in politics.

Woman: follower, weak, soft, sensitive, emotional, dependent, polite, gentle, faithful, and sweet, one who is not trustworthy, likes to gossip, jealous, mother and wife, whose main tasks are to raise children, cook, clean, take good care of the family, preserve the culture, good listener to parents and to the husband.

We ask workshop participants to further consider:

What will happen to boys when they grow up with these belief systems, training, and education? They answer, "They will be very confident, have lots of freedom, be leaders, will not be able/willing to listen, particularly to women. They will be self-centered, have lots of ego, be very controlling and possibly very violent."

What will happen when girls grow up with these belief systems and training? They answer: "They will become dependent, have no confidence, have low self-esteem, have narrow worldviews, be good followers, have lots of fears and worries. Their place will be in the kitchen and if they work outside the home their jobs will be in support or service-related work. Their role in public will be as good followers."

Buddhist women and men from many countries in Asia grow up in this culture. These belief systems are reinforced through training and education from different institutions such as the family, village lifestyles, temples, schools, the mass media, workplaces, and politics. Adult women, no matter what class, educational background, or ethnicity, internalize that they cannot live their lives alone, that they need husbands to be their leaders and protectors once they leave their parents' homes. To reinforce this belief system, being a single woman or a widow is a taboo. For women married to abusive husbands, it is very difficult to think about leaving their relationships because of the messages in their heads and all around them. In addition, their fear is understandable, because the reality is that a patriarchal society does not provide support systems for women who decide to leave a marriage. Even parents uphold patriarchal culture by not supporting daughters who leave abusive marriages and by not accepting them back. It is particularly difficult for women with children to leave marriages because of economic and cultural conditions. Many of the women with whom we work tell us that they choose to stay in an abusive relationship because they want their children to have a father.

Male Dominance over Buddhist Institutions

The most significant influence of patriarchy within Buddhism is the refusal or the reluctance of the monks and religious institutions in Tibetan schools and most Theravada Buddhist countries (except Sri Lanka) to allow women full ordination in spite of the Buddhist feminist movement on this issue over the last decade. The Buddha allowed women full ordination more than twenty-five hundred years ago on the grounds that women are equal to men and have the same potential to attain enlightenment. When the first Thai woman was ordained as a novice in 2002, there was very strong resistance from the monks, the religious institutions, and the state. The Thai religious institution's reason for not allowing the ordination of women was that there was never a female monk lineage in our country. This is the same reason that the religious leaders in Burma, Laos, Cambodia, and Tibet in exile give to women.

Within patriarchy, the refusal of female ordination causes further suffering for women. In northern Thailand parents expect the son to pay gratitude to them by taking temporary ordination. That action alone satisfies the parents' expectations and is his responsibility as a son. The ordination ceremony will be very grand and lots of money will be spent. At the time of a parent's funeral, sons may be ordained a day before the cremation so that they can walk in front of the funeral procession to pull the cord leading their parent's coffin. Thus, parents believe that when they die they can hang on to the yellow robe worn by their ordained son to lift them up to a higher realm. Because women cannot be ordained and because of the gender roles designed by patriarchal culture, a daughter's responsibility is to take care of the economic and welfare needs of the parents as long as they are alive. This is a huge and long-term responsibility since many Buddhist countries do not have good social welfare for their older citizens. In the north of Thailand this culture leads many poor women from rural areas into the sex industry.

The Education of the Monks

When a man wears the robe and has his head shaved, his status and power is further lifted up. In Thailand, most monks come from poor families and take ordination as a way to climb the social ladder. The community, the religious institutions, and state agencies provide the monk with food, accommodations, money, and other benefits. After ordination monks are supposed to be trained and supervised for five years under their "Upatcha," the senior monk who ordained them. This, however, is not generally practiced. If some monks go to a Buddhist university the subjects they learn are mostly Buddhist intellectual academic study and a few other secular subjects. In general, monks in many Buddhist countries are neither educated in social issues nor capable of applying what they learn to respond to contemporary social problems, particularly violence against women.

When monks do not practice meditation they are further removed from developing wisdom, a key to understanding suffering and cultivating compassion towards people who are in oppressed situations, as women are. Men in robes with power, privilege, and unquestioned leadership roles can be socially unaware, ignorant, and lacking compassion. Thus, they become an important factor that causes and sustains violence against women.

The examples cited previously show how patriarchy, the foundation for the culture in many Buddhist countries in South and Southeast Asia, has helped establish a deep-rooted misogyny, discrimination, and control over women within Buddhist institutions. When we ask women in workshops which root causes have the most influence in creating violence against women, they emphasize the culture of patriarchy and religion.

THE THIRD NOBLE TRUTH: The Awakened Society and the Cessation of Women's Suffering

Before the Buddha passed away he said that Buddhism would continue and flourish if it was taken care of by four groups of people: ordained men and women, and lay men and women.

From his words it is clearly understandable why Buddhism is currently facing a crisis and in many communities no longer carries the essence of the Buddha's teachings. The oppression of women within Buddhism is one of the main root causes of the crisis. The awakened society must go back to the Buddha's vision of the four groups of people equally involved in sustaining Buddhism. These four groups of people need to share power and leadership roles in using resources, teaching, leading rituals, interpreting, and making meaning of the Buddha's teachings as they are relevant to lived experience and society. The solution to the evils I have described in this chapter can be found in the central teachings of Buddhism. As seen in the other chapters of this book, religions function as cause but can also function as cure for violence against women.

In an enlightened society, women, both lay and ordained, are respected for their values, their religious leadership roles, and their spiritual experiences. These positive images of women can be found in mass media, literature, temple art, religious texts, and rituals. Women and young girls have access to Buddhist educational institutions and meditation practice, thus supporting them to take teaching roles. Women and girls have their own temples where they feel safe, respected, and supported, and where spiritual assistance is provided to women who are experiencing suffering. Young girls have more choices and will be supported if they choose to live a monastic life, either for the short or long term.

In this awakened vision, Buddhists are actively involved in social work. Monks, nuns, and lay men and women are living in harmonious, trusting, and respectful relationship with each other. Violence against women and other forms of violence in society are reduced. Girls, boys, women, and men have more choices, space, and freedom in deciding their lifestyles. Boys, men, and monks are not living in fear, hatred, or disconnection from themselves and others—particularly women.

THE FOURTH NOBLE TRUTH: The Paths to the Cessation of Women's Suffering

The Fourth Truth is generally called the Eightfold Noble Path: the vision and knowledge that lead to peace, insights, and enlightenment, a state of the end of suffering. The Buddha discovered this path through his practice and then taught it for forty-five years. This is the essence of his teaching and it is composed of eight categories: Right View, Right Thinking, Right Speech, Right Action, Right Livelihood, Right Effort, Right Mindfulness, and Right Concentration. These eight categories are interconnected and each helps cultivate the others. The eight categories aim to promote and perfect the three essentials of Buddhist training and practice: wisdom, ethical conduct, and mental discipline.

Wisdom Paths

The first two paths comprise wisdom and consist of right view and right thinking.

RIGHT VIEW. The Buddha taught that right view means *the acknowledgement of the Four Noble Truths—that there is suffering, there are root causes that lead to the suffering, there is cessation of suffering, and there are ways or paths to the cessation of suffering.* The right view means the acknowledgement of women's suffering and understanding the root causes of women's suffering. It means to believe that the cessation of women's suffering is possible once the root causes are removed, and the way to achieve that state is to follow the right paths.

Let us consider right view on the notion of karma. Karma means action, and the consequences of the action becomes causes of further action. Our present is a result of our past, and it will determine our future.

Gender-based violence is not a result of the previous life karma of an individual; it is a manifestation of the long-term accumulation of collective ignorance rooted in the socialization and internalization of patriarchy by women, men, communities, and society. In other words, it is because of the past and present ignorance practiced by people individually and collectively. Therefore, it is crucial that we make sure that we do not commit violence to ourselves and others and that we prevent others from committing violence to themselves and others.

Having the right view on interconnectedness will also mitigate violence against women. In Buddhism we believe that nothing exists by itself. Everything interconnects with many other things for existence. Violence against women is neither a personal problem nor an independent action, no matter how the patriarchal culture misleads us. The violence that individual women experience is a result of the structural violence whereby patriarchal society sets up the framework and the conditions that allow the violence to take place. Individual men, groups of men, or collective institutions acting against women are the result of the interconnectedness of various factors. Violence against women is an interaction of various elements, such as patriarchal culture, the lack of laws to protect women, media, economics, war, and conflict. Understanding the interconnectedness helps us see the problem from the bigger picture. With this understanding, when facing violence against women, it helps us not to find fault only in a particular perpetrator, whether it is an individual, group, or institution. Particularly when our actions are driven by anger or hatred, we can lose sight of the big picture if we only focus our energy and emotions on fixing, changing, or getting rid of one particular actor alone.

In order to remove the root causes of suffering we need to work at the individual and structural levels. When an individual creates new karma, such as stopping violence against women, it affects the structural level. When structural change takes place, such as the promotion of women's ordination, individual women's lives improve.

Finally, right view on nonself and impermanence helps us to understand that gender is socially constructed by human beings. One of the main teachings of the Buddha is nonself. The Buddha said that women, as well as men, have potential to attain enlightenment. This means that enlightenment is beyond gender. Therefore, being stuck in gender roles created by patriarchal ignorance is in itself an obstacle to enlightenment.

Patriarchy is socially constructed by society and like everything else it will cease once the conditions holding it up no longer exist. Impermanence helps us to be aware that as strong and deeply rooted as patriarchy is, it does not escape the nature of impermanence. Oftentimes we feel it has always been like this, so it will never change, no matter how much and how long we try. As activists we can get burned out and feel despair when dealing with the problem of violence against women. Holding to the truth of impermanence helps us not to forget that there is an end to this suffering. Impermanence, therefore, is a source of hope.

RIGHT THINKING. The Buddha taught that *right thinking means to think of not harming oneself and others and to think of ways to stop unwholesome deeds without ill intention.*

When thinking about the issue of violence against women it is important to first look at our intention and what it is in our mind. Right thinking comes from having the right view toward the suffering that others or we are facing. Right thinking is about having clarity and pure intention in our mind before or while taking action. It helps to ask ourselves: "What is happening? What causes this to happen? What right actions can I take? What are the aims of my actions? Am I doing this for myself, my ego, because it disturbs me, or to relieve the suffering of others?" Clear thinking comes from the mind that is calm and awake. Without right thinking we can make the situation worse. When we think with ill intention we will create the negative factors that will cause the cycle of suffering to continue or expand.

Ethical Conduct Paths

The next three paths are part of ethical conduct. They consist of right speech, right action, and right livelihood.

Right view and right thinking comprise the basic wisdom that we use as the foundation and guidance for our ethical conduct. Right speech, right action, and right livelihood offer skillful means to guide our actions when we deal with the issue of violence against women. The reason we have to act with skillful means is because we all are part of the dominant patriarchal culture and have internalized it deeply. In patriarchal culture we are trained to become a man or a woman, to think and act in the ways that the culture expects and trains us. Our thoughts and actions tend to become automatic, and we do not challenge or ask ourselves why.

If we are mindlessly acting without right thinking and right view we will naturally accept, ignore, or participate in the problematic system. For example, it is so common when we hear the story of a wife being beaten by a husband to think, "Oh, this couple does that all the time"(accepting it), or, "She must have done something wrong to deserve that"(participating in the system), or, "It is terrible! I wish that would not happen but I cannot do anything to help" (ignoring it). We need to address the problem with right view and right thinking so that our actions produce a clear and clean karma that will lead to reducing or ending the suffering.

RIGHT SPEECH. The Buddha taught that *right speech means avoiding false and rude speech, not saying things that cause disharmony and conflict, and not gossiping or engaging in meaningless chatter.*

Speaking up about any form of violence against women is speaking the truth. Particularly in domestic violence, when a woman reaches out and asks for help, we need not to traumatize her further by saying, "You must have done something wrong," or, "This is your karma." We have to challenge and educate monks, lay men, and women, when we hear them giving these messages to women.

We have to speak out about violence against women because both the man and woman suffer physically, mentally, and spiritually. The woman suffers from the violence and the man also suffers because he lives in anger, hatred, and ignorance. Both of them lose the ability to purify their body, speech, and mind, a path to attain enlightenment.

RIGHT ACTION. The Buddha taught that *right action is about not harming, not stealing, and not being involved in sexual misconduct.*

With this right action we will do whatever we can to stop violence against women and to help remove the root causes of violence that harm women and, ultimately, men. One of the actions we can take when helping a woman who has experienced violence is to offer her *deep listening.* If we do not have these skills we can ask others who do have listening skills to help. Listening is an art to be learned.

We want be mindful in our daily lives not to do anything that supports the continuation of violence against women. For example, when we see a company that uses women's bodies as sexual objects in their advertising, we can give that company feedback or we can boycott their products. We can refrain from consuming media or information that exploits women. We can educate our children about the impact of a mass media that depicts violence against women. Right action may include becoming involved in creating new laws to protect women and that take action against men and institutions that commit violence against women. Creating structural transformation might take the form of demanding that religious institutions and state agencies give women leading roles in religion. We can advocate for the implementation of mechanisms that require monks and religious institutions to be held responsible for violating women's rights and dignity. We can involve ourselves in educating both male and female monks and novices on gender issues and other relevant social issues. Reforming Buddhist education, training, and the process of ordination, particularly for monks, is a crucial action to help Buddhism become relevant to the modern world.

Especially important is action with understanding (wisdom) and compassion. To live our life based upon the Buddha's teachings is often described as being a bird with two wings, wisdom and compassion. There is a story of the Dalai Lama meeting with his friend, an elderly monk, who had left Tibet to join the Tibetan community living in exile in northern India after living twenty years in Chinese prisons and labor camps as a result of participating in a nonviolent protest against the Chinese government's occupation of Tibet. During those twenty years the monk faced immense suffering from brutality, isolation, and fear. When they met, the Dalai Lama asked his friend, "Were there ever times when your life was truly in danger?" The monk paused and answered, "There were only a few occasions when I faced real danger, and those were the occasions I was in danger of losing my compassion for the Chinese." The monk's action represents the heart of the Buddhist teachings—wisdom and compassion. His wisdom guided him to protest against the unwholesome deeds committed by the Chinese authorities to take over Tibet. But when they tortured him he responded to them with compassion, understanding that their action was done as a result of hatred, anger, and ignorance. He was in jail facing great physical suffering but his mind was in peace and freedom.

In the early years of my work I often felt angry, frustrated, hopeless, and isolated. It was not until I committed myself to Buddhist practice that I was able to deal with these emotional challenges more effectively. I have learned to understand the interconnectedness of wisdom and compassion that I need to have when facing any form of violence or resistance, particularly from men.

What helps me to understand their resistance is the awareness of the deep-rooted internalization of patriarchy in people's thinking and behavior. What helps me to be calm, patient, and aware of what is going on when I face resistance is the understanding that they, too, are victims of patriarchy. This understanding helps me to have compassion and loving kindness toward their suffering and ignorance, the same way I have for my father. I realize that it is not the person that is the problem I am working to change, but it is the deep-rooted patriarchal culture with which I am dealing. This understanding helps me not to take the adversity personally. I understand that while I demand from men their understanding, compassion, and loving kindness for myself and other women, the only way I will succeed is to give the same things that I demand from them. The transformation can only come from this understanding and compassion. We all suffer from the same violent culture.

Buddhism believes that everyone and every sentient being has Buddha nature, an awakening nature, a potential to attain enlightenment. When we believe that the perpetrators also have the seeds of enlightenment, also want peace and happiness, but, like us, have ignorance or make mistakes, we see no separation between us and them. We will have compassion and loving kindness toward them the same way we have toward ourselves when we are vulnerable. And we will do anything we can to help them realize their suffering and ignorance so that the seeds of awakening are growing in them.

RIGHT LIVELIHOOD. The Buddha taught that *right livelihood means to be involved in the livelihood that does not support killing, stealing, sexual misconduct, lying, and consuming toxic materials.*

With this path all forms of livelihood that support peace, safety, self-fulfillment, and respect of women are encouraged and promoted.

Mental Discipline Paths

The next three paths comprise the mental discipline. They are right mindfulness, right effort, and right concentration. Mental discipline involves training the mind rightfully when we take action.

RIGHT CONCENTRATION. We cultivate mental discipline through Samatha and Vipassana. Samatha meditation is the practice of concentration, stopping, and calming the mind. Vipassana means the ability to look deeply so that we can see clearly the very nature of all things: impermanence, interconnectedness, no separate self, and suffering.

RIGHT MINDFULNESS. Mindfulness helps us to be aware of our own mind because it is the mind that guides our speech and actions. This is particularly important for helpers, such as counselors, family members, friends, neighbors, medical people, religious leaders, healers, or concerned government officers, so as not to be trapped by our own internalized patriarchal belief systems. We have to be mindful and keep reminding ourselves not to replicate the dynamics of oppression when helping women.

Mindfulness aids helpers in reminding themselves to support women in a power-sharing way. It also helps create wisdom and inner peace, the core elements needed by helpers to work with women to end their suffering. Helpers can then work with women to first use the Four Noble Truths to understand the suffering that they have experienced. With understanding, calmness, compassion to self and others, and the ability to let go of past suffering, women survivors of violence can live in the present and have the wisdom to think about their future.

Working against a long and deep history of discrimination and oppression is very stressful and extremely difficult. And because of those challenges we often get angry and feel hatred toward the people, groups, or institutions that are involved in the oppression. Cultivating mindfulness practices will help us to not be overcome by the negative energy of bias, greed, anger, hatred, burn-out, and hopelessness.

RIGHT EFFORT. Wisdom guides us to learn why there is a problem and to know when and how to take action. Mindfulness, compassion, and loving kindness guide the way we act. These elements also help us practice letting go when the actions we take do not produce immediate results or meet our expectations, so that we will not lose our motivation, blame ourselves, or feel like giving up. Instead we let go of our attachment to the outcome.

After the three-month Buddhist Peace Building training, many women from Burma reflected how their new understanding of karma, the Four Noble Truths, and the daily mindfulness practices helped transform their suffering. One woman from the Shan state said, "Now I can forgive the Burmese soldiers who caused suffering to my family. And I understand why my mother become an alcoholic and I wanted to help her out." She also said, "a four-year-old girl was raped in my community, and everyone said it was because of her previous life karma, but now I understand that it was not a right understanding and we have to educate our community about violence against women and children."

Another woman who lives in exile in Bangladesh said, "I never knew of the Four Noble Truths before. If my people understand this teaching they will take responsibility for our social problem because it is not our previous life karma."

After the second feminist Buddhist counseling training in the northeastern part of Thailand, one of the women told me that she is now leaving her abusive relationship. She said, "I understand clearly now the real meaning of karma and the right view, and right thinking helps me realize that there is no need for me to continue to suffer in this relationship."

CLOSING

Violence against women has a deep connection with other forms of violence such as war, the use of violence by state agencies in suppressing citizens, and excessive police force in dealing with drug or crime issues. Human beings first learn to control and exploit each other within their own families. One of the most common forms of violence existing in every society is gender-based violence. When we accept, ignore, or feel powerless to deal with the violence in our family, then it is very easy for us to accept and ignore or feel powerless to deal with other forms of violence in society.

The Four Noble Truths awaken us to see the suffering of women, its root causes, and the ways to end it. The Eightfold Noble Path guides us to create an awakened society. Although we have not yet achieved the state of no suffering, by working and living our lives along this path we are already living an awakening experience. Awakening is about seeing and being, truly being.

10

"I will espouse you with righteousness and justice":
Domestic Violence and Judaism

LIORA GUBKIN

The family portrait on the screen shows two young, smiling boys with their parents, Marc Friedlander, a successful CPA and member of the local synagogue board, and Zitta Friedlander, a physicist and active member of B'nai B'rith Women, a Jewish women's service organization. The camera shifts to nineteen-year-old Adam Friedlander, speaking more than a decade after the portrait was taken. "Nothing indicated my father was an abuser," he says, "except for his words and his actions." Although a psychiatrist had been informed that Marc bought a gun and showed it to his children, the doctor concluded that a man with Marc's education and standing in the community would not use it. When Marc shot Zitta thirteen times in a parking lot while dropping off the children for an arranged custody visit, the psychiatrist was proved tragically mistaken. Zitta's friends at B'nai B'rith Women were among those shocked and devastated by her murder in 1988. Ultimately, one response to the loss was a new organizational mission: to eradicate domestic violence in the Jewish community. The March 2005 premiere of *When Push Comes to Shove, It's No Longer Love* at the Second International Conference on Domestic Abuse in the Jewish Community, sponsored by Jewish Women International (formerly BBW) was a moving testament to their progress. Adam appeared as one of five Jewish young adults featured in the short documentary on the subject of teens and "unhealthy relationships." The film also demonstrated how much work remains as the four women in the video tell heartbreaking and harrowing stories of how their search for the dream Jewish husband became a nightmare.

This essay uses the conference, "Pursuing Truth, Justice and Righteousness: A Call To Action—The Second International Conference on Domestic Abuse in the Jewish Community" (attended by more than five hundred advocates, rabbis, survivors, JWI members, academics, Jewish communal workers, social workers, and volunteers from thirty states and six countries), as a touchstone event to examine domestic violence in the Jewish community. The vignettes presented throughout this chapter answer two questions, contributing to this volume's multifaith examination of women, religion, and violence: First, in what ways do Jewish religious, cultural, and social norms enable or perpetuate a climate that allows intimate partner violence against women? Second, what aspects of Jewish tradition provide potential resources for critique, prevention, and healing?

"IT DOESN'T HAPPEN HERE": Recognizing and Defining Intimate Partner Violence

One out of every three U.S. women reports being physically or sexually abused by a husband or boyfriend at some point in her life.[1] The definition of intimate partner violence recognized by the U.S. Department of Justice covers physically violent acts of "rape, sexual assault, robbery, aggravated assault, and simple assault," and the U.S. National Crime Victimization Survey reported "691,710 nonfatal violent victimizations committed by current or former spouses, boyfriends, or girlfriends of the victims during 2001."[2] Eighty-five percent of these attacks were against women. A full 20 percent of violent crime against women in 2001 was intimate partner violence. In addition, one-third of female murder victims in 2000 were murdered by an intimate partner. These statistics present the horrific reality of physical violence among intimate partners, but physical violence is only one tool an abuser uses to control his victim.[3] In contrast to legal definitions of abuse, social definitions highlight psychological, economic, emotional, and sexual dimensions of domestic violence. Each may

---

1. Commonwealth Fund, Health Concerns across a Woman's Lifespan: 1998 Survey of Women's Health, May 1999. Cited in Michelle Lifton and Leigh Nachman Hofheimer, *Is There Really Domestic Violence in Jewish Families?* PowerPoint presentation, JWI International Conference, "Domestic Abuse in the Jewish Community," March 20, 2005.
2. Bureau of Justice Statistics Crime Data Brief, Callie Marie Rennsion, "Intimate Partner Violence, 1993–2001" (Washington, D.C.: U.S. Department of Justice Bureau of Justice Statistics, 2003).
3. Although men may be victims and women may be perpetrators, although same-sex relationships are not immune to intimate partner abuse, in the vast majority of domestic violence cases, a man is the abuser and a woman is the victim of abuse. In the context of this work on religion's role in violence against women, I will use the male pronoun to refer to the abuser and the female pronoun to refer to the victim.

play a part in the systematic attempt to control one's partner, and as survivors, activists, and case workers all attest, the underlying motivation for these forms of violence is a desire for the abuser to control his partner. This difference between legal and social definitions holds important consequences. To the extent that the legal system is a helpful resource, it responds primarily to isolated incidents of physical violence.[4] The power and control wheel developed by the Domestic Abuse Intervention Project of Duluth, Minnesota, in the 1980s is used throughout the world to recognize, name, and respond to the myriad forms of domestic abuse. It was developed through interviews with battered women in support groups who were asked to identify the ways they felt controlled and through interviews with men in batterer groups who were asked what specific tactics they used to create and maintain power and control in their relationships. Power and control occupy the center of the wheel, and the spokes radiating outward identify various tactics: economic abuse, including maintaining sole access to family income; male privilege; using the children, including threatening to take them away; minimizing, denying, and blaming; isolation; emotional abuse, including making her think she is crazy; intimidation, coercion, and threats. The rim of the wheel, which keeps the wheel together and in motion, is physical and sexual violence. Today one can find power and control wheels (on following page) adapted for the specific needs of teens, lesbians, and gays, Native women, people with disabilities, immigrants, and the elderly.[5]

What would occupy the spokes of a Jewish power and control wheel? When a room full of Jewish survivors and communal workers were asked this question, answers—some of which will be considered subsequently—flowed all too easily. Yet, the myth persists within the Jewish community, and even in the larger society, that "it doesn't happen here." Rabbi Susan Grossman called the community to account in her opening plenary of the Second International Conference on Judaism and Domestic Abuse: "Too long we believed 'not in our homes.' . . . We need people to tell their stories and for others to listen with compassion, believing that truth." This includes refuting stereotypes and misconceptions that prevent Jews from seeing that domestic violence "does happen here." Some of the most pernicious stereotypes are about Jewish women. The image of the Jewish

---

4. Hofheimer, legal advocate at the Washington State Coalition against Domestic Violence, refers to physical abuse as "the tip of the iceberg that breaks the surface of water" in cases of intimate partner abuse.

5. National Center on Domestic and Sexual Violence, "Wheels" Adapted from the Power and Control Wheel Model ([cited June 27, 2005]); available from http://www.ncdsv.org /publications_wheel.html. Used by permission of the Domestic Abuse Prevention Project, 202 E. Superior Street, Duluth, MN 55802, 218-722-2781, www.duluth-model.org.

POWER AND CONTROL WHEEL

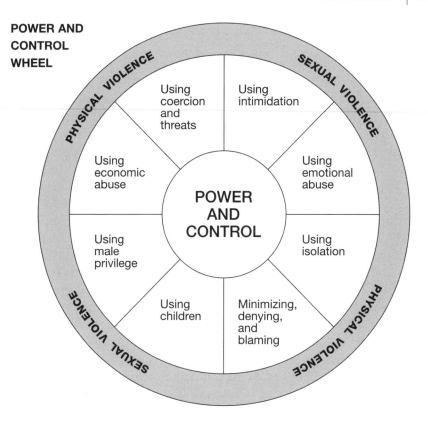

American princess (JAP) suggests that Jewish women are pampered and privileged, not battered and abused. As one advocate was informed: domestic violence for a Jewish woman means "the coffee isn't hot enough." Not only does the JAP image deny and belittle abuse, it also serves to blame the victim. If she is such an unbearable princess, then it is not his fault—she is too demanding, too much to take. If a Jewish woman is not dismissed as a pampered and privileged princess, she may be viewed as "the Jewish mother" (or mother-in-law) who rules the roost—both her husband and her sons—and could not possibly be dominated, controlled, and terrorized, since she herself is completely domineering. Stereotypes of Jewish women are most virulent, but Jewish men are not immune. Jewish men are seen as bookish, not physically strong, and thus incapable of inflicting physical harm. Besides, as another stereotype suggests, Jews use words, not fists—and what's the harm in words?[6] These images of Jewish

---

6. The question is rhetorical. Powerful elements of the power and control wheel such as coercion, threats, intimidation, emotional abuse, minimizing, denying, and blaming create wounds inflicted through language.

men also minimize and obscure the reality of domestic abuse in Jewish families.

In addition to gender-specific stereotypes, other damaging misperceptions relate to issues of class. Many people erroneously believe that domestic violence does not afflict wealthy or college-educated people.[7] David Rose, a Conservative rabbi and currently a member of Jewish Women International's National Clergy Task Force on Domestic Abuse, admits that he attended his first program on domestic violence in the Jewish community only because it was held in his synagogue. Reflecting upon attending that event in 1993, Rose says, "I couldn't imagine any of the successful women sitting before me as victims." However, an anonymous letter from a congregant in the room began his education about "the Torah of domestic violence." Rose's dedication to the issue is still the exception and his previous perception the norm, as class-based discrimination colludes with communal denial and adds to the difficulty for upper-middle- and upper-class women to recognize and name their experience. The yelling, pushing, and punching they endure is not abuse—it's "a communication problem." Furthermore, to the extent that their status, and sometimes even their sense of self, is dependent on a husband's income or standing in the community, they may be unable or unwilling to reveal the abuse to others. Weitzman argues that "what distinguishes upscale violence is that this wife isolates herself and keeps the abuse hidden as a direct result of her social class and the environment in which she has been raised and currently resides."[8]

In addition to pernicious stereotypes, there are also specific Jewish events and norms that contribute to denial and silence. For some Jews, the Shoah remains a trauma of such magnitude and consequence that no other

---

7. Embedded in this misperception that educated and prosperous men do not abuse is the assumption that Jews are educated and prosperous, a truth for some—but certainly not all—Jews. The most recent survey of the American Jewish community reports that the median income for the approximately three million Jews who identified as Jews by religion is $72,000; the median income for Jews who identified as Jews by birth but not religion is $58,000. Fifty-eight percent of all Jews are college graduates. Laurence Kotler-Berkowitz, et al., "The National Jewish Population Survey 2000–01: Strength, Challenge, and Diversity in the American Jewish Population" (United Jewish Communities and the Mandell L. Berman Institute—North American Jewish Data Bank, 2004). When reading these numbers, one must also ask who controls the money. "Although it may appear that Jewish women living middle- and upper middle-class lives have access to money, abusers often deny their victims access to the family's financial resources." Jewish Women International, "Key Findings from the National and Chicagoland Needs Assessments: A Portrait of Domestic Abuse in the Jewish Community" (Washington, D.C.: Jewish Women International, 2004), 10.
8. Susan Weitzman, *"Not to People Like Us": Hidden Abuse in Upscale Marriages* (New York: Basic Books, 2000), 103.

suffering can be spoken.[9] If the Holocaust is part of one's personal family legacy, speaking out can be especially difficult. Letty Cottin Pogrebin observed in her opening plenary that often "children of Holocaust survivors don't go public because they want to spare their parents further suffering."[10] Her claim was borne out during the survivor speakout as one social worker anonymously spoke of her own encounter with violence, her reluctance to speak, and her Holocaust-survivor mother's unwillingness/inability to hear the specifics of her daughter's trauma.

After the Holocaust, survival and safety are keywords of the Jewish community, and Jewish communal organizations regularly raise funds by highlighting threats made by outsiders, including the "threat" of intermarriage, in their appeal letters. Ending domestic abuse *within* the community, however, does not appear as a priority. Even when it is discussed within the Jewish community, often it is still about someone else. Orthodox Jews are certain that abuse exists in liberal Jewish homes that don't observe the commandments; Conservative and Reform Jews are certain abuse exists in Orthodox homes that are strongly shaped by traditional gender roles.[11] During a session on the role of clergy, attended by Jews representing a range of possible affiliations, interdenominational tensions lurked just below the surface when panelists were asked about a correlation between rigid gender roles and violence. Reform Rabbi

---

9. On this issue see Laura Levitt, "Intimate Engagements: A Holocaust Lesson," *Nashim: A Journal of Jewish Women's Studies and Gender Issues* 7 (spring 2004): 190–205. Similarly, there has been reluctance in many segments of the religious and scholarly communities to focus on gender-specific abuse that occurred during the Holocaust for fear that it would somehow minimize or trivialize the event. See Myrna Goldenberg, "Memoirs of Auschwitz Survivors: The Burden of Gender," and Joan Ringelheim, "The Split between Gender and the Holocaust," both in *Women in the Holocaust,* ed. Dalia Ofer and Lenore J. Weitzman (New Haven, Conn.: Yale University Press, 1998), for elaboration of this point. Friedman's analysis of survivor testimonies, however, suggests that sexuality was often an important dimension for survivors' own understanding of their experiences. Jonathan Friedman, *Speaking the Unspeakable: Essays on Sexuality, Gender, and Holocaust Survivor Memory* (Lanham, Md.: University Press of America, 2002).

10. Letty Cottin Pogrebin, "The Misery behind the Mezuzah: Domestic Abuse in the Jewish Community" (keynote address at Jewish Women International Conference on Domestic Abuse in the Jewish Community, Washington, D.C., March 2005, photocopy), 6.

11. On these interdenominational tensions, see Carol Goodman Kaufman, *Sins of Omission: The Jewish Community's Reaction to Domestic Violence* (Boulder, Colo.: Westview Press, 2003). Judaism includes four main denominations or movements. Orthodox is an umbrella term that refers to many different traditional groups. Conservative, Reform, and Reconstructionist are the more "liberal" movements within Judaism. There are also humanist Jews, as well as Jews who identify as Jews by birth rather than by religion. According to the 2000–01 National Jewish Population Survey, of the 46 percent of American Jews who belong to a synagogue 38 percent are Reform, 33 percent Conservative, 22 percent Orthodox, 2 percent Reconstructionist, 5 percent other types. Cited in Kotler-Berkowitz, "The National Jewish Population Survey 2000–01," 7.

Drorah Setel was quick to question the research and its applicability to Orthodox families. Orthodox Rabbi Mark Dratch urged everyone to focus on the goals we share, rather than focus on differences in views about gender and, thus, destroy the possibility for coalitions on the work that needs to be done. Conservative Rabbi Susan Grossman proposed a "litmus test" in response: "If a woman is afraid to articulate a desire to change roles," she suggested, "then it is not a safe relationship."

Recognizing domestic violence in one's own community remains difficult as many Jews, both secular and across the denominational spectrum, "are deeply invested in the idea that we are morally superior and less violent than other people."[12] More research is needed, but anecdotal evidence from Jewish and secular social service agencies along with the few studies we do have suggest that domestic violence occurs among Jews at the same rate as within the larger population.[13] As conference participant Rita Moskowitz, a lay leader of the Jewish community in Tulsa, Oklahoma, summed it up, "we need a Jewish/Yiddish way to name the problem."

SHALOM BAYIT: Marriage, Divorce, and the Peaceful Jewish Home

While a Jewish name for intimate partner violence may not yet exist, there is a name for the Jewish ideal. Literally, *shalom bayit* means, "peace in the home." In a household characterized by family harmony, husband and wife love, respect, and honor one another.[14] Sometimes the Jewish sources place responsibility for shalom bayit on both husband and wife, but often it is understood primarily as the responsibility of the wife who is "the foundation of the home."[15] The ideal of shalom bayit can be misused to

---

12. Pogrebin, "The Misery Behind the Mezuzah," 8.

13. Advocates within the Jewish community note a need for current research with larger samples than currently available. The most recent studies, the 2003 National Needs Assessment and Chicagoland Needs Assessment studies conducted by Jewish Women International, "were not designed to provide statistically significant data" but, in keeping with anecdotal reports from multiple sources, assert "domestic abuse is at least as common among Jews as it is in the general population" (7). For summaries of earlier studies see Amanda Sisselman, "Shalom Bayit: Peace in the Home; Whose Responsibility Is It?" (master's thesis, State University of New York, Albany, n.d.). See also Mimi Scarf, "Marriages Made in Heaven? Battered Jewish Wives," in *On Being a Jewish Feminist*, ed. Susannah Heschel (New York: Schocken Books, 1983), 51–64.

14. The traditional ideal of a Jewish home presumes heterosexual marriage and a goal of procreation.

15. See Sholom B. Wineberg, *Eternal Joy, volume 3. A Guide to Shidduchim and Marriage Based on the Teachings of the Lubavitcher Rebbe, Rabbi Menachem M. Schneerson. Chapter 3: The Wife and Shalom Bayis* ([cited April 22 2005]); available from http://www.sichosinenglish.org/books/eternal-joy-3/10.htm, for an example of a contemporary use of the classical sources. The terms "classical sources" or references to "the rabbis" most

hold a woman responsible for fixing a disharmonious marriage, compelling her to return to a man who batters. "Why Can't She Keep Shalom Bayis," a pamphlet from three organizations in the New York area, is targeted toward Orthodox Jewish families and directly critiques the role this concept continues to have in legitimating abuse and in preventing women from seeking help.[16] The pamphlet quotes Rabbi Abraham J. Twerski, M.D., whose work broke the silence surrounding Judaism and domestic abuse, especially in the Orthodox Jewish community.[17]

> Is shalom bayis her responsibility?
> Response: Shalom bayis is indeed a sacred concept, but it is the responsibility of both husband and wife that this is achieved. To say that the Torah advocates a woman sacrificing herself to tolerate lifelong abuse is unconscionable. This is hardly what the Torah wants. The Torah condemns human sacrifice. It is a mistake to think that the entire responsibility for shalom bayis rests on the shoulders of the wife.[18]

Some women perceive the practices and values connected with shalom bayit as the primary source for their devotion to God. Their religious obligations are fulfilled through their husband and children.[19] In tight-knit Orthodox communities a woman may decide not to seek help for fear it will prevent a good *shidduchim*, a marriage match for her children.[20]

These women wish a good match for their children, but even a good marriage is based on an inequality in Jewish law. Modern Jewish wedding ceremonies draw upon the understanding of marriage developed in the Mishnah and Talmud, rabbinic texts from the second to sixth centuries CE.[21]

---

often refer to the authoritative literature of the Talmud, written between the 2nd and 6th centuries CE, and later commentaries known as codes and responsa. Most Orthodox and many Conservative Jews refer to the Talmud as Oral Torah and consider it revelation given at Sinai at the same time as the Written Torah.

16. "Bayit" and "Bayis" are two transliterations of the same Hebrew word.

17. Abraham J. Twerski, *The Shame Borne in Silence: Spouse Abuse in the Jewish Community* (Pittsburgh: Mirkov Publications, 1996).

18. See Grace Jantzen's essay in this volume on the ideal of women's sacrifice.

19. There are three obligations (*mitzvot*) particular to women: making challah (the braided bread eaten on Shabbat); lighting the Shabbat candles; and observing the laws of family purity (*niddah*)—including attending the ritual bath after menstruation—which regulate sexual relations within marriage.

20. This point was made several times during the conference by people who work with women from large Orthodox communities in Baltimore, Israel, New Jersey, and New York.

21. The following explanation is indebted to the work of Rachel Adler whose work *Engendering Judaism: An Inclusive Theology and Ethics* (New York: Jewish Publication Society, 1998) offers a re-visioning of Jewish law in an attempt to transform the Jewish marriage ceremony into a covenant-making between equals.

A woman is acquired (*kinyan*) by a man, and that transaction is made holy (*kiddushin*). *Kinyan*, acquisition, is a legal concept derived from Talmudic property law, and it is the method by which a woman is transferred from one man—usually her father—to another, her husband. The rabbis place women, slaves, and fields in the same category and use biblical text to support the analogy noting that the same verb is used in Genesis when Abraham "takes" a field from Ephron (Gen. 23:13) and when a man "takes" a wife (Deut. 22:13). In the Talmud an exchange of money becomes the one acceptable method for a legal "taking" of a wife. One reason marriage is *kiddushin*—holy or sacred—is that the couple makes a contract to live according to the norms of the Jewish community and to build a Jewish home together, and their contract is witnessed by the community. In this sense, a marriage is kiddushin because the couple is joining a larger community. But kiddushin also means "to set apart," and the rabbinic development of kiddushin as an aspect of marriage was also meant to indicate that the woman is set apart; she is no longer available to other men. She is the property of her husband alone, and—unlike slaves or fields—she cannot be rented out or shared with others. The rabbis turn once again to the Bible for analogy and metaphor. *Hekdesh* is the term used for property that is "set apart" and earmarked as a pledge for the Temple. As the sanctified aspect of marriage comes to dominate the liturgy, the transfer of money in kinyan is reduced to a symbolic role. However, it does not disappear, and it is not rejected. As Adler notes, "while the purchase of the bride may have dwindled to a mere formality in the rabbinic transformation of marriage, her *acquisition* is no formality."[22] This symbolism is clear in the ceremonial actions of a traditional wedding. The groom places a ring on the forefinger of the bride's right hand and says, "you are hereby sanctified unto me with this ring according to the laws of Moses and Israel." The officiating rabbi then reads the contract, the *ketubah*, which lists the groom's obligations to the bride. Patriarchal marriage is now holy.

In traditional Judaism a woman cannot legally initiate termination of her marriage. Both the process and the document that render the *ketubah*, the marriage contract, null and void are called a *get*. The get must be freely given by the husband and freely accepted by the wife. The legal requirement for a get affects Orthodox and Conservative Jews and all Jews within the state of Israel, and refusal by some men to grant a get to their wives has resulted in the suffering of women who become *agunah*, chained women. An agunah cannot remarry; her children would be

---

22. Adler, *Engendering Judaism*, 176.

mamzerim, bastards and forbidden to marry according to Jewish law. In cases of domestic abuse, withholding a get is a powerful tool for control. Modern rabbis have recognized this connection. Chatam Sofer, the eighteenth-century rabbi whose students were the creators of ultra-Orthodox Judaism, said, "We do not force a wifebeater to grant a divorce because it's better to live in two than to dwell alone."[23] Fortunately, we do find dissenting voices in twenty-first-century Orthodoxy. Rabbi Tzvi Weinreb, executive vice president of Orthodox Union, also recognizes that the get can be misused to continue control and abuse: "When a man withholds a get, nine times out of ten he was also guilty of physical violence in the marriage. . . . We rabbis have a major role to play in exerting pressure. The rabbinate as a whole has tremendous power but we can't do it one at a time. We need to get together and say we won't allow him in any synagogue unless he gives the get."[24]

Unfortunately, as we see from the words of Chatam Sofer, Jewish tradition was not and is not unanimous on condemnation of either withholding a get or physical violence against a spouse. In *Silence Is Deadly: Judaism Confronts Wifebeating*, the definitive book on the treatment of domestic violence in Jewish law, Naomi Graetz organizes the vast range of rabbinic responses into categories that include acceptance of "lawful" wifebeating, rejection, denial, and apologetics. Acceptance of wifebeating under certain circumstances is a minority position, but it is held by several prominent rabbis, including Maimonides who said, "A wife who refuses to perform any kind of work she is obligated to do may be compelled to perform it, even by scourging her with a rod."[25] Although there is debate as to whether the rod is an instrument used by the husband or refers to the rabbinic court, Maimonides becomes precedent for later rulings that excuse physical violence by a husband against his wife. On the other hand, the majority position includes several strong condemnations of family violence, including these words from Rabbi Meir of Rotenberg in the thirteenth century: "A Jew must honor his wife more than he honors himself. If one strikes one's wife, one should be punished more severely than for striking another person. For one is enjoined to honor one's wife, but is not enjoined to honor the other person."[26] Commenting on the range of views presented and the social and historical conditions

---

23. Quoted in Pogrebin, "The Misery Behind the Mezuzah," 11.
24. Tzvi Hersh Weinreb, "A Rabbi's Notebook," *Jewish Action: The Magazine of the Orthodox Union* (Spring 5758/1998), 11–12.
25. Cited in Naomi Graetz, *Silence Is Deadly: Judaism Confronts Wifebeating* (Northvale, N.J.: Jason Aronson, 1998).
26. Cited in Graetz, *Silence is Deadly*.

that may have led to some of these decisions, Elliott Dorff, author of the Conservative Movement's responsa on family violence, concludes, "social conditions cannot constitute an excuse for bad law: rabbis in times past, and in our day as well, must take the responsibility to formulate law that is worthy of the moral mission embedded in the tradition from its earliest roots."[27]

MORAL MISSIONS AND PROPHETIC CHALLENGES

In his invitation to participate in the Religious Consultation project to write this book on women, religion, and violence, Daniel Maguire directed our attention to ways religions are implicated and complicit in violence against women as well as the moral resources within traditions. The title of the domestic violence conference, "Pursuing Truth, Justice, and Righteousness: A Call to Action," echoing the words of Jeremiah, points to the prophets as proponents of social justice, whose words can be marshaled in the struggle to move ever closer to a society that nurtures the flourishing of all humankind. Rabbi Michelle Fisher's session, "Engaging with Challenging Texts," one of the more than sixty workshops at the conference, showed a darker, more ominous side of the prophetic tradition. The second chapter of "Hosea," the topic of the session, reveals domestic abuse in Torah itself, although it has not often been recognized as such. Attention to Gomer's perspective, as Hosea's wife and the victim of intimate partner abuse, is a recent phenomenon. In this eighth-century BCE text, Hosea castigates the people Israel for breaking their covenant with God and worshipping other gods. In the opening chapter of "Hosea," God tells the prophet to take a wife whose behavior is understood to parallel Israel's, and, consequently, Hosea experiences the anguish God feels at her betrayal: "Go, get yourself a wife of whoredom and children of whoredom; for the land will stray from following the Lord" (1:2).[28] It is a truism for feminist scholarship that our experiences shape our reading and understanding of texts.[29] This point was made painfully clear to me as I studied chapter 2 of "Hosea" in a room with women who work with victims of domestic violence and/or are

---

27. Elliot Dorff, "Introduction," in Graetz, *Silence Is Deadly*, xx.

28. Under the subheading "The Marriage: An Act of Sympathy," Abraham Joshua Heschel argues that Hosea's marriage to Gomer was "a mirror of the divine pathos, that his sorrow echoed the sorrow of God" (56). Gomer's emotions are completely absent from the text, as are most of the actions of chapter 2; Heschel's presentation of Hosea's marriage jumps from 2:4 to 3:1 and concludes: "He will not forsake her in spite of her faithlessness" (53). Abraham J. Heschel, *The Prophets: An Introduction*, 2 vols., vol. 1 (New York: Harper Torchbooks, 1962).

29. See the chapter by Sa'diyya Shaikh in this volume for further elaboration of this point.

themselves survivors. One of these women described this passage of Torah as "an abuser's manual." As I looked around the room, I saw many other women give a nod of recognition to the truth she told. The following columns present several verses from chapter 2 alongside elements of the power and control wheel in an attempt to give visual voice to the insights presented by women whose life experience includes encounters with intimate partner violence.

VERSES FROM HOSEA CHAPTER 2	ELEMENTS FROM POWER AND CONTROL WHEEL
(4) Rebuke your mother, rebuke her— *For she is not My wife* *And I am not her husband—* *And let her put away her harlotry from her face* *And her adultery from between her breasts.*	**Using children** **Isolation**
(5) Else I will strip her naked *And leave her as on the day she was born:* *And I will make her like a wilderness,* *Render her like desert land,* *And let her die of thirst.* *(6) I will also disown her children;* *For they are now a harlot's brood,*	**Sexual violence** **Coercion and threats** **Physical violence** **Using children** **Blaming**
(10) And she did not consider this: *It was I who bestowed on her* *The new grain and wine and oil;* *I who lavished silver on her* *And gold—which they used for Baal.* *(11) Assuredly,* *I will take back My new grain in its time* *And My new wine in its season,* *And I will snatch away My wool and My linen* *That serve to cover her nakedness.*	**Economic abuse** **Male privilege** **Sexual violence**
(12) Now will I uncover her shame *In the very sight of her lovers,* *And none shall save her from Me.* *(13) And I will end all her rejoicing:* *Her festivals, new moons, and sabbaths—* *All her festive seasons.*	**Sexual violence** **Coercion and threats** **Intimidation**

In these seven verses we find all ten plagues identified by women as ways they experienced violence within intimate relationships. In the concluding verses of this tirade of abuse, God/Hosea makes clear he is punishing Israel/Gomer for making offerings to other gods and "forgetting me" (2:15). The next verse, however, brings an abrupt change in tone. After Hosea/God "punishes" Gomer/Israel, he speaks "coaxingly" and "tenderly" (2:16) and initiates a new relationship where he is no longer "master" (*baal*, which is also the name of a Phoenician or Canaanite god) but "husband" (*ishi*). With this shift, a new covenant is made. Hosea's description of the covenant evokes edenic imagery and is followed by words presenting a beautiful relationship, words that have become part of daily Jewish liturgy: "And I will espouse you forever: I will espouse you with righteousness and justice, and with goodness and mercy, and I will espouse you with faithfulness; then you shall be devoted to the Lord" (2:21–22).

Hosea's relationship with Gomer functions as a powerful, violent, and problematic metaphor for the relationship between God and the people Israel in the eighth century BCE. As lived metaphor, Hosea's life becomes "symbolic action" for the Israelites to make theological meaning out of their ongoing historical struggles.[30] One approach to this troubling text, used in several rabbinic commentaries, is to focus on the chapter as metaphor. For example, Ibn Ezra, the twelfth-century rabbi known for his grammatical analysis, contextual interpretation, and philosophical insight, reads the entire episode as an "interpretation dream" or allegory.[31] The actual, physical violence disappears as the God-Israel relationship subsumes the relationship between Hosea and Gomer. A variation on this approach is used in the 2004 Jewish Study Bible, which introduces the "metaphorical world of the book of Hosea." Ehud Ben Zvi, who authored the introduction to "Hosea," goes to considerable effort to privilege the metaphorical reading and the historical setting of the text, although he does acknowledge that "this imagery carries connotations that are very troublesome for many contemporary readers, and especially painful for those who cannot but associate their reading of the text with their, or their acquaintances', personal experiences."[32] At the Torah

---

30. See Carole Fontaine, "Hosea and a Response to Hosea," in *A Feminist Companion to the Latter Prophets*, ed. Athalya Brenner (Sheffield, England: Sheffield Academic, 1995), 40–69, for the role of symbolic action in prophetic literature.

31. Edward Greenstein, "Medieval Bible Commentaries," in *Back to the Sources: Reading the Classic Jewish Texts*, ed. Barry Holtz (New York: Summit Books, 1984), 213–59. See also A. J. Heschel, *The Prophets*, 53; Yvonne Sherwood, "Boxing Gomer: Controlling the Deviant Woman in Hosea 1–3," in *A Feminist Companion to the Latter Prophets*, 101–25.

32. Ehud Ben Zvi, "Hosea," in *The Jewish Study Bible*, ed. Adele Berlin and Marc Zvi Brettler (New York: Oxford University Press, 2004), 1144.

study session, along with chapter 2, Fisher gave us one midrash, a traditional Jewish form of biblical commentary, that explicated the metaphor. In the selection from *Midrash Rabbah* the rabbis begin by noting that although chapter 1 concludes with the sentiment, encapsulated in the name of Hosea's son, "you are not My people," chapter 2 begins with the affirmation that the people of Israel will be called "Children-of-the-Living-God." The rabbis take this shift to show how God loves Israel even when angry, and, therefore, "how much more [love] will God show them when God is pleased with them!" The midrash then changes the human subjects of the analogy altogether and recounts a story about a king who was angry with his wife and yet went to the marketplace to commission jewelry made of gold.

One could take some solace in the fact that this emphasis on metaphor —perhaps—suggests some discomfort with literal readings of the text. Following this line of reasoning, the violence is made metaphoric and NOT literal, rather than both literal and metaphoric, because the acts of abuse attributed to Hosea are deemed unacceptable behavior by a husband toward his wife, especially when the husband is a prophet. Ultimately, however, attempts to minimize the impact of the violence by naming it as metaphor are hardly satisfactory. In fact, they point toward a deep misogyny embedded in aspects of Israelite and Jewish society, texts, and traditions. Metaphor involves the representation of one thing by another. In this case, the idolatry of the Israelites is represented by the "whoredom" of Gomer, and the response of God is represented by the abusive tactics of Hosea.[33] As one participant in "Engaging with Challenging Texts" asked: "Why is it that the worst image the biblical text could envision for Israel was female sexuality?"[34] Fisher's handout prefaced these texts with the blessing for Torah study: "*Barukh Atah Adonai Eloheinu Melek HaOlam, asher kid'shanu b'mitzvotav v'tzivanu la'asok b'divrei Torah.* Praised are you Adonai our God, Ruler of the Universe, who has sanctified us with mitzvot, and commanded us to busy ourselves with words of Torah." Yet, how can we affirm a covenant so brutally coerced? There were no simple answers to this painful question. Graetz offered the observation "God needs to do *teshuvah* [repentance]." Others in the room rejected God altogether.

---

33. See Fontaine, "Hosea and a Response to Hosea," for discussion of scholarly debate on term status of Gomer.

34. For specific discussion of the power of metaphor in Hosea and its link to Jewish law, see Graetz, *Silence Is Deadly*, and Adler, *Engendering Judaism*. Renita J. Weems, *Battered Love: Marriage, Sex, and Violence in the Hebrew Prophets* (Minneapolis: Augsburg Fortress, 1995), and Gerlinde Baumann, *Love and Violence: Marriage as Metaphor for the Relationship between YHWH and Israel in the Prophetic Books* (Collegeville, Minn.: Liturgical Press, 2003), address the marriage metaphor of the prophets in detail beyond the scope of this chapter.

Theological questions persist as the second chapter of Hosea remains a significant part of Jewish liturgy and ritual. It is read every year in synagogues as the *haftarah*, the reading from the Prophets, in conjunction with the opening chapter of Numbers. Graetz points out that the set distribution of readings from the Prophets (haftarah) to accompany the weekly Torah portion reading in synagogue is a relatively recent development and says we have "ample precedent" to pick a different reading. She suggests this from the position of a self-described "product of modern Orthodoxy" and "strongly identified religious Jewish woman."[35] In Reform Judaism, the practice of choosing haftarah in keeping with modern sensibilities is well established. Setel shares Graetz's concern and goes so far as to suggest that "the 'pornographic' nature of female objectification may demand that such texts not be declared 'the word of God' in a public setting."[36] Others see the yearly reading as an opportunity to give a *drash*, a commentary on the Torah portion often delivered by the rabbi, specifically addressing domestic violence in the Jewish community.

Hosea is read yearly but evoked daily when a Jew puts on *tefillin*, biblical verses placed in a leather box that are worn each weekday morning in response to the command: "Take to heart these instructions which I charge you this day. . . . Bind them as a sign on your hand and let them serve as a symbol on your forehead" (Deut. 6:6, 8). As she wraps the leather strap that holds the box around her finger, she proclaims: "And I will espouse you forever: I will espouse you with righteousness and justice, and with goodness and mercy, and I will espouse you with faithfulness; then you shall be devoted to the Lord" (2:21–22).[37] Putting on tefillin is both a public and highly personal act, and how individuals reconcile the power of the ritual and the beauty of these verses with the violence that precedes them will vary. Long after the study session ended, I was haunted by the "abuser's manual"/Torah connection. I asked Fisher how she "engaged" this text, especially when she put on tefillin. "I try to recall it's not just a sign, or a *mitzvah*, or a betrothal I am reenacting when I wrap tefillin," she said, "It's also an obligation to remember and speak up about the context that those verses come from."[38] As for me, I can no longer unambivalently describe myself as "a Reform Jew whose tradition places strong emphasis on select words from the Hebrew

---

35. Graetz, *Silence Is Deadly*, xi.
36. Drora T. Setel, "Prophets and Pornography: Female Sexual Imagery in Hosea," in *Feminist Interpretation of the Bible*, ed. Letty Russell (Philadelphia: Westminster Press, 1985), 86–95.
37. Traditionally Jewish men wear tefillin, but the people with whom I discussed this issue were women who have taken on this daily ritual practice.
38. Michelle Fisher, letter to author, 13 April 2005.

Prophets"[39] without recognizing the words I choose *not* to select as "words of the living God."

PURSUING TRUTH, JUSTICE, AND RIGHTEOUSNESS

Torah is not monolithic. As we struggled with the legacy of Hosea, Jeremiah's words inspired those gathered together to remove the "abomination" of domestic violence from their midst, to engage in the task of *tikkun olam*, repair of the world, and strive toward an ideal of "truth, justice, and righteousness."[40] The work of tikkun olam occurs on many fronts: rabbis, social workers, activists, and advocates work tirelessly to educate the community, including other rabbis, and provide support—economic, emotional, and spiritual—to women who have suffered far too long in silence. Results from the 2003 Needs Assessment surveys conducted by Jewish Women International suggest that women are far more likely to turn to their rabbi for help if she or he has previously spoken about domestic violence. The accounts from rabbis who have spoken are astoundingly similar; once they broke the silence, they discovered—sometimes little by little, sometimes in a deluge—that, indeed, domestic violence "does happen here," as women from their congregations came for help. To speak out, however, and to not do further harm in an effort to help congregants, rabbis need training. Lots of training. For a little knowledge can be dangerous, especially if a rabbi tries to "fix" the relationship; minimizes the woman's concerns; says a rabbi cannot take sides; recommends couples counseling; advises the woman to remain for the sake of shalom bayit; or encourages the woman to leave without adequate safety planning. Several new training programs for rabbis by rabbis are currently under way. Rabbi Diana Monheit is currently working with New York Board of Rabbis to develop "*Sh'ma Kolenu* [Hear Our Voices]: A Clergy Domestic Abuse Prevention and Education Program." Monheit, along with twelve other rabbis, comprise the National Clergy Task Force on Domestic Abuse in the Jewish Community. It is a good start, but as Rose notes "this work takes great time and great patience."[41]

---

39. Liora Gubkin, "What Men Owe to Women," California State University, Bakersfield. February, 2005.

40. Ellen Umansky suggests that, in the nineteenth and twentieth centuries in the United States, Jewish women's organizations, more so than text study or public prayer, have often served as sites for Jewish women's spirituality. See Ellen Umansky, "Spiritual Expressions: Jewish Women's Religious Lives in the United States in the Nineteenth and Twentieth Centuries," in *Jewish Women in Historical Perspective*, ed. Judith Baskin (Detroit: Wayne University, 1998), 337–63.

41. "Plenary Session: Clergy: Leaders and Partners in Ending Domestic Abuse in the Jewish Community," Jewish Women International Conference on Domestic Abuse in the Jewish Community, Washington, D.C., March 2005.

Mark Dratch, an Orthodox congregational rabbi for the past twenty-two years, has ambitious plans. Dratch is leaving the congregational rabbinate to found JSafe: The Jewish Institute Supporting an Abuse-Free Environment. He envisions a certification program to provide training to a wide variety of Jewish institutions and organizations on policies and guidelines for abuse-free behavior, including effective responses to domestic violence. Just as the Orthodox Union stamps a product as kosher, so JSafe would certify that an organization is properly trained to combat abuse. Dratch speaks passionately of this work and the need for a communal-wide organization: "We have a systemic problem in the Jewish community," observes Dratch, and although "there is good work being done out there," there is currently no structure to disseminate and replicate successful programs. Dratch hopes to change that.

As more rabbinic-led programs get under way, social workers continue their efforts to reach clergy. Project S.A.R.A.H. (Stop Abusive Relationships at Home), which targets Orthodox women and Russian-speaking women in the state of New Jersey, has been training rabbis for ten years. An explanation of their approach presented by Esther East, founder of Project S.A.R.A.H., illustrates the "great time and great patience" required. Rabbis are difficult to reach, East notes. It is mostly a matter of time, and if they do not think domestic violence is a problem in their community, they are unlikely to allocate what little time they do have to the issue. Project S.A.R.A.H. often initiates contact with the rabbis through the rabbis' wives; in fact they are often included in the training, which is currently done jointly so that the rabbi and rebbitzin know they have heard the same thing.[42] Project S.A.R.A.H. sends a written invitation and follows up with a phone call. The program includes a respected rabbinic figure paired with a domestic violence expert. The program is free and food is provided. Topics are different for each session, and Project S.A.R.A.H. mails an audio tape to all the rabbis in the area who did not attend. When they first began working with the clergy, East notes, they would introduce rabbis to the problem of domestic violence and then tell them to "refer, refer, refer." Now, they realize rabbis will more often take it upon themselves to do something, so Project S.A.R.A.H. has developed training to give them some skills.

Of course rabbis are not the only leaders in the Jewish community. Project S.A.R.A.H. also provides training to *mikveh* attendants, women who oversee the ritual bath used by women as part of the laws of family purity. These training sessions focus on listening skills and boundary sup-

---

42. In the Orthodox communities targeted by Project S.A.R.A.H. rabbis are married men.

port as attendants occupy a potentially intimate place within the communal structure, especially in Orthodox communities. Lay leaders also have an important role to play in domestic violence education. Kehilla Community Synagogue, a congregation in Oakland, California, affiliated with the Jewish renewal movement, for example, developed a comprehensive policy "on the prevention of and response to abuse" for its community. The document presenting policy guidelines begins with two epigraphs: "on the day when God made humans, they were fashioned in the image of God" and Rabbi Arthur Green's claim, "The realization that every human being is God's image makes an unambiguous demand upon us." These are followed by a preamble, a statement of intention, which begins, "With the adoption of these policy guidelines we acknowledge the reality of abuse in our community. We seek to eliminate it and to promote the process of healing."[43]

Eliminating abuse may be beyond our reach, part of the ongoing, never-ending task of tikkun olam. In the meantime, many survivors, social workers, rabbis, and lay people have turned to private and communal ritual resources within Jewish tradition to promote the process of healing. Sometimes, the simplest of rituals can hold great power. *Mi Shebeirach*, the prayer for healing recited each Shabbat, serves as one site for healing. Joseph Potasnik, executive vice president of the New York Board of Rabbis, adds a reference to domestic violence directly into the traditional prayer with a special mention of "those who are hurting whose words we may not hear, words we should hear." The weekly recitation of this prayer reminds the community that domestic violence is a reality, and it affirms the willingness to hear, believe, and help those who suffer abuse in their homes.

In addition to the weekly ritual of Shabbat, Judaism has a rich yearly holiday cycle, which can also offer resources for support and healing. Shalom Bayit, an organization working to end domestic violence in the California Bay Area, has developed a calendar of rituals coordinated with the Jewish holy days in order to make holidays relevant to survivors: March brings Purim and the opportunity to explore images of the "good woman" and the "bad woman" through study of Vashti and Esther; July brings Tisha B'Av, a holy day focused on destruction, loss, and grieving.

September/October brings Sukkot. The *sukkah*, symbolic of the protection God gave through temporary shelters while the Israelites wandered in the desert for forty years, is a shelter of peace. October is also

---

43. Kehilla Community Synagogue, Oakland, California, "Policy Guidelines on the Prevention of and Response to Abuse in Kehilla Community Synagogue" ([cited July 12, 2005]); available from http://www.kehillasynagogue.org/abusepolicy.htm.

domestic violence awareness month, and celebrations of Sukkot at Shalom Bayit consider "the concept of home as a shelter of peace" and also help people to understand "that this seemingly lovely concept is simply not reality for anyone being abused in [her] own home."[44] December brings Chanukah—a holiday that celebrates light, freedom, and miracles. Naomi Tucker, executive director of Shalom Bayit, created a candle-lighting ceremony that honors miracles particularly relevant to survivors of domestic abuse:

> It is a miracle that women who are battered can gather enough strength to fight back, to leave, or even just to make it through another day. It is a miracle that a person can experience such horrors and somehow retain who she is on the inside, somehow piece herself and her life back together again, somehow continue to hold down a job or take care of her children, somehow remain a loving person.

All who are gathered for the candle lighting then recite, "In honor of the miraculous strength and courage of all battered women, we light the sixth candle."[45]

Of all the holidays that can speak to the struggle for liberation from abuse, Passover resonates most strongly. When Alison Iser was struck by the parallel journeys from slavery toward liberation taken by the Israelites and the women she met in her role as a battered women's advocate, she began the conversations that would eventually lead to an annual seder, a Passover ritual meal, solely for women who have experienced domestic abuse, and the publication of *A Journey towards Freedom: A Haggadah for Women Who Have Experienced Domestic Violence*. The Passover seder held in the Seattle area every year in a new location known only to participants serves as both a healing site for the women and an educational tool for the Seattle Jewish community. The mere presence of a seder for women who have been or are currently abused provides an opportunity for rabbis and lay people to learn about domestic violence. Although general community members are not allowed to attend, they may help make the seder special by creating gifts, such as a *matzah* cover or seder plate, for the women. Through these gifts, the women also learn there are members of the Jewish community who care about their well-being. Perhaps even more important, the seder allows the women to form Jewish

---

44. Rebecca Schwartz and Naomi Tucker, "Healing from Domestic Violence: Suggestions for Jewish Ritual Themes" (Oakland, Calif.: Shalom Bayit, 1996).
45. Naomi Tucker, "Candle Lighting Ceremony" (Oakland, Calif.: Shalom Bayit, n.d.).

community with each other. *A Journey towards Freedom* relates the process of creating a community in the context of the seder with the words of one survivor:

> I shed unexpected tears upon hearing someone else's story. Another woman who also believed that her situation was unique. Another woman who thought that she too had a weakness that somehow caused her to be victimized. And now, together, she and I cry because we realize we are not victims, but rather, somewhere along the way, we became survivors. We are not so unique that we need to feel alone.[46]

Words from survivors, written during pre-seder writing workshops over several years, are incorporated into the traditional telling of the journey from slavery toward liberation. The haggadah, however, does not attribute passages to any individual author. The editors explain their choice in the introduction to the haggadah: "As we, seder participants, go around the table and take turns reading paragraph after paragraph of our collective Haggadah story, the separations between battered and nonbattered women are diminished, reminding us of the Passover message that none of us are free until we are all free."[47]

These words take us to the core moral resources of Jewish tradition. Jews are commanded: "Remember you were a slave in Egypt," and remembrance includes living a life shaped by the ethics of that memory. Although the ethical insights of Jewish tradition were first elaborated by men from the vantage point of their experiences, a growing group of women educated in and dedicated to Jewish tradition—women including Fisher, Iser, Monheit, and Tucker—read and write these words for themselves, place their experiences at the center rather than at the margins, and compel others to recognize their inclusion as agents of Jewish history and tradition. In the most optimistic of times, when surrounded, for example, by hundreds of women (and men who are their allies) dedicated to the eradication of violence against women, we see the possibility of *tikkun olam* and of a Judaism that unequivocally recognizes the worth of women, as well as of men, and enables the flourishing of both.

---

46. Alison Iser et al., *A Journey towards Freedom: A Haggadah for Women Who Have Experienced Domestic Violence* (Seattle: FaithTrust Institute, 2003), 26.
47. Iser et al., *A Journey towards Freedom*, iv.

11

Sexual Violence in the Catholic Church

MARIA JOSÉ ROSADO-NUNES
REGINA SOARES JURKEWICZ

"When women are perceived as less than human, the consequence is violent abuse."[1]

In 2003 UNIFEM, an institution of the United Nations, called for presentations and projects that centered on the theme of violence against women. At Católicas pelo Direito de Decidir (CDD; "Pro-Choice Catholics"), we decided to propose a study of the sexual abuse of women by priests in Brazil. The inspiration for this study came from information not previously released in the country about violence suffered by nuns in various parts of the world, including Brazil, in which pregnancy resulted. Access to this information was made possible after the American journal *National Catholic Reporter* released the results of a study about these cases, a study that had been commissioned by the Vatican. The results of this investigation, however, surpassed expectations when they found cases in twenty-three countries, including Brazil.

When we approached the hierarchy of the Catholic Church to learn of the specific results from Brazil—that is, where the cases were found, who the nuns were, what happened to them, and what the subsequent policy of the church had been following the revelation of these abuses—the only response we received was a denouncing of the report. It was attributed to overzealous authors. The information was called into question and any abuse was denied. We found, therefore, that it would be practically impossible to know exactly what had happened in Brazil to

---

1. Mary Ann Rossi, "The Legitimation of the Abuse of Women in Christianity," www.women priests.org; accessed 17 July 2004.

the nuns mentioned in the *National Catholic Reporter* as having been sexually violated by priests. We had learned, however, via the press, of acts of sexual abuse committed by Catholic priests against girls and women in Brazil. We proposed to UNIFEM a study of these cases instead. At the same time Regina Soares Jurkewicz, a member of the CDD board, embarked on her own study of priest sexual abuse for her doctoral dissertation in religious sciences. This chapter includes some of the results of her investigation and study.[2]

THE STRATEGY OF HIDING

The limited amount of literature that could be found about sexual violence committed by priests was limited to the abuse of minors.[3] Abuse of women and sexual violence[4] by priests were rarely objects of study and were virtually ignored by the media until the last few years. This abuse has been regularly and systematically denied or hidden, as much by the church hierarchy—bishops and priests—as by nuns, the parish community, law enforcement, and even the victims, until the time came to publicly disclose and condemn it.[5] The complex mechanisms by which this abuse is hidden reveal a great deal about cultural and religious disciplinary practices. These even include sermons understood to be part of the practices—such as those which show "men" and "women" to be radically different in their nature and assigning to men an inevitable sexual drive that is, because of its inevitability, acceptable and forgivable.

---

2. The study consisted of the gathering, classification, and selection of material found in the national media about cases of sexual abuse by priests of women and girls. Of the twenty-one cases reported in the news, two were chosen for further analysis. The cases involved twenty-one girls and adolescents (ages nine to fifteen) and four women. Interviews were conducted with persons involved in these cases. We do not provide specific details of these cases, but refer to them throughout this study. This empirical study was conducted under the supervision of Regina Soares Jurkewicz.

3. A. W. Richard Sipe, *Sipe Report: Preliminary Expert Report*, s.d. (2003), found at www.richardsipe.com; accessed on 26 April 2004; Gino Nasini, *Um espinho na carne: má conduta e abuso sexual por parte de clérigos da Igreja Católica do Brasil*, 2nd ed. (São Paulo: Santuário, 2001); Pepe Rodriquez, *Pederastia en la Iglesia Católica: delitos sexuales del clero contra menores, un drama silenciado y encubierto por los Obispos* (Barcelona: Ed. B, 2002).

4. While there is a difference between the two terms—abuse and violence—for facility we use them interchangeably.

5. The terms "victim," and "survivor of abuse," which is more commonly used in the United States, refer to persons involved in cases in which the accused were found guilty in the courts. When we speak of "accusers," we are referring to girls and women who have disclosed being victims of abuse or sexual violence, but whose perpetrators have not been found guilty in the court system. In these cases, the women who disclosed abuse are treated as "accusers" and not as "victims." In this text, however, we do not make the distinction and use the two terms interchangeably.

The testimony of Richard Sipe is significant: "After I was ordained in 1959, I learned that some priests had sex with adults and even minors, and to some degree this behavior was taken for granted by church authorities. Yet, an atmosphere of crisis regarding this issue did not exist. The secret world of sexual activity, including sexual activity with minors, was known by the Catholic hierarchy and, though considered unfortunate and morally wrong, was accepted as an inevitable and easily forgivable failure of some priests."[6]

In the case of the Catholic Church, we see an elaborate strategy of denial and concealment as a means of dealing with cases of abuse. Pepe Rodriguez details this strategy by outlining "Ten Basic Steps," common and universal, that have been adopted by the church hierarchy to hide clergy delinquency:[7]

1. Discrete investigation of the occurrence: By way of oral reports, the church authorities are informed of the situation.
2. Attempt to discuss the situation with the victim: After admonishing the priest, there is an attempt to convince the family that the abuser has been punished and is very sorry, persuading the family not to press charges in the courts so as not to hurt the church's image.
3. Hiding the abuser's actions: The attempts to impede the abuser's case from becoming public include the transfer of the abusing priest, suspension of benefits offered to the family, and attempts to suborn the victim and family.
4. Reinforcing the means of concealment: When the case finally becomes public and social and media pressures become stronger, or judicial proceedings commence, the church hierarchy adopts an expedient ruling against the abuser. In many cases, this is limited to the transfer of the priest to another diocese, parish, or even country.[8]
5. Attempt to deny the facts or to show the case as an isolated occurrence: If it cannot be denied, it is treated as an exceptional case.
6. Public defense of the abuser: Church officials place emphasis on the personal merits of the priest, his dedication to the church, and his repentance, always with an appeal to the Christian ideal of forgiveness toward the repentant sinner.

---

6. Sipe, *Sipe Report*, accessed on 26 April 2004.
7. Rodriquez, *Pederastia en la Iglesia Católica*.
8. One case reported in the newspaper O *Estado de São Paulo*, on 14 June 2005, confirmed this strategy: the father of the victims (two minor girls, sisters, ages fifteen and sixteen), reported the sexual abuse of his daughters in January of this year. The church's reaction was merely to remove the priest from official religious duties. Only in June of the same year was the case made public and court action taken. See O *Estado de São Paulo*, 14 June 2005, section A, Vida&, 16; idem., 15 June 2005, section A, Vida&, 19.

7. Public denouncing of the victims: The victims are marginalized, making them partially responsible for the abuse.
8. Attributing the report as an attack on the church: Officials blame political and ideological enemies of the church for publicizing the abuse, claiming that these enemies are using social forces as a means of dismantling the religious institution.
9. Negotiation with the victim: Church leaders offer material compensation for victims, in the hopes of silencing them and keeping them from reporting the priest.
10. Protection of the abuser: Because of the evidence of guilt, church officials develop a plan to protect the image of the priest.[9]

These ten steps reveal the principles that govern the social and religious differentiation of women and men. Underlying this process is the attribution of guilt to the women, and the victimization of the men, reaffirming the superiority of the men.

In the cases made public in Brazil, this strategy is clearly followed. There is a tendency, not just on the part of the church hierarchy, but also by those who know the facts or are in some way involved in the case, to conceal the abuse, to denigrate the women and girls,[10] and to justify the defense of the abuser. Some of the interviews in this study are, to say the least, revealing.

An attorney representing an accused priest said in an interview, "the priest in question is a dignified man who speaks several languages, including German, is dedicated to charity, a university professor. He has used all of his earnings to purchase food for the poor and this type of conduct has enraged the jealousies of local politicians, who see the priest as a potential rival. In response, what happened was that two or three young ladies came forth saying that they had had sexual contact with the priest."[11]

This type of speech discourse creates a negative image of the girls, calling them dismissively "young ladies." At the same time, the priestly image is depicted of a man of distinction, like those found in the works

---

9. Marie M. Fortune, "Conduta imprópria do clero: abuso sexual nas relações ministérias," na revista *Concilium*, 252 (1994/2): 159. She makes note of these same procedures in the reaction of religious institutions. Their goal is: "To protect the transgressor from the consequences of his bad behavior; keeping secret the abuse perpetrated; preserving the façade of worthiness and normalcy of the institution."
10. The marginalization of these women, transforming them into unworthy types, is clearly shown in the words of Father José Maria Costa, a counselor in the Family Ministry department of the CNBB: "There are many women who sit in the front row during mass, cross their legs and provoke the baser instincts of the male priest," *Folha de São Paulo*, 4 July 2005, Cotidiano section.
11. Soares Jurkewicz, field notes.

of Bourdieu.[12] The priest's cultural and social position is elevated and separate, impeding him, as it were, from having close contact with these "young ladies" from a different social class. Statements such as these demonstrate the asymmetry of gender and social class that exist between the accused and his accusers. Such a situation repeats itself in every case of abuse about which we were able to obtain information.

One of the victims expressed perfectly this inequality of social position that creates a certain credibility on the part of the accused: "I always trusted him. It was the way he spoke, I could accuse him but who would believe me? People always believe that it was the woman's fault. They can believe that he is capable of it, but only because she threw herself at him. He gave in to her temptation . . ." (Interview 10).[13]

On the other hand, the same attorney cited previously blamed mandatory celibacy of priests as the culprit for these "indiscretions": "Celibacy is responsible for many indiscretions, because celibacy translates into a prohibition of one's own innate self . . ." (Interview 6). Yet, in other moments in the same interview, he tries to show the dignified nature of the accused priest and the insignificance of the victims, while at the same time implying that both the women and the priest are deserving of respect.

Likewise, the community is concerned that a possible trial against a local priest will hurt the city's image. An attorney for one of the NGOs that supported the victims in their complaint expressed a concern about the city's desire to maintain its image untarnished by the behavior of one of its local priests. He says: "There were two movements: one to preserve the image of the local people and the city, of which they (the women) would be tarnishing the image of the city and of one important person in the city . . . and the other was the moral questions that revolved around them" (Interview 1). According to this statement, the veracity of the case is not called into question; what local townspeople said was that the women were guilty of moral failings. What bothers the community is not so much that abuse had occurred, but rather the public incrimination of the priest. By making the case a matter of public concern, the city appeared in many national newspapers and magazines in a negative fashion. For the local residents, the preservation of the city's "good reputation" and that of its lead-

---

12. In the ideas of Pierre Bourdieu, the possession of economic and cultural capital provide the value of "distinction" in developed societies. Social differences are built, therefore, on the possession of these forms of capital. On the other hand, the greater the difference in relationship to the holding of economic wealth and cultural position, the greater the distance between the social actors. See *La distinction: critique sociale du jugement* (Paris: Ed. De Minuit, 1979).

13. The numbers given to each interview correspond to their classification in the original research.

ers and citizens, among them the accused priest, was endangered by the accusations. There is a commonly held notion that "the priest is a priest, but also a man," and because of his human nature he is subject to the temptations of "young ladies" who are looser in their moral conduct. The accusation of the priest is considered more threatening to the priest than the actual occurrence of the abuse and the sexual violence, which, if not publicly exposed, would be able to continue in silence, without a "blemish" on the good reputation of the community and its residents.

In the same interview mentioned above, the attorney returns to the negative reaction of the local community, in light of the charges: "The city knew that the abuse happened and this bothered everyone a great deal . . . to reveal that which many believed should not be divulged. There was a negative undercurrent . . . there was one person in one of the meetings who spoke clearly of this: 'we wished it was a lie!' When she spoke those words, she revealed two things: she knew that the allegation was true, but she wished that it were not; second, she wished that people did not know, that it had never been revealed to the public, she wished it had been a lie. . . . This comment came from one person who worked in the agency for social policy."

The same person said in an interview: "From my contact with the victims and with the local population, my feeling is that for many the public nature of all of this tore at the very fabric of the social order that had been in place in the city. Furthermore, because it was a religious figure, a professor, someone who had been a great strength to the poor in the city . . . in short, someone beloved by many, it hurt a lot of people" (Interview 1).

The logic behind this is the exact same as that which led the ecclesiastical hierarchy to defend the institution. The image of the church has to be preserved, even with the appearance of a certain degree of tolerance of those who do not live up to the institutional standards—in this case, celibacy—or of those whose behavior is morally condemnable. In a religious institution founded on the principle of separation of clergy and laity, in which all of the religious authority falls on the former—the clergy—a unified defense of the institution is necessary for the preservation of this hierarchical structure.

Continuing in this same vein, everything is done to "avoid scandals." Many consider the public accusations of the girls and women to be far more scandalous than the abuse and violence. In this kind of thinking, silence is the best way to preserve both the institution and the local community. It is not just the church hierarchy that wishes to avoid public disclosure of cases that involve ecclesiastical leaders, but also parishioners, faithful Church members, and the local population.

Even the accusers described this perception that their abusive experience touched on a delicate subject that should never have been revealed: "There were people in my own parish who found out . . . they already knew something about the case, but when I went to work, no one spoke to me . . . no one wanted to get involved, no one cared . . ." (Interview 11).

For the local community wishing to preserve its image, the revelation of this case also brought the fear that other such cases of abuse and violence, previously kept under wraps, would come out. "Sexual abuse of minors in this city is common," said one judge, in a conversation with one of the interviewers. The interviewer asked the judge: "Is it possible that the community's opposition to these young women might be because, if this case moves forward, it could bring to light others?" She responded: "There are far too many cases in this city that have been covered up" (Interview 4).

BRAZIL AND THE UNITED STATES—A CLOSE COMPARISON

If we examine closely the procedure adopted in Brazil and in the United States to deal with Catholic priests who have been involved in cases of abuse and sexual violence, we find that in the latter, a better approach for punishing the guilty and supporting the victims was put in place. In Brazil, the case is quite different due to a lack of institutional policy for dealing with the problem.

Marie M. Fortune, an expert on inappropriate sexual conduct by Christian church clergy in the United States, has said:

> Thorough research on the sexual involvement of U.S. clergy with members of their congregation does not exist. A study done in 1984 did offer some significant data: 12.67% of the clergy members studied had confessed to having had sexual intercourse with a member of their church. An astounding 76.51% of the clergy in the study offered that they knew of a fellow minister who had had sexual relations with a member of their church (Blackmon, 1984). But the study that is most revealing, and gives us a better idea of the depth of this problem, was undertaken by the lay membership. The research into sexual molestation in Christian congregations by laity is just as limited as the aforementioned studies among clergy. In 1985, the United Church of Christ in the United States asked the female membership of its clerical community if they had had any experiences of sexual molestation or inappropriate sexual behavior on the part of the senior ministers, etc.: 47% responded in the affirmative. Another study commissioned by the United Methodist Church in 1990 found that 77% of its female clergy

had experienced sexual assault when they were serving as assistants and students. Despite the majority of offending ministers in the cases discovered being heterosexual males and the great majority of the victims being heterosexual females, it is clear that neither gender nor sexual orientation precludes someone from the risk of sexual transgression or from the possibility of being tricked into having a relationship with a minister or counselor.[14]

In 1976, Richard Sipe released the results of a study conducted in the United States, in which he found the following: 6 percent of all Catholic priests had had sexual relations with minors. In his preliminary report, referenced above, Sipe identifies a series of phases in the United States through which secrets were exposed and acts of sexual abuse of minors by priests finally came to light:[15]

First Phase: The Interface of Psychiatry/Psychology and the Problems of Catholic Clerics

In the late 1950s and early 1960s, treatment left the closed system and entered into the psychiatric system. Psychiatry and psychology were used to treat the offending cleric, contain the scandal, and placate the legal system if the cleric ran afoul of the law. Victims and their families were usually reassured by church authorities and subsequently ignored. The sexual problems of Catholic clergy were subsumed under the umbrella of other psychiatric problems, especially alcoholism.

Second Phase: The Advent of Reporting Laws

In 1962, the first reporting laws were passed. By 1968 virtually all states had reporting laws. In 1974, federal legislation mandating the existence of reporting laws in each state was passed. Such offenses were required to be reported and church authorities were mandated reporters in each state. The 1974 federal legislation made reporting laws a mandatory requirement for the receipt of federal aid.

Third Phase: The Fusion of Psychiatry/Psychology and the Opening of Catholic Treatment Centers

In the late 1960s and early 1970s, a number of Catholic treatment centers specifically for priests and religious officials opened, all coinciding

---

14. Fortune, *Conduta imprópria do clero*, 153–54. Fortune limited her study to cases of sexual abuse committed by Christian church clergy in their role as counselors.

15. The date presented by Sipe refers specifically to clergy sexual abuse of minors. Sipe, *Sipe Report*, accessed for this study on 26 April 2004.

with a growing awareness among Catholic bishops and religious superiors that sexual and moral/spiritual problems had psychological dimensions. [Sipe] observed that as these facilities opened, referrals of priests with sexual addictions increased. Awareness of the dimensions of the problems presented by sexual addictions expanded as psychology and psychiatry broke through the barriers of secrecy as victims and perpetrators became willing to talk more openly about their experiences.

Fourth Phase: Victims of Priest Sexual Abuse/the Bishops' Response

While on the one hand the North American church hierarchy sought the use of sophisticated treatment techniques for the treatment of Catholic priests and religious who had acted out sexually with minors, on the other hand the victims who reported misconduct to Chancery Offices, bishops, and religious superiors consistently report that they were seen as traitors and disloyal to their church. Victims and their families were deceived, confused, ignored, disbelieved, or discouraged.

Fifth Phase: The Secret System Is Breached

In the period from 1985 to 1992, there was a growing sensitivity to the realization that Catholic bishops and religious superiors could be involved in concealing disclosure of criminal activities by Catholic priests and religious. The media revealed cases involving credible evidence of cover-up on the part of numerous bishops and other church superiors: transfers to avoid scandal, lack of supervision, and active concealment of crimes came to light. For the first time, some victims of abuse by priests who became aware of the news coverage realized that they were not alone. This knowledge empowered some of these victims to come forward. A growing mass of people who had been violated began to share some of their experiences with psychologists, psychiatrists, spouses, parents, friends, and attorneys.

In Brazil, as was stated in the beginning, there are still very few studies about sexual abuse by Catholic priests. One of the rare studies done was published in 2001, as the product of a doctoral dissertation in pastoral theology by Father Gino Nasini: *A Thorn in the Side—Poor Conduct and Sexual Abuse by Priests in the Catholic Church of Brazil.*[16] Also unknown are the types of ecclesiastical actions taken to find the women and children who are victims of this type of abuse in Brazil. There are two treatment facilities for priests who suffer from psychological

---

16. Nasini, *Um espinho na carne.* This study was conducted among the clergy and was performed to find out what paths were being followed to deal with this problem.

problems, alcoholism, and the like. One might presume that priests who had committed sexual abuse might be treated in these centers, but that type of information is unavailable.

One Brazilian bishop, when asked about the existence of some type of plan of action on the part of the Catholic Church to deal with sexual abuse committed by priests, responded:

> There are reports and research, recently ordered by the Commission for the Vocation and Ministry of the Brazilian National Conference of Bishops, to be conducted by competent professionals . . ." (Interview 5). The same bishop confirmed: "In the first place, the number of reported cases is almost insignificant. The accusations by and large have not been confirmed. There are maybe five to ten cases, unlike in the United States. One can easily see how the media exploits the issue, promoted by opportunists and by those interested in taking advantage of embarrassing situations. A document by the U.S. Conference of Bishops seems to go in the direction of not confusing an accusation with actual proven guilt, accompanied by condemnatory action. All accusations must be rigorously backed up in order to be considered proven. In second place, the orders must follow the line of a firm and decided choice in favor of celibacy, embracing the sacrifice in turning oneself over to God in service of the people and containing an inner peace, harmony, and happiness, as characteristics of a special consecration of life. Nevertheless, we religious men and women have to live within the context of a completely sexualized society, which relies on the individual desires and props up the tyranny of pleasure and power as symbols of modernity . . . (Interview 5).

In this study, various arguments that were used traditionally by members of the ecclesiastical hierarchy of the church in order to respond to cases of sexual abuse by the clergy dictate the following: an understanding that the number of cases is irrelevant; the exploitation by the media that divulges these untruths; a refusal by the church to recognize the difficulties in treating questions relative to sexuality; the unconditional insistence on celibacy; and the modern context of casting blame falls upon an eroticized society.[17]

---

17. In conclusions released in 2004 from research conducted in Brazil, 41 percent of priests studied revealed that they had been intimately involved with a woman at some time in their religious life. The release of this study prompted reaction on the part of the Brazilian National Council of Bishops, who cast doubt on the interpretation of the data and reaffirmed the credibility of their priests, stating that the majority of them keep the promises

Although found in another context, this conflict between the church and modern society appears in materials published by a Brazilian journal with national circulation. In that journal, Cardinal Renato Martinho, president of the Pontifical Council for Justice and Peace, denounced "the existence of an anti-Christian lobby" in the world. According to him, "these lobbyists are full of both money and arrogance. They comprise a holy inquisition. They place the Catholic Church and other Christians in the witness chair."[18]

In Brazil, cases of abuse and sexual violence in the Catholic Church gained visibility because of actions by the media. We can assume that the number of cases about which the press had knowledge is actually far less than the number of actual cases that have occurred. There are no mandatory notification laws. In most of the cases, it is the obligatory notification that leads to immediate denial. As long as there is not a registry of all cases, the ability to hide those cases will continue to exist.

OVERSTATED VIOLENCE BY "HOLY MEN"

One of the hypotheses tested in this study had to do with the resistance of women to disclose sexual violence committed by religious authorities. The women resisted in disclosing the abuse largely because of a holy aura that accompanies the figure of the priest, making it difficult for them to be seen as the perpetrators of sexual abuse because their symbolic power masks their position as aggressors. The women also knew that they might be seen as opportunists as much in the judicial process as in public opinion, or even in the eyes of their own families.

One priest, in one of the cases in the study, took the side of a female victim when he said: "The fact that I am a priest, or an attorney, or some other public person, lends a certain degree of credibility, and makes it so that I am placed in a position that is more protected from future consequences. Even public opinion is more likely to defend those who have power . . . making a priest untouchable . . . and when one speaks of religious power there is another factor that is more . . . respected by others, because of religion . . . a moral power almost always has more authority than any other type of power . . ." (Interview 4).

---

that they have made to live celibately. At the same time, their strategy included a process of discrediting the study, even though it had been conducted by an organization in which the church had confidence and was at one time affiliated with the Brazilian National Conference of Bishops and with the Religious Conference of Brazil. The Catholic hierarchy released a statement alleging that this particular study spoke of "relationships with women," and that that did not necessarily signify relationships that involved sex.

18. *O Estado de São Paulo*, section A, Lifestyle, 14, 19 October 2004.

An attorney who had followed one of the cases said, along the same lines, that attributing a sacred nature that emanates from the figure of the holy priest leads to the relationships of power that permit the establishment of situations of violence. She said: "This case is very similar to the type of incest abuse that occurs in families. There exists a relationship of power where one of the figures is a father-figure, likeable and trustworthy. One is abused by this figure but must keep the abuse secret for some reason that the father figure explains. I think that this god-like quality exists very strongly when we look at the relationship that one has with the priest. It is a position of respect and he was in the position of power and authority. If he said that intimate relations were okay then they were considered to be sanctioned. He is all-knowing, he is learned, he has power. It is a relationship of one-sided power, because it is a relationship between a priest and his parishioners, or employees . . ." (Interview 7).

The Brazilian researcher Rita Laura Segato, a specialist in violence against women, clearly defines the social position of the man as a determinant for his abusive attitudes. What she explains about men in general, *a fortiori*, is especially true of priests: "A man enters the social scene with a certain air of authority and control which is, in and of itself, violent. . . . 'If the *other* does not subordinate herself in deference to my position, I cannot occupy the position that I hold.' A man cannot take his place unless the woman is willing to submit to him in that position, an act that sometimes manifests itself as affection, love. 'If I do not receive this, I must usurp my position.' This is manifest in sexual crimes, the likes of which are a form of forced submission that cannot be made romantically."[19]

The testimony of one of the witnesses is an example of this: "He took advantage of his status, his sacred calling, of being a priest as if being a priest was a different kind of man, better, as if his abuse was not really a sin. . . . Even though the Church says that sex is a sin, if it is a priest who does it, it's not a sin. He said this a lot to many other people. . . . To admit that you had been abused is brave . . . imagine if the perpetrator is a priest, who to many people does not sin. Those who disclose are lying, that is what many people think. In the imagination of these people the Church is a sacred institution, it is holy, it is an institution that you can trust" (Interview 9).

These testimonies recognize that the priest holds a different place socially due to his influence and his potential abusive power. There is in each of these a critical view that recognizes the line that power can cross in the relationship between the priest and his parishioner. We have found in in-

---

19. Rita Laura Segato, "Qualquer homem pode se tornar um aggressor," interview, found at: www.aids.gov.br/imprensa/NoticiasImpressao.asp; accessed on 9 June 2005.

terviews with those who have disclosed sexual abuse by priests that one can observe that the sacred image of the priest in many of them: "I believed in the priests and saw some of them like a father. My parents are separated . . . I also thought that priests could not sin and they did everything right, just like a parent. After all of this happened, I thought: they are not like that. . . . I think people often see the priest as a holy figure, always believing that they are religious and that they are closer to God than others. . . . One only observes the priest, he does not see the man that exists underneath the priestly garb . . . he doesn't understand that the priest can do things wrong, he can sin as well . . ." (Interview 10).

The power dynamic established between an offending priest and his victim really crosses a line that the "sacred" figure of the priest should not cross. The testimonies reveal, on one hand, just how much the sacred nature of the priest can actually protect him, making him somehow immune to any sort of association with violent acts. The very women and girls who had been involved in the situations of abuse recounted how they had never on their part questioned their relationship with the priests. The closeness and intimacy, which in other relationships might have led one to suspicion, were interpreted by these women as expressions of friendship, caring, and tenderness. All of the victims in the cases examined in these studies maintained very close ties with the priest, performing duties in the chapel, the parish, or the parish residence.

One of them explained:

> He was a priest, and I am not going to not trust the priest. There was one day that he asked me to go and clean up one of the meeting rooms in the church, it was on the other side of the church. I went to clean up the room and he followed me over there. He hugged me and then groped me. . . . I did not want to think anything was wrong because he is a priest. I could not think badly of the priest . . . because up to that point I completely respected him because he was a priest, and I was a good Catholic girl. I did not want to imagine why he grabbed me the way he did. I did not know about the other girls. . . . A priest to me was a different type . . . a good Catholic like me; he wasn't holy, but he was a person who dedicates himself completely to the Church and to God. He would not have the evilness within himself to do this sort of thing . . . he just couldn't. At that moment I realized that he was capable of doing this, that he was just a normal person. (Interview 11)

The testimony of each of these victims is evidence that, in their imaginations, they had constructed a holy image of the priest. He was seen by them as a special being, because of his closer connection with God. Therefore, they could not even imagine him being a possible sexual predator. His role as a priest masks his personality and intentions. The sacred aura in which he is clothed, that which comes from on high, makes him immune to any sort of suspicion. How can you accuse someone who is symbolically so powerful? Who would believe that his holy man is a perpetrator?

One particular story of a woman who disclosed is significant. Even her father, as well as the local community, immediately doubted her word. There was a social distance that separated the priestly image from reality that immediately made her suspect:

> My father, the first time that I told him everything, did not believe me. He said that I was making it up, that it was just in my head, that I was imagining things, that the priest was just playing around. But a priest should not be playing around in this kind of manner. Then there began to appear other stories, other people, and he began to see that I really was telling the truth, that there really was something terrible that had happened to me, you know? From that point on, he began to believe my story. . . . Even with friends and neighbors it was like that. . . . On the surface the priest appears to be very good. He is a good person. Of course, no one would believe me, a woman against a priest. No one was ever going to believe and that was what happened, no one believed. As much as I though about it [pressing charges], I did not understand that it was still going on. The lawyers never called me again. I thought that it was over. (Interview 11)

IS IT WORTH IT TO MAKE A PUBLIC DISCLOSURE?

What would lead women or girls to disclose their abuse if they immediately became discredited and despised by society?

It is not easy, as demonstrated above, to disclose abuse or sexual violence. It is even more difficult when the object of this accusation is a religious authority. It is a known fact that women who finally bring themselves to disclose their abuses often find themselves in humiliating circumstances, sometimes facing threats by the abuser. In the cases analyzed, the initiation of the disclosure process did not vindicate the girls and women who had suffered abuse. In one of the cases, disclosure was made by the mother of two girls who had been systematically abused. The priest had compensated the girls with money and food because the girls' circumstances were of extreme poverty. There was a great degree of jealousy among the girls and also with other girls who had "visited the priest." They were all neighbors and lived in the same poor neighborhood. One day, a mother of two sisters got tired of the bickering between them. Hers is the story of a woman worn down, very poor, nervous, and who was frequently drunk. She went in search of the police chief and she disclosed the priestly abuse. One of the local counselors explained to us: "The chief believed her and went to investigate. . . ."[20] It is interesting how this counselor emphasizes the fact that the police chief believed the story of this woman. In this particular case, the disclosure came from someone who did not have anything to lose. She was a poor, drunk, old woman. To her, the power of the religious institution did not frighten her in the least.

In another case study, that of an ex-nun, someone who had already ended their formal relationship with the religious institution is the central figure in making certain that the accusations took place. She lives in a rural camp and participates in a social movement among the poor, those without jobs and homes. She brings the women together and convinces them to disclose their abuse. This is what she told us in an interview:

> I scheduled a room that the archdiocese workers use and we were in there, just us. We sat down and I listened to the women and this is what I told them: 'I think that we need to do two things: We need to find an attorney, and we need to make a public disclosure in the police station in the special victims unit. . . . He struck woman A, she had marks . . . the problem is that they did not make the report within 24 hours, and so she did not have visible signs of the abuse.' . . . [A]t the time, I was not that smart and I was moved by my immaturity and rage. I said to the women: 'We have to get together and go after him, we have to do that. We have to do what justice is failing to do.' I was actually suggesting that a group of women go out; we would grab him, we would beat him and castrate him. He would never be able to hurt anyone again. We would not kill him, we would castrate him. And so, because I did not have a better strategy . . . no one would support me. . . . If the NGO had not come in and given aid, I don't know what would have happened. We had no support. Where would we have found someone to support us? (Interview 9)

It is not easy to confront the dominant, masculine religious power. One needs a very strong feeling of indignation.

Do the women and girls who had been violated believe that is was worthwhile to disclose their abuse?

---

20. Soares Jurkewicz, field notes.

Let's take a look at their testimonies:

[T]o me, if it was just me, I would not have reported. I really wouldn't have, because my family suffered, I suffered, you know, it is hard to be remembered just for this. . . . But since it wasn't just me, there were three more girls . . . if I did not do something and there ended up being more people who suffered like I did that was my thinking: that I am not going to report so that I do not expose myself . . . everything would be the same . . . with them holding it all in. . . . On the one hand, it was worthwhile because the media covered it so much . . . before I would look in the mirror and see a bitter person. . . . I did not know if people would help me or criticize. After I spoke out, of course there were others who condemned the priest's actions and made terrible accusations . . . but now I can look at myself in the mirror and say: I do not have anything to hide. . . . The Church tried to hide as much as it could . . . but if the Church sees that there are so many cases like mine. . . . (Interview 10)

Was it worthwhile to disclose? Look, if I knew that the Church would punish him or they would kick him out or not let him perform mass, I would say yes. But now, knowing the Church is not going to take any measures. . . . (Interview 11)

The ex-nun who encouraged the women to disclose reports on the positives and negatives:

I think that P. would say that it was worthwhile, because it got results. She got good mental health care. She became a new person, she was freed from her problems, went on to have a normal life. After two years of therapy, she has started to date again. She isn't afraid anymore. Now V., who was married to a man who beat her like an animal, the last time that she went to report, she had been beaten a number of times with a stick and had to stop at the hospital . . . how could she say that it was worthwhile? The guy was not convicted, what benefit was there for her in this? She did not receive any benefit at all, it was not worth the pain. If she had remained quiet, she probably would have been beaten less. The situation with the women is this, those that find support and are able to get back up, they will believe that change is possible. And A., what is she going to say? It was worth it? It wasn't worth it to her, she just got stressed out. Her husband found out, she was threatened, lost her job, what was worth it? They said this to me, and even blamed me to some degree, saying: you made us go out on a limb. (Interview 9)

The effects of the violence that these women suffered in their personal lives is significant. In addition to the suffering that accompanies the abuse, there were other harms in consequence of having disclosed their abuse. They were persecuted, sworn at, even had rocks thrown at them, in the street and at school. Some of them had to move to another city. Some of them will carry with them psychological traumas forever, feeling guilty and afraid.

An analysis of the empirical data collected up to this point allows us to confirm one of our hypotheses. Sexual abuse that occurs in the Catholic Church has one demonstrated fact: the strength of symbolic religious power makes it difficult to disclose, by creating fear and guilt. On the other hand, disclosure is the only way to find solutions that will minimize the problem. A hidden crime that is never revealed will never be punished.

CONCLUSION

As we arrive at a conclusion, we must first examine empirically the cases of violence that have been studied, in particular the category of "isolated cases." Contrary to popular thought, these are model cases, in the sense that they reveal a structural and systemic nature of violence perpetrated against women in society and in religious spaces. As Fiorenza notes, this violence cannot be considered "as isolated cases or as unusual behavior, but must be viewed as normative practices . . . and they should be placed on a continuum of masculine power and control over women and children."[21] Such a "continuum" allows us to see one of the root causes, the devalued image of the woman that infects all religions. So many feminist thinkers, whose works would be too numerous to name here, in the areas of philosophy and theology and social sciences, have come to show to what degree the cultural baggage of conception and childbirth for women turns them into beings who are destined by their biology to remain in certain social positions. As strange as it might seem in the beginning of the twenty-first century, these misogynistic assumptions tracing back to Aristotle, Augustine, Thomas Aquinas, and other Christian thinkers—the idea of women as *defective males*—continues to pervade our culture and inspire our thoughts and discourse.

In Catholic thought, this way of thinking of women as biologically subjected to their sexual roles, and therefore, inferior to men, continues

21. In *Concilium* (1994/2): 10.

to be reaffirmed in various documents that have come out of the "Holy Roman Catholic Church" in the last few years, as Patrick Snyder shows, analyzing the following pontifical documents: "Even though it is not explicitly stated, one is led to question up to which point the thinking and teachings of John Paul II are influenced by the androcentric cultural commentaries of Augustine and Thomas Aquinas."[22]

Commenting on the work of this author, Louise Desautels says: "After two decades, in response to feminist criticisms, John Paul II focused an incredible amount of energy on defining the woman, once and for all, and denying her any kind of future evolution of role, or accompanying future social changes. For the Pope, the woman is strictly a mother, in both the biological and spiritual sense, in the image of Eve and Mary. From this 'immutable truth' there results a reaffirmation of the traditional position of the Church: there will be no future ordination of women, contraception and abortion will continue to be banned, and women will submit to their husbands, etc."[23]

According to Snyder, in the text cited above: "John Paul II clearly defines maternity, once and for all, as the nature, the dignity, the calling, and the final temporal and spiritual place of the woman."[24] He concludes: "Everything is really quite heavy when one speaks of the dignity and calling of the woman, in John Paul II's teachings, as in those of his predecessors, as a means of reflection that would change the theological thinking about the woman, her biological identity, and her physical sexuality is closed to further discussion; in a way, more or less, a woman finds herself cut off, so to speak, from the real world in which she finds herself, not even an eternal figure, not Eve, not Mary, but as a human being defined by one path that is ever-changing."[25]

This structural inequality attributed to the Catholic thinking about men and women sustained the possibility that the actual physical body of the woman continues to be an object of violence. This inequality establishes immediate hierarchical relationships and relationships of power, opening up a space that facilitates the perpetration of abuse. "One's social place depends upon one's anatomy—masculine or feminine. The feminine is associated with social scenes of lesser value than the respective as-

---

22. Patrick Snyder, "Le Féminisme selon Jean Paul II: Une negation du déterminisme corporal de la femme." Text presented at the Colloque International: la Recherche féministe dans la francophonie. État de la situation et pistes de collaboration, 1996, 11.
23. Patrick Snyder, "L'église et les femmes," www.acfas.ca/decouvrir/v23-1.html; accessed on 9 June 2005.
24. Snyder, "Le Féminisme selon Jean Paul II," 10.
25. Ibid., 12.

pects that are masculine. There is no real reason or material condition that can explain this difference."[26] Women are attacked simply for being women. In the construction of the docile, submissive "feminine body," women are destined to the realization of their biological role, maternity, and this places women in a risky situation. The "specific nature" of women, making them eternally feminine, ends up submitting them to the violent will of men. It is "natural" that men "possess" their women. If such a statement can appear anachronistic and identified with the thinking and practices of centuries ago, then as Joseph Ratzinger, currently Pope Benedict XVI, cites in a text in 2004: "It is understood in a certain sense the role that Genesis details to us for the woman, in her most profound and original state of being, she exists for 'the other.'"[27] It is not by accident, Joanne Carlson Brown states, that "violence committed against women has a greater likelihood of being revealed to the world in situations in which the teachings and practices of the Church legitimate an inferior role for women in relationship to men."[28]

We wish we could end this chapter with the affirmation that an end to this violence is in sight. But how can one do this, when the main thinking of the highest order in the most powerful church in the West is against it? How can we do that when every three seconds a woman suffers some act of violence in the world? How can we do that when, up to the end of 2004, more than three hundred women had been kidnapped, raped, tortured, and executed in the city of Juárez, Mexico, alone, and when this feminicide has not caused worldwide indignation? There is hope, however, in that the veils are being lifted and the widespread, hierarchically managed cover-up is finally being exposed to the cleansing glare of sunlight. In this there are glimmers of hope.

26. Segato, *Qualquer homem pode se tornar um agressor*, accessed 9 June 2005.
27. "Letter to the Bishops of the Catholic Church on the Collaboration of Men and Women in the Church and in the World," #1, 31 May 2004.
28. Joanne Carlson Brown, "Em respeito dos anjos: Violência e abuso sexuais," in *Concilium* (1994/2): 33.

Conclusion The Role of Religion in Violence against Women

ARVIND SHARMA

How might one conclude a book on violence perpetrated on women in the name of religion?

PERSPECTIVE

As one reads chapter after chapter about how religions have been implicated in violence involving women, one becomes aware of the danger of overkill. In order to better focus on the role of religion in this respect, one needs to look at the whole picture. Only by doing so will we be able to assess the role of religion correctly and avoid the pitfall of overdetermination. The points that follow may seem, on the face of it, revisionist in nature but that is not the intention underlying their presentation. The intention is to nuance the discussion of violence against women in order to make it more cogent in terms of the role played by religion. The following points are noteworthy in this respect.

Statistics

Although the existence of violence against women cannot be doubted, the incidence of such violence is open to debate. Such incidence is usually presented in the form of statistics. A 1993 Statistics Canada survey concluded that one out of two women had "experienced at least one incident of violence since the age of 16," and that "one third of the victims complained of threats so severe that they feared for their lives." It has, however, been pointed out that Statistics Canada is, in this case, "misrepresenting its own data: the figures here refer to perpetrators, not to victims. It is not that 34 percent of *women* fear for their lives. . . . It is that 34 percent of those *partners* who were complained about made the women fear for their lives."[1] The Canadian Panel on Violence Against Women (1993) "claimed that 98 percent of Canadian women are sexually violated"[2] as against the more usual figure of one out of three suffering such a fate.[3]

The problem with statistics is that the extent of the problem represented by them has an implication for the manner in which it might be solved. As Christina Hoff Sommers notes, if the "average male is a serious threat to women, then a massive make-over of American society would be called for. If, however, 2%–3% of men are abusive, then we need to target that group. . . ."[4]

Another problem with statistics is their comparative character, and sometimes lack of it. The Canadian survey of 1993 was a single-sex survey and thus has been criticized as potentially partisan. The point is that violence against women might need to be seen in the light of the level of violence that characterizes a society in general. In one notorious case, although a 1997 survey disclosed that 46 percent of women and 18 percent of men resorted to violence, only the latter figures were first released. The former figure was released only after the case was exposed and after three years of pressure.[5] The figure is counter-intuitive, but according to another Canadian figure, based on a study conducted by the University of Alberta, 12 percent of husbands and 11 percent of wives were victims of domestic violence.[6]

Such past or future findings do not necessarily go against the assumption of the book; what they seem to indicate is that that there could be a subculture of violence against women in the midst of a more general culture of violence. The book then addresses ways of dealing with this subculture.

Role of Religion

Even if the general impression of substantial violence against women worldwide is statistically confirmed, the issue may need to be nuanced further when it comes to the role religion plays in it.

I hold in my hand, for instance, a book entitled: *Violence: Opposing Viewpoints*.[7] It contains a chapter devoted to domestic violence. The

---

1. Paul Nathanson and Katherine K. Young, *Legalising Misandry* (Montreal: McGill-Queen's University Press, 2006), 362.
2. Ibid.
3. Scott Barbour and Karin L. Swisher, *Violence: Opposing Viewpoints* (San Diego: Greenhaven Press, 1996), 139.
4. Nathanson and Young, *Legalising Misandry*, 360.
5. Ibid., 363.
6. Ibid., 356.
7. Barbour and Swisher, *Violence: Opposing Viewpoints*.

book, however, contains hardly any reference to religion; the word does not even figure in the index. A chapter devoted to causes of violence contains the usual suspects: media, genes, family breakdown, criminal justice system, drug trade, and even capitalism—but it contains nothing about religion. This illustrates the point, through oversight, that many other factors beside religion could contribute to violence. The fact that other factors could lead to violence does not, of course, mean that religion is off the hook; it does, however, mean that it may be keeping company, even if it is bad company.

Traditional Religion

Even when we talk of religion it needs to be clearly understood that in this book we deal with traditional religion and not fundamentalist religion. It is a widely held view in the field that fundamentalist religion aggravates the problem of violence against women and this is an important point to explore. This book, however, engages the various religions in their traditional version in the context of violence against women.[8]

Secular Factors

If religion is taken into account as a factor contributing to violence towards women (understood traditionally rather then fundamentally), then the question arises: Do secular factors also play a similar role? If, for instance, patriarchy is understood as a secular historical development in human history that preceded the rise of world's religions, then this has major implications in assessing the role of "religion" in this context. As Christine E. Gudorf observes in the very first chapter in this book: "Patriarchy preceded the origins of even the oldest of the contemporary world religions, so that contemporary religions came into being in cultures already imbued with patriarchy, a patriarchy that had often been legitimated by prior religious traditions now extinct" (pages 12–13). These other elements may have to be taken into consideration before the proper role of religion in the situation can be determined.

What About Ideologies?

Another general factor that needs to be borne in mind has to do with how surrogates to religion fare in the context of violence against women. One has in mind here the ideologies of fascism and communism, for instance. The latter is particularly relevant, for it claims, at least in theory, to abo-

---

8. For the role of fundamentalism, see Arvind Sharma, ed., *Fundamentalism and the Position of Women in World Religions* (forthcoming).

lition all discrimination and presumably violence against women, just as many religions, at least in theory, often abolish sex distinctions at the soteriological level. It might be instructive to compare their record with that of religions. For instance, did the communist countries succeed in eliminating violence against women? The communist revolution in China was also presumably a harbinger of such equality but it is now learned that the communist party maintained a special cadre to entertain Chairman Mao, whose members boasted of having contracted syphilis from him! One way of broadening the bandwave would be to consider the violence of women under various "worldviews" rather than just "religions." According to Ninian Smart, the similarities between religions and certain ideologies such as nationalism or Marxism were so compelling that they should be studied in an integrated manner, and ought to be referred to in the same breath as "worldviews," rather than being set apart as "religion" and "ideology." The proposal, although not adopted here, is an important one and suggests another point for investigation. The difference between religion and ideology is usually said to turn on the presence of the transcendent dimension in the former and its absence in the latter. Thus Marxism dispenses with a transcendent referent, but places history, it might be said, virtually in the same role in an essentially immanent ideology. This raises the question: Do transcendence and immanence, as philosophical categories, relate to the issue of violence towards women in the same way, or do they possess different implications in such a context? This point too is not pursued in these pages but might be well worth pursuing elsewhere.

POINTS IN COMMON: Karma and the Creation Stories

Now that the parameters of the scope of this investigation on the role of religion in the violence directed at women have been set out, one might move to a consideration of the religions themselves. Before one does so, however, it might be worthwhile to pause to take a look at a clustering that seems to emerge once these essays are perused. That is to say, some common points seem to underlie the presentation of some of these traditions, points around which several religious traditions cluster. Two points are particularly noteworthy in this respect. The first is the doctrine of karma, and the other is creation stories.

More than one paper alludes to the use of karma, in religious cultures familiar with that idea, to rationalize violence towards women. Such rationalization takes several forms. The violence could be blamed on a woman's bad karma, or the promise of her generating good karma by putting up with it might be held out. It becomes even more powerful as an explanation when these various aspects are made to cohere. As David Loy notes (page 56):

Obviously, this understanding of karma and rebirth has important implications for much more than the Thai sex industry. The connections with other types of physical and structural violence against women could also be discussed, as well as many other nongendered consequences regarding the rationalization of racism, economic oppression, birth handicaps, and so forth. Karma is used to justify both the authority of political elites, who therefore deserve their wealth and power, and the subordination of those who have neither. It provides the perfect theodicy: there is an infallible cause-and-effect relationship between one's moral actions and one's fate, so there is no need to work toward social justice, which is already built into the moral fabric of the universe. In fact, if there is no undeserved suffering, there is really no evil we need to struggle against.

This brings to mind a similar description of karma as a perfect theodicy by Max Weber in the context of the caste system. One was born in a particular caste on account of one's own karma in a past life, and by doing one's caste duty in the present life, one ensured birth in a higher caste in the next life. It is interesting then that such an interpretation of karma could be adduced both to justify caste discrimination and discrimination against women. In this sense it perhaps has a parallel in a particular interpretation of the idea of "calling," if one's calling is defined as the place one finds oneself in as a result of God's will, which one should pursue to conform to God's will.

The situation as presented in the preceding text may be described as one of karmic deadlock, but the deadlock is broken somewhat differently in Hinduism and Buddhism. The Hindu counterargument has typically been that karma impels but does not compel. Or more formally, that karma is of three types. The first is called *pràrabdha* (destiny), or that karma that has begun to produce its results. Different from this is one's *sancita* (accumulated) karma, which is the karma one has accumulated but that has not started to produce its effect. It is like karma in the storeroom, if *pràrabdha* is like the goods involved in a transaction. Different from both is *kriyamàõa* or *àgàmi karma*, or the karma one has yet to perform. This includes the karma of present and future actions.[9] These are comparable to the goods one is going to buy and sell.

From the point of view of this triptych, the problem with the earlier interpretation of karma is that it identifies all karma with *pràrabdha* and

9. M. V. Nadkarni, *Hinduism: A Gandhian Perspective* (New Delhi: Ane Books India, 2006), 42–44; Arvind Sharma, *Classical Hindu Thought: An Introduction* (New Delhi: Oxford University Press, 2000), chap. 12.

leaves no room for the other two forms of karma—specially of the *kriyamàõa* or *àgàmi* kind. The condition one is born in may be the result of past karma, but the doctrine does not imply that one must remain stuck in it—otherwise what is *kriyamàõa* or *àgàmi* karma for?

The karmic deadlock is broken in Buddhism somewhat differently. Therein it is emphasized that whether any outcome is the result of one's karma or due to natural or socioeconomic factors can only be determined by the Buddha's insight.[10] This has a direct bearing on the case of Buddhism in Thailand. One cannot prima facie blame one's involvement in sex traffic on one's karma—it could very well be a sign of societal malaise rather than personal bad karma.

The other recurring them is that of the creation stories, which play a role in determining one's attitude towards women not only in Judaism, Christianity, and Islam, but also African traditional religions, wherein Dogon cosmology in West Africa is invoked in justification of female cutting. Echoes of such an etiological justification may also be heard in Veena Talwar Oldenburg's account of the role of Sita in Hinduism.

One needs to bear in mind here that these stories can be rewritten. That this would hardly be an innovation is indicated by the presence of two tellings of the covenant account and the two tellings of the Genesis account. There is also an *ânanda Ràmàyaõa* in classical India, in which Sita is glorified over Ram, for instance. Narrativity need not always involve fixed normativity.

RELIGIONS: Simultaneously Demeaning and Empowering to Women

Two leitmotifs that underlie the discussion of violence towards women in several traditions were lifted up for special attention in the previous section, namely, karma and creation stories. In this section we shall proceed by looking at each band of the rainbow coalition of world religions. A central point that emerges from such a survey is the unsurprising one that almost all religious traditions contain elements that demean women on one hand and empower them on the other.

Mutombo Nkulu-N'Sengha thus draws attention to the central role of female cutting for the Gikuyus of Kenya. He cites a line from a book by Kenyatta, the former president of Kenya, entitled *Facing Mount Kenya* to the effect: "the real anthropological study, therefore, is to show that clitoridectomy, like Jewish circumcision, is a mere bodily mutilation which, however, is regarded as the condition sine qua non of the whole

---

10. T. W. Rhys Davids, tr., *The Questions of King Milinda* (Delhi: Motilal Banarsidass, 1965 [1890]), part I, 193–95.

teaching of tribal law, religion, and morality" (page 139). There is also a reference, however, to the African allegory of the cave from the folktales of Ghana. Ananse collected all the wisdom of the world in a gourd, which he wanted to hoard up at the top of a tree, but he had tied the gourd in front of him as he climbed. When his son, Ntikuma, pointed out his lack of wisdom in tying the gourd to his front rather than at the back, he threw it down in a fit of anger. It broke and people took away what they could. This explains "why there is so much wisdom in the world, but few persons have more than a little of it and some persons have none at all."

Liora Gubkin uses the second chapter of Hosea to reveal domestic abuse in the Torah itself in the context of Judaism, but she also alludes to Jeremiah's words to engage in the task of repairing the world (*tikkun olam*).

Grace Jantzen deals with Christianity, as also John Raines. Thus, on the one hand, women are linked with the devil because Eve was the first to sin. On the other hand, an alternative understanding is also suggested, which may have positive implications in relation to women, such as an organic understanding of the garden. John Raines focuses on how the sacrificial metaphor has weighed more heavily on women, but he also demonstrates how the prophetic heritage of Christianity could be a redeeming factor.

The chapter on sexual violence in the Catholic Church by Maria José Rosado-Nunes and Regina Soares Jurkewicz also needs to be placed here, as an illustration of how easily an obsession with control of women slides into exploitation of women, compounded all the more by the fact that it is perpetrated by priests who convert their charisma into miasma. Once again one needs to experience the redemptive power of the prophetic tradition: "Whereas the pre-writing prophets challenged individuals, the writing prophets challenged corruptions in the social order and oppressive institutions."[11]

Sa'diyya Shaikh points to the various verses of the Qur'an (2:1228; 4:3; 4:34) that have apparently had negative implications for women. But she also records how battered women have built their lives, calling it "*tafsir* through praxis" or "embodied *tafsir*," by drawing upon the ethical resources of this tradition and endorses the position adopted by Riffat Hassan in such a context.[12]

Veena Talwar Oldenburg discusses the crucial role of Sita in shaping the sensibility of Hindu women, specially as found in the *Ramcharitmanas* of Tulsidas (c. 1532–1623). This text has been declared by the eminent au-

---

11. Huston Smith, *The World's Religions* (San Francisco: HarperSanFrancisco, 1991), 291.
12. Riffat Hassan, "Feminism in Islam," in Arvind Sharma and Katherine K. Young, eds., *Feminism and World Religions* (Albany: State University of New York Press, 1999), 248–78.

thority Sir George Grierson to have "been far better known today in North India than the Bible is in any country of the West."[13] And yet, as she notes, "Sita's refusal to go back to Ram after he abandons her in the forest can also be interpreted as an endorsement of modern divorce" (page 172).

David R. Loy and Ouyporn Khuankaew address issues pertaining to the position of women in Buddhism and point to a particular understanding of the doctrine of karma and monastic discrimination against women as negative elements in the situation. At the same time, Loy offers a more salutary understanding of the doctrine of karma and Khuankaew offers a wonderfully original formulation of the Eightfold Path.

Hsiao-Lan Hu refers to the problems posed by the four teachings, imaginatively extending the concept of *san-chiao* to include not only Confucianism, Taoism, and Buddhism but also the Legalism of Han Fei Tzu; she also applies the Confucian doctrine of the Rectification of Names (*cheng-ming*) to these teachings themselves. As Terry Woo notes elsewhere, "the paradox is this: feminism also wants peace and stability; and Confucius too was asking for a complete revolution from the greed, disloyalty, licentiousness, and violence of his times."[14]

IN CONCLUSION

The wheel turns full circle as one returns to the first chapter by Christine Gudorf. This chapter presents a general overview of the theme and notes that "the vast majority of male aggression, even violence, is aimed at other men, not women" (page 17). It also refers to the dimorphic view of the sexes as socially constructed. We are thus encouraged to emerge now from our immersion in violence against women to take a look at the larger landscape once again. The two relata—men and women—how do they relate? Does the relationship at times overwhelm the relata? This could happen when human rights discourse fails to distinguish between men and women, even when this distinction needs to be taken into account. Do the relata interpenetrate to a certain degree? After all, men and women both possess testosterone and estrogen, although in different proportions. The book examined the element of violence in the relationship, specially when directed by one relata towards the other, thereby contaminating the relation. The bad news is that religion has to role a play in it; the good news is that if it is a part of the problem, it can also be a part of the solution.

---

13. Ainslie T. Embree, ed., *The Hindu Tradition* (New York: Random House, 1966), 249.
14. Terry Woo, "Confucianism and Feminism," in Sharma and Young, eds., *Feminism and World Religions*, 115.

Index

239